Talent Crunch

Talent Crunch

Issues and Perspectives

Edited by

E Mrudula

2010

Icfai Books

The Icfai University Press

TALENT CRUNCH: ISSUES AND PERSPECTIVES

Editor: E Mrudula

First Edition: 2010
Printed in India

Published by

The Icfai University Press
52, Nagarjuna Hills, Punjagutta
Hyderabad, India – 500 082
Phone: (+91) (040) 23430–368, 369, 370, 372, 373, 374
Fax: (+91) (040) 23352521, 23435386
E-mail: info@icfaibooks.com, icfaibooks@icfai.org, ssd@icfai.org

ISBN: 9788131407967

Editorial Team: Jyothi E, Aruna Y and Neelima A
Quality Support: V Sandhya Srikanth and S Sirisha

Contents

Section III

Impact on Industries

Section IV

Global Perspective

Overview

Talent is the power of an organization. Talent refers to the skills, and competency. There is a misconception among the organizations while referring to talent. Some refer to talent as people. But it actually means what human capital possesses. Talent, in the true sense, means the proficiency that an individual possesses. It is the intelligence, ability, and creativity to lead people. Many organizations have also recognized that there is more than what they do to attract, motivate and retain the human capital.

On the one hand, organizations are finding ways of attracting more human capital by applying more attractive strategies. Shortage of skilled manpower is becoming an emerging issue in many countries as well as organizations and that is called Talent Crunch. It is the main block that is being faced by many today. It is specified as the lack of skilled workers/manpower. It refers to the shortage of individuals exceeding the organization's expectations. It is referred to as being more than lack of productivity and innovation. This crunch in talent leads to diverse results – slows down the organizational growth, brings down productivity, and also leads to leadership problems. The problems are observed to be on the higher side in IT industry though they are prevalent in Aviation, Animation and retailing industries in regard to this problem. Factors like demographic factors, environmental factors, high salaries, working environment, poaching, ageing workforce, meritocracy, lack of proper educational facilities and so on are encountered and it is high time that governments and employers took effective steps to overcome this problem. It is also an observed fact that countries like India and China that are having a huge population are also facing this problem.

This book "Talent Crunch: Issues and Perspectives" is an attempt to find out what the real reasons behind this shortage are and what the possible ways in which governments and employers can tackle this problem are. It contains reputed article on the topic. This book discusses strategies HR managers implement in overcoming this deficiency. Experiences of sectors—IT/BPO, Aviation, Tourism and Advertising in overcoming this problem and the steps they have taken in overcoming them are also discussed in this book. It further presents the experiences of countries like China, India, Europe, US which, in spite of having a huge population and a good skilled manpower, face this problem of shortage and also the steps the governments of those countries have taken to overcome it.

This book has been split into four sections. Section I introduces the topic of talent crunch and examines the causes, the challenges and the possible solutions to the problem. Section II deals with issues, the governments and the employers are likely to encounter and gives a hint of solutions. The third section discusses the impact of talent dearth on industries and presents the current scenario in various sectors. The fourth and final section focuses on the global perspective of the issues.

Section I: Introduction

In today's business environment, it has become essential for organizations to attract and retain talented workforce, as there exists a hiatus between the demand and supply of competent employees. Lack of talented workforce is one of the serious crises that the present day organizations face. It is, therefore, necessary for governments and organizations to play an active role in overcoming this crunch. The first article titled **"Talent Dearth – Causes and Solutions"** by *E Mrudula,* apart from examining the reasons for the paucity of talent, discusses the steps governments and employers have to take to overcome this ubiquitous phenomenon. In the later part, the article, elucidates how individuals can be encouraged and enabled in confronting this talent shortage, with examples of some companies that have encountered this problem and the strategies they have adopted to overcome it.

The second article **"Workforce Crisis: How to Beat the Coming Shortage of Skills and Talent"**, by *Ken Dychtwald, Tamara J Erickson* and *Robert Morison,* discusses the emerging shortage of talents and skills in organizations. They also say that this perplexing problem can be tackled using three cohorts – mature, mid-career and young workers. The authors have presented many examples of corporations which have already adopted various ways to engage the diverse workforce. The world, according to the authors is gripped by three phenomena – baby boom, longevity boom and the birth dearth and a reality – the workforce crisis. Leveraging the mature, rekindling the mid-career and retaining the young by way of flexible retirement schemes and simplifying the regulations in pension and benefit law are the challenges faced by organizations today.

The third article titled **"Retaining Talent: Challenges to HRM"**, by *Vineet Tandon,* discusses the attrition rate of employees in any organization. We are able to find more employees joining and leaving their workplace. The talent crunch adds to the worry of HR managers who are only left with the option of scratching their heads and singing no mercy's all time hit. As a HR manager, one must be able to find out the real reasons behind the talent crunch. The article discusses the scenario of skilled and unskilled labor in two upcoming sectors. The article also discusses the possible reasons of increasing talent crunch –

Changing lifestyles, dearth of motivation, increased expectations, increasing opportunities, decreasing loyalty towards organizations and job misfit.

The fourth article titled "**It's 2008: Do You Know Where Your Talent Is? – Why Acquisition and Retention Strategies Don't Work?**" written by *Robin Athey*, discusses the range of emerging talent crisis. It also compares the traditional talent management process with the model developed by Deloitte. The article cites that only those companies that win the hearts and minds of their top talent will be able to deliver value over both the short and the long terms. The game is changing in other ways as well. Jobs are no longer static. Companies must continually train and develop employees if they are to keep pace with the speed and complexity of technological innovation. Individuals need greater flexibility in their career paths, and organizations need greater flexibility from employees. People must connect across businesses, divisions, and regions in ways that promote high quality decisions and fast execution. Critical talent is scarce, and about to become much scarcer because of two looming trends: the retirement of the Baby Boom generation and a growing skills gap. Firms like Microsoft, Southwest Airlines, and SAS Institute are exemplary in the way they nurture and manage critical talent.

Section II: Issues

The fifth article "**Poaching: The Best Talent Worldwide – Tools and Approaches Ranging from Aggressive to Passive**" by *John Sullivan,* explains that Poaching talent is not a new approach, but has been deployed around the world for ages particularly in US and Eastern Europe. Poaching talent is the practice of proactively targeting and hiring top talent away from competitor or top firm with the intention of securing skills or capabilities faster, mitigating high-level talent losses due to attrition, damaging competitor's ability to achieve strategic objectives. The article discusses the three dominant poaching strategies which include – Direct Sourcing, Third-party poaching and Attract them with "Honey". It further discusses the six categories that power the "attract them with honey" strategy – Employment branding, Employee referrals, Event recruiting, Magnet hiring, Boomerang hiring and Internet. It further says that the war for talent is expanding and those with the most to lose need to understand the tools and approaches used by the competition.

The sixth article titled **"Meritocracy: Responding to the Myth"** by *Mike Hyter,* discusses an experience of the interactions of the author with senior level executives about their organizations human resource practices. The author mentions that he often keeps hearing about the organizations as true "meritocracies", where the gifted are at the top as a result of a fair process. The irony is that women and professionals of color in those same companies are far from fair to them. They feel that the developmental opportunities and promotions are not based on merit but are reserved for those who play the game and special treatment is given to those few at the expense of the others. In most companies, the best of intention's and diligent efforts of dedicated managers and HR professionals of assessing and rewarding talent is flawed. It is also an observed that it is in the best interest of the organization that they make attempts to correct the flaws.

The seventh article titled **"Workforce Ageing: The Challenges for 21st Century Management"**, is by *Margaret Patrickson* and *Rob Ranzijn.* It focuses on the employment policies for older workers in the new world of work. Currently, governments throughout the developed world are concerned about the impact of ageing workforces in the near future, after Baby Boomers retire. Managers have the opportunity and responsibility to take measures to prolong the working lives of their older employees. The need to develop new HRM practices for older workers is already urgent and will soon become critical if organizations wish to survive.

The eighth article titled **"Mismanagement of Talent: Employability and Jobs in the Knowledge Economy"** is by *Phillip Brown* and *Anthony Hesketh.* This article is a review of the book that examines the assumptions about education, work and labor market in a 'Knowledge' economy. It further raises the question whether 'Knowledge Based Economies' lead to significant increase in the demand for highly educated knowledge workers. Can expansion of higher education and policies aimed at increasing diversity overcome enduring inequalities in the allocation of job and life chances? It also tries to answer questions like whether the employers believe that there is an expansion of talent pool or more intensive "war for talent" (WfT). The value of human capital has become more important than tangible assets. It is therefore important to acquire great talent, since the differential value created by most knowledge workers is enormous. Excellent talent management has become a crucial source of competitive advantage.

Section III: Impact on Industries

The ninth article "**Employee Attrition in the IT/BPO Sector in India: Cost and Consequences**" is by *Sagar Chakraverty.* This case study discusses the reasons for huge talent crunch in IT/BPO sector. It discusses the monetary loss faced by the industry due to attrition and also the consequences faced by it due to this crunch. There was a heavy exodus of employees from one organization to another especially in the information technology (IT) – business process outsourcing (BPO) sectors in India and the biggest challenge for the HR managers was to retain employees. The battle for head hunting had become fierce and the organizations adopted all possible means to recruit the available talent pool. The rampant practice of poaching and bulk recruitment with lucrative offers, were important catalysts to accelerate the high attrition rates.

The tenth article "**The Indian Aviation Scenario – Shortage of Skilled Human Resources**" is by *E Naveen Kumar.* This article discusses the various perspectives of the shortage of crucial human resources in aviation industry and the need for more training establishments in the industry. The article also discusses the bottlenecks in pilots' shortage and the measures to overcome them. Flying as a pilot is one of the most exciting and challenging careers successfully accomplished by a chosen few. The airline industry is classified into six major segments: Majors, flag-carriers, cargo airlines, independents, low cost carriers (LCCS), regional, and leisure. Emergence of private players such as Kingfisher, Spice jet, Go air, Indigo has marked a boom in the aviation industry. Inefficiency and insufficiency of infrastructure coupled with shortage of skilled workforce threaten to derail the plans of dozen odd new airlines waiting in the wing. Even though the government has restricted one of the major indicators of pilot shortage – Poaching, there are still miles to go before addressing the problem.

The eleventh article **"HR Issues in Advertising Agencies in India"**, is by *Shalini Govindan*. It emphasizes that high attrition rates and the stressful work environment are the stepping problems in the advertising industry. The advertising agency is primarily involved in planning and creating ads for its clients. The agency conducts market research to understand the product, brand, the consumer, the consumer's relationship with the brand, customer preferences, etc. the advertising industry is facing a talent crunch and is unable to attract good creative talented work force. One of the imperative problems plaguing ad industry is constant job-hopping, and increased departure of high profile personnel from one agency to another[1] . To retain the best talent and protect them from the prying eyes of poachers is one of the biggest challenges that the HR executives face, considering the high attrition rates in the industry. Also the HR personnel need to frame policies that are in line with practices that are followed by service industries like software or financial services to fight poaching and job-hopping.

The twelfth article **"Employment Scenario and Human Resource Strategies in Tourism Industry"**, is by *H Rajashekar* and *Suresh Poojary*. It discusses the current scenario of the tourism industry. It discusses the obstacles to attract and retain the workers in the tourism industry due to its complex nature of tourism employment. The most significant features of the tourism industry are its capacity to generate large-scale employment and its ability to employ a large number of women and young members of the workforce. Untrained, unmotivated, underpaid and unorganized labor force bears a high turnover in the industry and even the standard practice of HRD is found lacking here. Career Advancement and career planning with good practice of HRMD must be designed to retain the employees, thereby, avoiding the problems of poaching and talent crunch.

Section IV: Global Perspective

The thirteenth article **"Talent Deficiency Syndrome®: Who Moved My Talent?"** by *Vineet Tandon,* discusses the issue of Shortage of skilled talent that is becoming a major problem in India. The article defines and describes the term **"Talent Deficiency Syndrome"**. It also discusses the reasons for the sudden shortage and the need to overcome talent deficiency. HR managers and headhunters are scouting for talent like crazy, and doing everything to overcome the Talent Deficiency Syndrome.

China's enormous pool of low cost manpower had enabled it to develop as a manufacturing base for companies across the globe. However, since 1998, the situation seems to be fast changing with China facing a shortage in the availability of skilled manpower. Experts predict that this would lead to an increase in the cost of available manpower and therefore increased costs for businesses. They fear that this would result in China losing its competitive advantage as a low cost manufacturing base. However, some experts are of the opinion that the shortage of manpower is merely a temporary phenomenon and China would continue to be a low cost manufacturing base. The fourteenth article **"China's Rising Cost of Business: The Human Resources Factor"** by *Souvik Dhar,* helps in understanding China's competitive advantage as a low cost manufacturing base because of the availability of low cost manpower and the reasons for increase in manpower cost since 1998. The case provides scope to discuss whether China would lose its competitive advantage as a low cost manufacturing base for global companies.

The fifteenth article **"Forecasting Labor and Skills Shortages: How can Projections better Inform Labor Migration Policies?"**

by *Christina Boswell, Silvia Stiller* and *Thomas Straubhaar,* and summarized by *Rajarshi Ghosh,* discusses the EU states which are experiencing serious skills and labour shortages in a number of sectors, despite persistently high rates of unemployment. Among the most widespread have been the shortages of highly qualified workers in IT, and employees in the health sector, as well as consumer and commercial services (Germany), education, health and social services (Sweden), construction (France), or engineers and teachers (the UK). These shortages can hamper productivity and growth, or can undermine targets in the provision of education, healthcare or social services. In most cases, such shortages are not caused by an aggregate shortage of labour, but can be attributed to problems of mismatch between labour demand and supply.

The sixteenth article "**Addressing the Challenges of an Aging Workforce: A Human Capital Perspective for Companies Operating in Europe**" by *Eric Lesser, Carsten Hausmann* and *Steffen Feuerpeil,* focuses on the impact of changing demographics from the European perspective and the way the companies across Europe and worldwide are developing innovative solutions to address this issues. Over the last several years, the focus of Europe has changed from preventing age discrimination to mobilizing the aging workforce. Two important factors have promoted the trend toward early retirement in European countries. First, the combination of state pension plans, coupled with early retirement and other social programs have made it relatively attractive for individuals to retire early. Firms need to take a proactive approach to address demographic changes, both within their organization and across their labor markets, to avoid issues that could significantly hamper companies in the industrialized world.

The last article "**The Aging of the US Workforce: Employer Challenges and Responses**" is by *Ernst & Young.* It is a survey that best understands aging workforce as an issue that results in workforce shortage. Retirements in organizations lead to brain drain. Corporate

America clearly understands, that it will definitely face workforce shortage as retirements are increasing and so it is focusing on resources as an immediate issue. The main purpose of the survey is to understand how organizations are approaching the issue, whether organizations are identifying older workers that may be lost as they retire and how to determine the programs to retain employees, so that their wisdom is transferred to the next generation.

Section I

Introduction

1

Talent Dearth – Causes and Solutions

E Mrudula

In today's business environment, it has become essential for organizations to attract and retain talented workforce, as there exists a hiatus between the demand and supply of competent employees. Dearth of talented worforce is one of the serious constraints that the present day organizaitons face. It is therefore, necessary for governments and organizations to play an active role in overcoming this crunch. Apart from examining the reasons for the paucity of talent, the article also discusses the steps governments and employers have to take to overcome this universal phenomenon. In the later part of the article, it elucidates how individuals can be encouraged and enabled in confronting this talent shortage with examples of some companies that have encountered this problem and the strategies they have adopted to overcome it.

"The global talent crunch is going to happen, and there's nothing anyone can do to stop it."

– Deloitte's Diotte.

Introduction

Talent is generally perceived as synonymous with the entire workforce of an organization. However the term actually refers to what people possess within themselves i.e., their abilities, skills and knowledge. Attracting and retaining talent has been one of the most challenging problems the organizations have been facing. Organizations recruit human capital based on skills and experience, as they together with intellectual capital form an important part of the organization. Companies attract and retain them through their attractive schemes and rewards. In today's competitive environment, it is essential for organizations to select the best and employ only those individuals who exactly fit the positions that are vacant rather than recruiting the individuals just to fill up the vacant positions. On the other hand employees too seek only those jobs that not only provides them with financial security but at the same time have meaningful career development.

It is widely accepted that economic prosperity of any country depends on having a well-educated and highly skilled workforce. In today's competitive world the most common problem organizations are facing is 'Talent Crunch', which is also referred to as lack of talented/skilled personnel. War for talent has been increasing and this has an adverse impact on organizations, viz., escalating up costs, inhibiting organizational growth and even creating leadership problems. Of late, the issue has been assuming alarming proportions. Structural changes in organizations are the most important factors that are making this talent even more critical. The main reasons for the paucity of skilled personnel include – lack of financial investment, lack of skills required, demographic shift (migration, ageing workforce), poaching, meritocracy[1], lack of educational facilities, outsourcing etc.

Generally, there are two ways of looking at this shortage. First, there is a shortage of potential workers with specific skills. Secondly, non-availability of persons having specific skills as required by employers. Both kinds of shortage are different but often they both result in lack of supply and demand of labour (Julie Ann McMullin, Martin Cooke with Rob Downie, 2004). According to Manpower

[1] Meritocracy is a system of government or other organization based on demonstrated ability (merit) and talent rather than by wealth, family connections (nepotism), class privilege, cronyism, popularity (as in democracy) or other historical determinants of social position and political power.

Inc. shortage of any kind can be addressed either by reducing the demand or increasing the supply. While reducing the demand is made possible by automation, outsourcing, computerisation, and increase in the supply is achieved through migration, training, off shoring, flexibility and optimising the workforce. This shortage may be result of technological changes, environmental changes and others. It may also be due to differential wage rates and educational qualifications. This shortage in talent in turn is making the job of HR managers also more difficult. With the increasing shortage of skilled manpower, HR managers are only left with finding answers to only one question – "Where do these employees go?" According to Anita Ramachandran of Cerebrus: "I see the talent crunch continuing for another two years at least and companies will continue to have to come up with their own training programmes." Since many organizations are realizing that people are the most important asset of organizations and its success. Organizations are on the lookout for the talented pool of employees to achieve and sustain competitive advantage. It is imperative that governments and employers have to play key role in overcoming this shortage.

Sectors Where Talent Crunch is Predominant

Sectors that are facing the problem of acute shortage of talented employees include IT industry, entertainment, BPO, KPO, aviation, animation etc. In IT industry, though the demand for IT professionals has skyrocketed during the last two decades the attrition rate in this industry is hovering 22%. According to NASSCOM, by 2010, India would face a shortage of 5,00,000 IT professionals. Companies started spending 3%-10% of their revenues on training. Some IT companies like Wipro, Satyam and iGate are using Restricted Stock Options (RSUs) as their effective retention and motivational tool[2]. The efforts which the companies put in, to retain their talented and most experienced employee's shows that the employees have better bargaining power. In other words, it can be said that "war for talent is shifting the balance of power from companies to employees."[3]

The aviation sector is also witnessing shortage of aviation crew, and an additional 2,000 pilots, 10,000 engineers and logistics staff will be required to

---

2 Retaining talent, Priyanka Vyas, *Hindu Business Line*, December 18th, 2006.

3 The War for Talent Heats Up by Richa Govil, Group Manager, Infosys Technologies, October 13, 2006.

fill up the positions generated by the proposed fleet induction. The other industries that are facing severe shortage of skilled manpower are retail and healthcare (biotechnology) industries. Even KPO industry is facing severe talent crunch. The analyst has overestimated the number of skilled workers is India, which is not confronting the estimates. According to the research made by UK research firms, KPO sector may arrive at a size of $5 billion with 1,00,000 people by 2010, which is far away from the projections that have been made earlier as $12

Animation Industry Faces Talent Crunch

It seems that a talent crunch has engulfed most of the sunrise industry—BPOs, KPOs and now, animation. Not long ago, animation was not a rage among career-oriented people, but now it seems to be going through what BPOs experienced earlier. Animation is now emerging as a lucrative career option. According to Nasscom estimates, the animation market in India is pegged at $250 mn. With a 30% annual growth rate, the market is expected to touch $900 mn by '09. Hyderabad-based Nipuna Services, the BPO arm of Satyam Computers, feels that the industry is capable of generating revenues worth $70 bn by '08 globally. According to Raman Madan, regional-manager —animation and desktop video, Southeast Asia and India, Autodesk Media and Entertainment, about 3,000 people are employed in the animation sector in India and the demand is for about 10,000 animators. The reason for the talent crunch, industry observers say, is the absence of animation from the curriculum as a structured course. Also, there are very few training institutes such as MAAC and Maximus, who provide some technical education to aspiring animators. MAAC, an animation training studio, which has about 35 centres across the country, produces 2,000 animators annually. Sachin Bhatnagar, technical head, MAAC, says that big names like UTV, Crest Animation, Prana Studios, Rhythm and Hues, DQ and Prime Focus recruit from their campus. For a fresher to enter this industry, he should be equipped with basic qualities such as creativity and the ability to visualise content on paper, apart from technical expertise. Animation houses are gung-ho about recruiting freshers. UTV Toons has started campus placements from this year. "Unfortunately, many who join this industry are not serious. They come with a perception that they will only be creating some colourful characters. But this is not the case," says Jyotirmoy Saha, VP—animation business development, UTV Toons. He says that people who want to make a career in animation should know that this is not an industry where one can make quick buck. Naresh Jhangiani, head—HR, Nipuna Services echoes a similar sentiment. He says that youngsters who want to join this industry should take it seriously, because a lot of effort goes into the conceptualisation of a character before transforming it into an animation. Career growth in this profession is completely based on the performance of an employee. A fresher can join an animation house at a junior/trainee level with a monthly salary of Rs 8,000-15,000 and can become a character animator or a modelling expert in three-four years. The salary at this level will range between Rs.25,000 and Rs.35,000. One can also earn as much as Rs 1 lakh a month if he has experience of seven years.

Source: Economic Times, May 24th, 2006.

billion with 2,50,000 people. This is due to low employability and increasing number of jobs are not in line with the number of skilled workers[4]. The other sectors like IT, Advertising, Tourism and Aviation are covered elaborately by way of individual articles.

Role of Government in Overcoming Talent Crunch

This problem is not only confined to individual organizations or industries as a whole. Even countries, which have huge population like China and India, are also facing talent shortage. It is important for governments to take active role in overcoming this risk of talent crunch. They are facing this problem over and above what anyone can comprehend. It is necessary for it to rework on the educational facilities that are provided and make them more job relevant. Students who have completed their education from high-quality institutions may be deficient in skills and knowledge required by the organization. Though most of the institutions have English as the medium of instruction, still there is a dearth of individuals who have sufficient skills and ability. Some times because of the opportunities running dry in the home country, there is a scope that talented individuals go abroad. In such case, it is important for the employees to relax their immigration policies to attract the most talented and highly qualified workforce. According to the Bureau of Labor Statistics, by 2010 the US will face shortage of 10,033,000 workers. Even Canadian labor workforce is going to face shortage by 2020[5]. Ageing of workforce has increased the concerns of countries like Japan in facing the problem of talent shortage. Though Canada can compete with other developed countries like US, Europe it is still facing this problem of looming shortage due to lack of suitable talent, wage levels, inadequate training and educational facilities. According to Manpower Talent Shortage Survey, 66% of Canadian employers are under pressure to find qualified personnel.

Many countries like Germany, Canada, Britain and France have made it easier for skilled workers to obtain visa, more work permits and more incentives. A non-demographic shift is also one of the reasons for talent crunch. It is happening

[4] Talent crunch may dim KPO sector prospects , Neha Kaushik, *Hindu Business Line*, August 7th 2006.

[5] How talent crunch is faced by countries like India, China, EU and US is discussed in detailed in the same book in Section-IV wherein it also discusses the role played by the governments of respective countries to overcome the problem.

more because of the baby boomers occupying half of workforce. Whatever may be the reason, it is also better for governments and organizations in including more baby boomers, as they are highly skilled and experienced in view of the fact that they are not having good number of young workforce to replace them. Immobility is making the talented workforce stay at their home countries without moving to places where there is opportunity for high career growth. Government should also improve most of their educational systems and infrastructures. They should provide more incentives for improving educational facilities in rural areas. They should also improve their vocational and educational training facilities and bring them in, line with the country's requirements. According to Manpower it is also necessary for government to include private agencies to look for skilled and talented workforce and provide them good and enhanced training facilities. It claims that many countries like Australia and China has engaged manpower as an outsourcer for recruiting talented workforce and at the same time provides them training services.

Role of Employers in Addressing Talent Crunch

As in the case of governments, other employers have also to play equally important role in addressing this problem. It so happens that employers find good workforce but at the same time they may face more turnover rates. It is important for them to concentrate on not only recruiting the skilled manpower, but at the same time provide them with all benefits that best makes the employees to fit in that organization with the right job that matches their knowledge, skills and abilities. The organization that lack good educational and training facilities have to turn themselves into learning organizations. Companies like Wipro and Satyam have started their own learning centers for their employees learning and development and at the same time they are providing training to their employees. Employers, should also concentrate on hiring underemployed, unemployed, disabled persons, and older workers by creating right environment and providing adequate training facilities to enable them to play active roles in their organizations.

It is also important for employers to encourage older workers to continue their working life in the same organization but reduce their share of stressful work by engaging them in less stressful works like training new young workers, which inturn will increase productivity level of skilled workers. This is possible by way of automation. To put it in a nutshell, employers should provide employees with good training facilities, flexible work environment, rewards for their achievements, bonuses, and help in striking balance between their work and home in order to achieve an overall career development. IBM is one such organization which provides such environment at the same time provides them with benefits that best helps its employees outside work. Survey conducted by SHRM reveals that the share of companies that are taking special measures in attracting and retaining the best workforce has increased from 35% in 2004 to 49% in 2005.

Role of Employees

It is also necessary for individuals (employees too) to play an active role by remaining in responsible positions with required and updated skills to compete for jobs and stay in the same organization for a considerable period of time. Individuals have to realize that it is high time for them to have the right skills and acquaint themselves with latest developments in their field of specialization through training and development. Employees who have joined the company right at the time of incorporation may have the right skills and knowledge to do their job. However, they need to take an initiative to update themselves, where ever and whenever necessary, with the latest skills and expertise to survive in the same organization even after a decade. They have to review their career plans, their interests and see that it matches the role they are playing in the current organization and if necessary take the help of their human resource department for training and counseling. These days many companies are providing variety of training facilities both for freshers as well as for those who have already been part of the organization, so that they can have a thorough knowledge of the job and its process. Infosys has started providing four types of training to its employees: technical training, quality process training, personal effectiveness and management development program and infosys leadership systems[6]. It has also received "Excellence in Practice Award" which rated infosys as the best in providing training to its employees. In 2005 infosys started "Infosys U" to further strengthen its training facilities to employees. Experienced employees may upgrade themselves with the process that now exists in the organization, which helps them in

[6] Infosys Technologies – Training for Retaining, Ruchi Mankad, IBS Ahmedabad, 2006.

completing their work fast and at the same time increasing their productivity and reaching their goals.

Conclusion

To minimize this crisis of talented personnel, organizations have started implementing effective strategies to deal with new face of talent management. Hema Ravichandar, strategic HR Consultant, expects three key trends to emerge in 2007: Remote working and related practices like flexi time and satellite hubs; retention bonuses; and the recall of retired professionals in the face of inadequate middle management maturity (Rajiv Shirali, 2006). Besides, even governments are revising their educational systems and rules, which best suit the talented workforce and making them stay at their home country, instead of going global. Even HR managers, who play an important role in overcoming this crunch, are taking an initiative to provide attractive benefits to employees.

(E Mrudula is working as a Consulting Editor at Icfai Books.)

References

1. A Anand, "Competing for Talent: The War Intensifies", *MBA Review,* February 2007.
2. Ruchi Mankad, "Infosys Technologies – Training for Retaining", Icfai Business School, Ahmedabad, 2006.
3. Priyanka Vyas, Retaining talent, *Hindu Business Line,* December 18th, 2006.
4. The War for Talent Heats Up by Richa Govil, Group Manager, Infosys Technologies, October 13, 2006.
5. Confronting the Coming Talent Crunch: What's Next? , Manpower Inc., 2006.
6. The battle for brainpower, *Economist,* October 5th 2006.
7. Talent Shortages Give Organizations a Handicap, Kellye Whitney.
8. Rajiv Shirali, "Important lessons for HR Managers", December 28th, 2006.
9. Labour Force Ageing and Skill Shortages in Canada and Ontario, Julie Ann McMullin and Martin Cooke with Rob Downie, Canadian Policy Research Networks Inc., 2004.

2

BOOK REVIEW

Workforce Crisis: How to Beat the Coming Shortage of Skills and Talent

Chitra Mukunnan

The book focuses on optimum utilization of three cohorts—the mature, the mid-career and the young workers—so as to avoid the crisis of the shortage of skills. The demographic and related trends that will affect corporations and their workforces have been covered in this book. The three cohorts have different skills to enhance the organizational effectiveness.

The authors, Ken Dychtwald, Tamara J Erickson and Robert Morison, in the book *Workforce Crisis*, have cautioned the organizations on the emerging shortage of talent and skills. This perplexing problem can be tackled by focusing on the three cohorts—the mature, the mid-career and the young workers. They gave many examples of corporations who have already adapted various ways to engage the diverse workforce. After many years of research, the authors have narrowed down on some innovative strategies for rewriting the "employment deal" and leveraging the talent of the people.

The world, according to the authors is gripped by three phenomena—the baby boom, the longevity boom and the birth dearth, and a reality—the workforce crisis. The shortage of skills coupled with shortage of workers is alarming. The labor market, like any other stock market, is volatile and can move in unprecedented directions. Workforce disruptors like diversity in gender, ethnicity, education, family, aspirations, loyalty are not only dynamic in nature but also impact differently. Many organizations ignore the shift in paradigm rather than address it and prepare for the transformation. Managing workforce supply and demand carries greater magnitude, urgency and complexity than ever before. Proactive "smart organizations" being aware of the challenges, make necessary adjustments in time. They improve business performance, cost structures and employee retention, by adopting effective management techniques and employment practices suitable for today and tomorrow. Hence, business leaders of today must focus on a coherent and forward looking workforce strategy to hire and maintain the best talent during turbulence and shortage. By considering workforce as supply, demand and opportunity, organizations can leverage demographics to strengthen relationships with customers and enhance their own capabilities.

In the era of ageless workers, it has become imperative that organizations should become multi-generational. The book elaborates on the necessity of engaging the three cohorts—the mature, the mid-career and the young workers. The authors have elucidated the ways to hold the attention of the three cohorts. When an employee is less than fully engaged in work—energy, focus and contribution are left on the table—the productivity is lost, never to be recovered. The profiles of the three cohorts are strikingly different and hence there is no "blanket strategy" applicable to engage them. The mature workers who have rich experience and knowledge and want a shift in their trajectory remain more focused. They strongly believe that age is no bar for accomplishment as the jobs are becoming less physically strenuous. The sandwiched, ripe mid-career workers are yearning for a change as their careers have stalled; pressures of work have become doubled, and work by itself has become a routine. It will be beneficial to companies to turn these unfocused employees into reenergized employees as shortage of skills and labor is inevitable. The restless young workers, who were not given proper responsibility, want to contribute immediately, grab responsibility, collaborate in decision making and manage their own performance. Organizations invest time and effort in grooming them but without an iota of guilt complex, these youngsters are always on the look out for a better deal. For retaining this digital workforce, apart from retention tactics, organizations will have to become more flexible to meet the changing needs, expectations and aspirations of the young blood.

Leveraging the mature, rekindling the mid-career and retaining the young are the challenges that are faced by organizations. Organizations must have unbiased hiring practices and should embrace a culture that acknowledges mature workers. The leadership potential of mature workers cannot be ignored. They are also keen on improving their own skills. Workforce strategy and execution of the same is necessary to optimize the services of mature workers, as it is their ability that matters and not the age. The strategy must begin with the hiring of the mature workers, bringing them in a flexible retirement scheme and simplifying the regulations in pension and benefit laws. The authors have given a thirteen-action formula to leverage mature workers. To rekindle the passion for work and reenergize the mid-career workers, apart from career changes, mentoring roles, sabbaticals and expanding leadership development, the authors have also recommended a nine-action plan. In order to avert a major shortage of skills and labor due to boomer retirement, organizations have to act swiftly by systematically retaining and recruiting people. Retention of young talent is a must and it is also a challenge. It is through rapid incorporation, continuous retention and with an easy return policy, the young can be lured to contribute and stay in the organization. Apart from the three 'S's (Say, Stake and Stimulus) and the three 'R's (Responsibility, Recognition and Respect), they must also have an attentive management, able to understand their attitude and their way of life to nurture and keep them engaged. Their thirst for learning cannot be ignored and they are always on the hunt for new opportunities. Excelling at retention is a key success factor for any organization. The authors have very explicitly mentioned the action to be taken to retain the young go-getters who are so different from the mature and the mid-career workers.

The need to establish an employment deal with the three cohorts is also covered. The importance of tailoring working arrangements to suit the requirement of the employees is also emphasized. All the three cohorts like flexible working arrangements with flexible time, reduced time or flexible place but for different reasons. Flexible work arrangements can entail many levels of change—managerial, organizational, operational and cultural. To put the system into practical effect which has in-built job satisfaction, employee engagement, employee commitment, help in retention, and the nature of work has a huge role to play. This arrangement has to be carefully implemented, for an employee adapting to a flexible working can have a cascading effect on the working of other employees in the organization. To bring the success, the authors have listed out ten levers—policy, employee commitment, management commitment, workforce planning, technology, training and orientation, teamwork, decision-making, communication, and information dissemination—which have to be assessed and examined in importance and performance to determine the true fit and what actions should be taken to succeed. The authors are confident that, by assessing the situation, pursuing the business goals, establishing pragmatic policies and practices and by enabling the transition to flex-work, organizations will be able to reap the benefit of business.

In the survey conducted by the authors, employees expressed their desire to learn but the opportunities to learn are rarely provided by the employer. Hence, to get rid of this misnomer, it is imperative that employers must provide scope for an employee to learn. Organizations should incline towards becoming a learning organization. The differences in learning styles of the three cohorts are very pronounced and organizations must realize this and thus make delivery of learning methods flexible. Organizations should make learning experiences as a means of bridging generation gap, fostering mutual understanding and sharing knowledge, which will lead to organizational cohesion. Though organizations can adopt their own ways to become learning workplaces, yet the authors have listed out some approaches and actions that could be implemented for success.

Performance management, is to identify, assess, motivate and reward employee performance with an emphasis on recognizing top performers. The performance management system should also be flexible and responsive to the needs and styles of employees and employee segments. There are several litmus tests to gauge a performance system for its transparency, accuracy and other relevant qualities. Though all factors of performance management are important, the authors have dealt upon only compensation and benefits—the core of all performance management system. Compensation and benefits awarded should be customized to meet the needs of the young, the mid-career and the mature workers. The preferences of the three can vary depending on the age, generational attributes and where they tend to be in their careers. Though customization for each employee is good and the best, it may not be practicable. The limitations can be overcome by employee segmentation, proper combination and integration. To bring about optimal performance, the rewards and benefits of working should be clear, fair and accessible by tying it to measurable performance. The four basic actions suggested by the authors can maximize the effectiveness of compensation and benefits.

Importance of analyzing workplace and anticipating the needs of the employees is also stressed. When work lacks elements like stimulation, variety, edification, connection, control and value, employees tend to recast their roles. A satisfied worker need not be an engaged worker, for, satisfaction does not equal engagement. While satisfaction is about sufficiency, engagement is about commitment and passion. Hence, all employers must go a step further and ensure that the employees are not only satisfied but also engaged. Work design makes or breaks productivity and good work design mixes human skill and automation to get the best of both. Companies should enrich and enlarge jobs. An apt workforce information and assessment will help to identify the need, attitudes, aspirations and satisfaction levels. This will help in proper segmentation of the employee and thus employee performance and potential can be harnessed. Opportunistic inquiry of new hires, failed hires, departing employees, mature workers and high-potential employees can enlighten the employers on how to make work more meaningful and thereby engage employees. A proper segmentation—age wise, generation wise, life stage wise, lifestyle wise, and work stage wise—will foster better engagement. The workforce analysis is an ongoing process and involves five basic steps—diagnose, assess, review, envision and move forward. Workforce crisis can be averted by setting strategies that will provide the right management practices ahead of the point of necessity and reap the short and long-term benefits of superior talent supply.

Book Excerpts

13 Action Formula to Leverage Mature Workers

- Develop a mature worker strategy by setting specific goals for mature worker retention.
- Assess recruiting channels and explore non-traditional sources.
- Review job descriptions and remove tacit references to employee age.
- Review and adjust interviewing and hiring practices.
- Review and adjust human resources practices generally.
- Build a reputation as an active recruiter and a good employer of mature workers.
- Assess mature workers' interest in flexible retirement.
- Adjust pension calculations and employee benefits.
- Establish a systematic retiree-return program.
- Institute procedures for career deceleration.
- Articulate the desired public policy and legislative changes.
- Lobby policy makers and legislators directly.
- Work with the union leaders.

This book focuses on the impact on the labor force due to the retirement of the baby boomer generation. This can, according to the authors bring about a skill shortage, which can be overcome by a multi-generational employment approach by the organizations. Just recruiting is not the answer to the problem of skill shortage. By identifying the aspirations, needs, desires of the three cohorts and then leveraging, rekindling, and retaining them through flexible working arrangements, innovative learning opportunities and creative compensation and benefits program, the coming shortage of skills and talent can be obviated.

(Ken Dychtwald, a visionary on the lifestyle, marketing and workforce implications on an aging population, is the founder and CEO of Age Wave, a firm focused on maturing workforce. Tamara J Erickson is an executive officer and member of the board of directors for The Concours Group, a management consulting, research, and education firm. He is an advisor on the organizational and strategic implications of the changing workforce. Robert Morison is an executive vice president and the Director of Research of The Concours Group.)

(Chitra Mukunnan, Facuty Member, The Icfai Business School, Chennai.)

3

Retaining Talent: Challenges to HRM

Vineet Tandon

With the economy experiencing robust growth, the role of HR managers has become more arduous. The challenge of acquiring new talent and retaining the existing talent is only going to intensify. What's the road ahead for HR managers?

Remember the song in the movie, Titanic—"Every night in my dream I see you". Now this is just the song most HR managers are singing today, which if we rephrase will be like: "Every night in my dream I see some people leaving the organization and I am again calling my headhunter to fill in the newly created gap". Well it may not rhyme like a song, but one can put oneself in an HR manager's shoes to know what he is going through.

The attrition rate of employees in organizations is alarming. Take any industry, any sector, any organization and you can find more than enough examples of employees joining and leaving their workplace. All this adds to the worry of HR managers who are only left with the option of scratching their heads and singing No Mercy's all-time hit—"Where do you go?"

As a HR manager, one may be able to find out as to which company an employee may be joining, but many other questions like why do employees not

Source: Effective Executive, April 2006.

stick to one company? Why do they leave? etc., remain unanswered forever. Hence, the regular merry-go-round of hiring and training continues.

Present Scenario

The Sensex is at an all-time high—Q3 results across the sectors have shown impressive performance; markets have been booming with IPOs queuing up; and consumer confidence is becoming rock solid. It can only get better and better. Everywhere there is a wave of optimism and the economy is expected to grow at the rate of around 8%.

With India becoming the cynosure for global giants, the boom across sectors is going to create a sure-shot supply crunch of talented workforce. So the challenge for today's HR managers is not only to fill the demand for emerging job openings but also to retain the existing workforce. HR managers have to gear up to retain their workforce, or face the consequences of losing their valuable manpower.

Let's look at the scenario of skilled labor in the two upcoming sectors:

Retail Industry

Analysts point out that the domestic retail industry has an estimated market size of $202.6 bn, which is expected to grow at a Compounded Annual Growth Rate (CAGR) of 30% in the next five years.

New forms of retailing such as departmental stores, hypermarkets, supermarkets and specialty stores are evolving and the share of the organized retail industry is likely to grow from its current 2% to 15-20% over the next decade.

This retail boom is expected to translate into eight million new jobs over the next five to six years.

Animation Industry

According to a forecast by NASSCOM, the digital content industry would reach a size of Rs.10,000 cr, in 2008, employing over 1 lakh people. It further pegged the revenue per employee in this sector at $15,000 and average offshore salary at $7,000 by 2008.

The same is the story across sectors. Be it IT/ITES, Pharmaceuticals or Aviation, the supply and demand of skilled labor is going to be a major concern for HR managers in the days to come.

Manpower Employment Outlook

Manpower, which conducts surveys of employers on a quarterly basis, expects robust hiring across sectors, in the fourth quarter with the greatest expectations reported by services employers (+45%)—the most optimistic for the second consecutive quarter—followed by employers in Finance/Insurance/Real Estate (+43%); Public Administration and Education (+43%); Mining and Construction (+39%); and, Manufacturing (+38%). Net Employment Outlook for the Wholesale and Retail Trade sector is expected to be +33% while the same for Transportation and Utilities—relatively the least optimistic—-has a healthy outlook of +32%.

While the above figures are indicative of the fact that many jobs will be available, equally true is the fact that demand for skilled labor will shoot astronomically. Retaining skilled employees will be a major concern for the industry and a formidable challenge for HR managers.

Moreover, executive movements are not just at any specific tier of management. Right from the management trainees to senior level management, executive movements are prevalent. Gone are the days when people used to stick to one organization for their entire lifetime. Today, being in an organization for more than a year means either the person is not really ambitious or something else is wrong.

A look at the people movement section of the website *www.exchange4media.com* reveals that around 40 executive movements took place in the month of January 2006 alone. Almost 45 executive movements were reported for December 2005. Here I would like to clarify that people movement listed on this website are all high-flier and top-rung executive movements. Also, these movements have primarily taken place in media/advertising and telecom sectors alone. One can easily imagine the number of middle-rung and lower-level executive movements that would have taken place during this period across other sectors and other levels of corporate hierarchy.

Why is this Happening?

Let's look at some of the possible reasons of increasing executive movements:

Changing Lifestyles

Lifestyles have changed considerably since the past. People prefer to break away from the monotony of doing the same job over and over again. Now, it's about new jobs every coming year, new responsibilities, and new work environments. People today think fast, act fast and change their jobs faster. I once read a powerful statement which said: "In today's world you have to run faster to remain at the same place." Nowadays everyone is in a rush. While some are busy climbing the corporate ladder, others are busy trying to prevent them from reaching the top. And mind you, all this is happening in a 24x7 environment!

Death of Motivation

I still remember the motivation theories we were taught in Organizational Behavior during our MBA tenure. While motivation theories have evolved from Maslow's Hierarchy of Needs to Equity Theories of Motivation, my personal opinion is that there is no such thing called motivation. Everyone is looking for a better deal. Therefore, may I suggest that we should have something called "the Deal Theory of Motivation," according to which whoever gives the best deal takes away the best talent. No matter what the job context or job content is, offer the best deal and your corporate headquarters will be buzzing with the best brains in the industry.

Increased Expectations

Executives' expectations have grown manifold. While one might have just passed out of college and joined a company as a management trainee, the expectations are already skyrocketing. He not only wants the best salary in the industry but also likes to have a corporate laptop, mobile connection, and club memberships. It's not whether the above expectations are reasonable or not, it's about whether your company can offer the same or not. So, while an executive may join you for a better salary, he may also leave you for a better opportunity offered next month. (Deal theory again!)

Increasing Opportunities

Another prominent reason for executives leaving a company is the rise in opportunities. Have a look around and you will find plenty of opportunities. While earlier job opportunities existed only in traditional industries, today, a large number of opportunities exist in non-traditional industries as well. People are no longer restricting themselves to becoming a doctor or an engineer or just a plain MBA graduate. People are increasingly opting for varied career options. Today, we have SPA managers, lifestyle experts, fashion designers, image consultants, nutritionists and what not. Besides, a lot of people are working in the corporate environment for a period of few years just to gain experience and establish contacts only to start their own ventures a few years down the line. Therefore, no matter what the perks your company offers, people will stay in the organization only till they want to; thereafter, no deals will work for them.

Assignments Abroad

People still have a fancy for overseas assignments and anyone getting a better prospect and opportunity for an assignment abroad will more often than not accept the offer. People today are looking for international exposure, and any such exposure will help them expand their network and vision besides having a pay package in terms of dollars. And who is not going to cherish such an opportunity!

Decreasing Loyalty towards Organizations

Employee loyalty towards the organization has decreased considerably. Executives today are only loyal to their career and future prospects and loyalty towards organizations is hardly existent. Whatever the reason, decline in loyalty is one of the challenges not many HR managers will be able to solve successfully.

Job Misfit

Another reason for executive movements is the job misfit. Sometimes in an effort to fill the gap, people are recruited fast without taking into consideration the job and competency fit. It only results in loss of man-hours and repetition of the whole process. While such cases of job misfit can be minimized by careful selection of candidates, clarity of role and career objective is also needed on the part of the person seeking a job. Executives sometimes join a company to get a brand name on their resume rather than for the work they are supposed to do.

Besides the above cited reasons, there could be many other reasons for executive movements. Some would like to have an MBA degree from a university abroad and would like to discontinue with the job, while others might just do it for want of a better salary. While some may discontinue to start something on their own, others might want to take a break, only to return after a period of time. The reasons will vary from person to person; however, the concerns for HR managers will continue to exist.

So, is there a way out? I remember the title of Robert Schuller's book: Tough Times Never Last, But Tough People Do. It's certainly a tough time for HR managers, but they've got to be tough enough to overcome the challenges. Here there are two challenges for HR managers: Attracting the best talent, and retaining the best talent. Let us look at these separately.

Talent Acquisition

There is a limit to which one can source good talent. With the economy booming and supply for talented skill sets being limited, there is going to be a supply crunch. So how does one match up to the demand for skilled labor? There is little HR managers can do to spruce up the supply of talented workforce. This as a whole needs participation from the industry as well as the government. No industry operates in vacuum, and therefore, to ensure that the industry gets a dedicated workforce, all the players need to play a collaborative role.

Unless the demand for talented workforce is tapped by training and educating the upcoming generation, there will only be poaching of talent. Also, there is a limit to which the "Deal Theory of Motivation" will work. No corporate can endlessly go on giving more and more perks and skyrocketing pay packages. After all, the very purpose of corporate survival is to make profits! There is a need to draw a balance between what is just and what is unjust. So what should the HR managers do for talent acquisition? Well, they should try to increase industry and academia interface so as to make sure that there is a ready supply of talented workforce for the future corporate requirements.

Corporates should come forward and create customized programs for training students and executives. More and more academic and industry interface must be organized and opportunities for on-the-job training should increase. The government should also try to facilitate the process of increasing educational opportunities, but the process will remain incomplete without the industry collaborating with the academia. Unless and until a collaborative effort is made by the government, academia, and industry, it is difficult to create a pool of knowledgeable workforce and transition to a knowledgeable economy will remain a distant reality.

Talent Retention

While talent acquisition needs collaborative effort from the industry, the academia, and the government, talent retention is a corporate prerogative. Companies need to design systems and processes, which will make people love their organization. But why will people love their organization when they place themselves above anything else? It's true that people think of themselves first, but it's equally true that most of us have basic fundamental needs.

While salaries, perks, challenges, designations, and foreign assignments may drive people for sometime, most of the people also seek stability for themselves. Therefore, an HR manager needs to identify and create systems and processes that will retain employees. More often than not, most jobs tend to become repetitive, and therefore, job escalation (assigning newer responsibilities) is something that HR managers need to look at. However, any new responsibility or task needs to be in sync with individual personality and expectations. Therefore, competency mapping (for proper selection of employees) along with personality-JD (Job Description) adjustment will go a long way in helping HR managers.

(Vineet Tandon is working as Senior Communication Analyst at Oracle Corporation. He can be reached at vineet.tandon@gmail.com)

4

It's 2008: Do You Know Where Your Talent Is?

Why Acquisition and Retention Strategies Don't Work

Robin Athey

Globalization is a force for both collaboration and competition. It is also proving to be a contest for resources—natural and human. In an age in which growth is largely a product of creative and technological advancements, companies that want to dominate their industries must be able to attract and retain talented employees. They must also engage people like never before if they want to innovate and grow. Only those companies that win the hearts and minds of their top talent will be able to deliver value over both short and long terms. Companies must continually train and develop employees if they are to keep pace with the speed and complexity of technological innovation. Individuals need greater flexibility in their career paths, and organizations need greater flexibility from employees. People must connect across businesses, divisions, and regions in ways that promote high quality decisions and fast

execution. This article presents the scope and range of emerging talent crisis. It also compares the traditional talent management process with the model developed by Deloitte.

Despite millions of unemployed workers, there is an acute shortage of talent: science educators to teach the next generation of chemists, health care professionals of all stripes, design engineers with deep technical and interpersonal skills, and seasoned marketers who understand the Chinese marketplace. Resumes abound, yet companies still feverishly search for the people who make the difference between 10 percent and 20 percent annual growth, or between profit and loss. Critical talent is scarce, and about to become much more scarce because of two looming trends: the retirement of the baby boom generation and a growing skills gap.

By "critical talent," we refer to the groups and individuals that drive a disproportionate share of their company's business performance and generate greater-than-average value for customers and shareholders. A company's critical talent possesses highly developed skills and deep knowledge—not just of the work itself but also of "how to make things happen" in the organization. Without these people, organizations could not achieve their strategies. (See Box, "Who is Critical Talent?")

Who Is Critical Talent?

The nature of critical talent varies by industry or organization. In large pharmaceutical organizations, for example, "blockbuster drugs" are the engine to fuel growth. In 2004, Pfizer's top 10 products each generated more than $1 billion in sales. Needless to say, Pfizer pays particular attention to the researchers and clinicians who drive this development.[1]

At $24 billion FedEx, one analysis suggested that the couriers who pick up and deliver packages might be more critical than the pilots who fly the packages through the night. The couriers have direct contact with the customer and must make continual decisions that impact the efficiency and effectiveness of the supply chain, such as how to reconfigure a route and how long to wait for a customer's packages.[2]

We are not necessarily referring to the "A players" or senior executives who command the highest salaries. More often we're talking about employees who

> Research suggests that a company's "stars" are the first to be poached by competitors and are less likely to stay. Moreover, a study of investment banks found that when imported from elsewhere, stars rarely sustain their performance in the new organization.[3]

don't end up in the annual report. They include the scientists and clinicians who discover and develop the blockbuster drugs that fuel pharmaceutical companies' growth. In the oil industry, they include the geologists and petroleum engineers who find and extract oil. In manufacturing, they include the machinists who perform precision manufacturing to Six Sigma standards. And in retailing, they may be the inventory managers who get the right good in the right stores at the right time.

When the knowledge and skills of critical talent become scarce, recruiting wars erupt. Many leading companies fight these wars differently. They do not succumb to bidding wars, knowing that the "star" who chases high offers will be out the door as soon as the next higher one rolls in. Nor do they bribe talent to stay, knowing that monetary incentives do not foster long-term commitment; worse still, they can mask discontent that infects others. Rather than focus on acquiring and retaining talent, talent savvy organizations support their key people on the issues they care about most: doing work that engages them, learning how to do it even better, encountering fresh challenges, and interacting with people in positive ways.

Firms like Microsoft, Southwest Airlines, and SAS Institute are exemplary in the way they nurture and manage critical talent. They go to surprising lengths to help these employees tap into their core skills and passions. They expect continuous learning and growth and know that the most important lessons don't take place in the classroom, but on the job. They also understand that positive relationships raise the performance of critical talent to new levels.

Crunch Time for Critical Talent

In just a few years, two emerging trends will force organizations to start paying unprecedented attention to their critical talent. The first is the retirement of Baby Boomers, the first crop of which will retire in 2008. Their impact will soon be felt. In automotive manufacturing, for example, up to 40 percent of managers will be eligible to retire within the next five years. In the public sector, countries such as Canada, Australia, and the United States could lose more than a third of their government employees by 2010. Retirees are also draining much of the working blood out of health care, with shortages of nurses and pharmacists particularly acute.

> CEOs of successful companies are worried about the dwindling supply of talent. They are twice as likely as CEOs of less successful companies to cite the "availability of managers/executives" as a top concern.[4]

Meanwhile, many schools are having trouble meeting the demand for qualified candidates. They struggle with limited capacity, obsolete educational models, declining educational standards, and a general shift among students away from "hard skill" disciplines, such as science and engineering. In fact, the US Department of Education estimates that 60 percent of all new jobs in the 21st century will require skills that are possessed by only 20 percent of the current workforce.[5]

> **The Rise of Talent Markets**
>
> CEOs rely heavily on finance and marketing. Yet these "decision sciences" are relatively new.[6] Finance sprang forth from accounting with the rise of capital markets. Similarly, marketing evolved from sales with the increasing sophistication of customer and product markets.
>
> Today, talent is the scare resource, giving rise to talent markets. Yet there is no "decision science" to help leaders optimize their talent decisions. John Boudreau at the University of Southern California and his research partner Pete Ramstad argue that this is a critical step in the evolution of HR. HR executives often define their efforts in terms of policies and programs. Instead, they must provide analytical insights and support to help leaders *improve* their talent decisions, not just *implement* them.[7] We agree.

The Sad Statistics of the Global Labor Pool

By 2008, a wealth of skills and experience will begin to disappear from the job market. The first members of the Baby Boom generation will turn 62, which is the average retirement age in the large, developed economies of North America, Europe and Asia. Over the next 15 years, 80 percent of their workforce growth will occur among people 50 years or older. By 2050, 40 percent of Europe's total population and 60 percent of its working age population will be people over 60.[8] With mounting pension obligations and shrinking workforces, Germany, Italy,

> "We are about to face a demographically driven shortfall in labor that will make the late 1990s seem like a minor irritation."
>
> – Anthony Carnevale, Former Chairman of the National Commission for Employment Policy.

Spain, and Japan could face economic crises. As management guru Peter Drucker has suggested, the confluence of a bulging aged population and a shrinking supply of youth is unlike anything that has happened since the dying centuries of the Roman empire.[9]

Four industries in particular will suffer a mass exodus of employees: health care, manufacturing, energy, and the public sector. The Australian health care system, for example, expects 31,000 vacancies to go unfilled by 2006. The United States sees a shortage of more than 1 million nurses by the year 2012. More than 80 percent of US manufacturers face a shortage of qualified machinists, craft workers, and technicians. The magnitude of the situation has prompted the National Association of Manufacturers to warn its members that they may soon face a serious labor crisis.[10] As these and other industries compete for talent, they will constrain the available supply for others.

The shortage of workers is not just one of retiring Baby Boomers. A massive skills gap makes it worse. A staggering example is occurring in science and engineering. In the United States, colleges will graduate only 198,000 students to fill the shoes of 2 million Baby Boomers scheduled to retire between 1998 and 2008, according to NASA projections. Likewise, the Bureau of Labor Statistics projects that more than 300,000 of the 1.3 million new IT jobs to be created between 1996 and 2006 will go unfilled.

Why won't colleges fill the skills gap? The problem is one of waning student interest, institutional capacity, and the quality of education. Not enough students in large developed economies are pursuing science and engineering. While 42 percent of students in China earn undergraduate degrees in science and engineering, only 5 percent of US students do so. In Germany, once celebrated for its streams of innovation and Nobel Prize winners, the number of engineering graduates has declined by almost a third since 1995, to about 36,000—one-tenth the number produced by Chinese universities. The waning interest among German students was one of the motives behind Siemens' recent decision to turn

> SAS's CEO Jim Goodnight is passionate about educational reform. He remarks that in the United States, "All corporations should get involved in the school system. The future of our country is in producing highly educated people. Otherwise we'll lose our high-tech jobs to India and China." So far, the action behind his words has resulted in SAS in School, Internet-based software for classroom use, and the establishment of a private school that he hopes will be modeled for its small classes and *extensive use of technology.*[12]

to Beijing to develop its new cell phones.[11] This trend will likely continue, fueling the rise of global talent markets.

In other areas of specialized education, such as information technology and nursing, schools simply can't meet demand. Faculty shortages in computer science departments, for example, have reached crisis proportions, seriously curbing the supply of qualified job candidates.

Figure 1: Projected Change in the Working-Age Population (15-64) 1970-2010 and 2010-2050

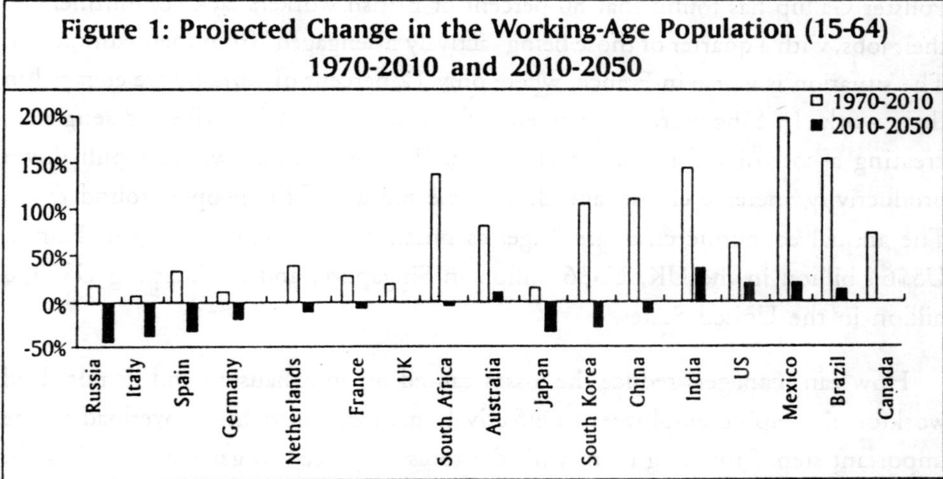

The workforce outlook in Europe and parts of Asia is worrisome. Economic growth may be signifcantly hampered by a shrinking workforce in the coming years. The situation in the Americas appears better. But consumer demand is projected to grow as the overall population ages. Organizations seeking a piece of that growth may feel pressured to achieve higher performance with fewer people.

Perhaps the most disturbing factor of all, though, is declining educational standards. Many schools are not keeping pace with the increasing complexity and rapid technological change facing organizations today. Others are simply not graduating enough students. In the United States, only 70 percent of high school students graduate, and only 32 percent leave high school qualified to attend four-year colleges. For African-Americans and Latinos, the graduation rate is about 50 percent, and less than 20 percent have the qualifications necessary to continue their education at the college level.[13]

The result: fewer and lower-quality workers, especially in areas that require high levels of skill and education. Large organizations that wish to expand and strengthen their employment base at home may have to take it upon themselves to close the skills gap.

The Disengaged Employee

Waves of downsizing, employer demands, job disenchantment, and technologies that keep employees plugged into their jobs both day and night have taken their toll. If recent surveys are an indication, more than half the workforce is fed up. Pollster Gallup has found that 80 percent of British workers lack commitment to their jobs, with a quarter of those being "actively disengaged" from their workplaces. The situation is worse in France, where only 12 percent of workers are engaged in their work. In Singapore, 17 percent of the work force is actively disengaged, creating a corrosive force in organizations.[14] Disenchanted workers pull down productivity, increase churn, and darken the morale of the people around them. The annual economic costs are huge: as much as 100 billion Euros in France, US$64 billion in the UK, US$6 billion in Singapore, and a whopping US$350 billion in the United States.[15]

How can managers reduce the losses caused by an exhausted and demoralized workforce? Helping employees to effectively manage information overload is one important step. Providing them with the tools they need to get their job done in the most effective way possible is another. Redesigning jobs and working conditions are other important interventions, along with ensuring that key people are effectively developed and well-deployed. But a crucial and often overlooked source of disengagement comes down to workplace relationships. Emerging research suggests that workplace toxicity may trump other factors when it comes to employee morale and performance. The first step in tackling workforce discontent may involve looking in the mirror. The number one reason for why people leave depends upon the relationship with their boss. Rather than dive headlong into technology based solutions to ameliorate work overload and stress, organizations may want to kick off their talent strategies by first examining the deployment and development of the people tasked with leading others.

Shortcomings of Current Approaches to Managing Talent

When labor gets tight, most organizations hunt for external candidates to fill their most critical jobs ("acquisition") and try to convince current employees to stay ("retention"). These companies offer money, perks, and new challenges. But this is more of a knee-jerk response than a clear strategy. Sometimes it works. But more often it delays, or even fuels, the inevitable churn of good people. (See Figure 2, "The Traditional Talent Management Process.")

In particular, companies place too much attention on "acquiring" talent, the front-end of the process. The typical US company spends nearly 50 times more to recruit a $100,000 professional than it will invest in his annual training after he comes aboard.[16] In part, this is understandable. It is far easier to phone an executive search firm or post openings on a Web site than it is to "grow" someone into a position or to deal with the internal politics of redeploying people from within.

Figure 2: The Traditional Talent Management Process

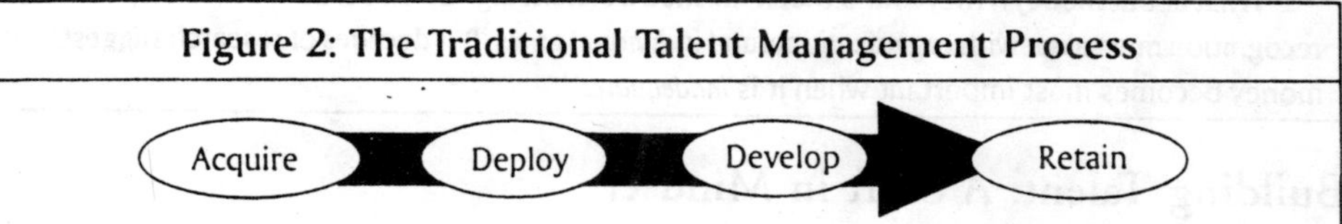

Organizations focus their energy on "acquiring" and "retaining" critical talent—especially when talent is scarce. This focus on the end points is problematic for many reasons. To begin, the resulting process is linear because employees are often ignored once they are recruited into an organization or project. As such, they can become pigeonholed without the opportunity for redeployment. Instead, individuals need flexibility to try on new roles and organizations need flexibility to shift to marketplace demands. Attraction and retention are important metrics, or outcomes. But to be effective, talent management strategies must be built around the thingsthat generate the most value and matter most to employees—the "customers" of this process. That is, their development and deployment—and connection to others.

Source: Deloitte Research, 2004.

But such shortcuts are costly. The average cost to replace an employee is one and a half times his/her average salary. New candidates can take a year or more to master their jobs. Moreover, a company that focuses on external talent can erode the commitment of internal candidates who perceive a bias against them.

Common retention approaches are problematic, too. Often, they are driven by simple metrics such as employee turnover. But while churn at a company may fall from 10 percent to 5 percent from one year to another, it may hide the fact that critical employees are pouring out the door. Furthermore, the numbers say nothing about why people leave. In exit interviews, those leaving frequently resist giving the true reasons for their departures for fear of burning bridges. Finally, turnover does not measure people's commitment to the company. When jobs are scarce, it is easy to retain a noncommitted workforce.

As a result, by focusing on the end points of managing talent (acquisition and retention) rather than on the middle ones (deployment and development), organizations ignore the things that matter most to employees. When this happens, companies set themselves up for inevitable churn, which becomes especially hazardous in a tight labor market.

A Conference Board study asked employees what they expected from their employers. The top three responses were: 1. Interesting, challenging work 2. Open, two-way communication 3. Opportunities for growth and development.

What about money? They found that it finished a distant eighth. This makes sense. Rewards and recognition must align with organizational and individual goals. But decades of research suggest that money becomes most important when it is *inadequate.*[17]

Building Talent: A Shift in Mindset

A growing number of successful companies, such as Microsoft, Southwest Airlines, and SAS, are taking more than their fair share of the talent marketplace and cultivating high performers in key positions through a very different method. Rather than starting with recruiters, they first look inside to match employee experience and aspirations to the company's evolving strategic needs. This doesn't mean that they ignore external talent. They take recruiting seriously, in large part to achieve ambitious growth targets. But their historically low turnover rates let them spend much less time battling churn—and a lot more time outmaneuvering the competition.

As the competition for critical talent heats up, organizations must rethink the ways they manage these people. To begin, they must identify the segments of the workforce that drive their current and future growth. Then, rather than focusing on metrics and outcomes ("acquisition" and "retention"), they must concentrate on the things that employees care about most: *developing* in ways that stretch their capabilities, *deploying* onto work that engages their heads and hearts, and *connecting* to the people who will help them achieve their objectives. By focusing on these three things, attraction and retention largely take care of themselves. In the next three sections, we will describe how this model of *develop, deploy,* and *connect* really works, and why it helps companies generate superior performance.

Figure 3: The Develop-Deploy-Connect Model

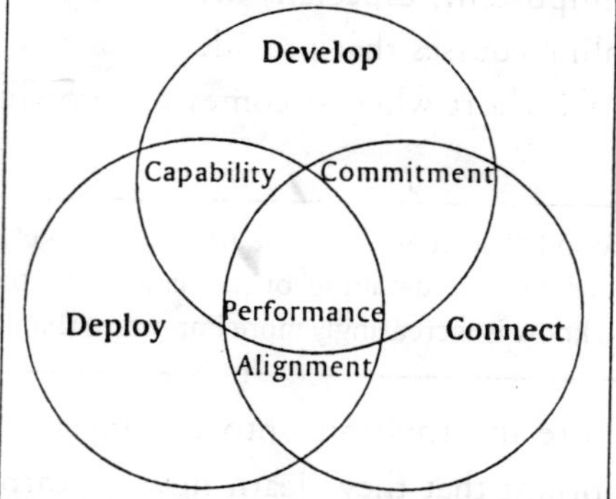

The Develop-Deploy-Connect model should be at the core of an organization's talent strategy. By focusing on these three elements, organizations can generate capability, commitment, and alignment in key workforce segments, which in turn improve business performance. When this happens, the attraction and retention of skilled talent largely take care of themselves.

Source: Deloitte Research, 2004

By "develop," we mean providing the real-life learning employees need, to master a job. We don't mean just traditional classroom or online education. As importantly, we mean the "trial by fire" experiences that stretch their capabilities and the lessons they learn from peers, mentors, and others.

By "deploy," we mean working with key individuals to (a) identify their deep-rooted skills, interests, and knowledge, (b) find their best fit in the organization, and (c) craft the job design and conditions that help them to perform.

By "connect," we mean providing critical employees with the tools and guidance they need to (a) build networks that enhance individual and organizational performance, and (b) improve the quality of their interactions with others.

Develop

The vanishing supply of talent will force many companies to take a hard look at how they develop key people. Gone are the days when companies were satisfied to find loyal, hardworking candidates. Instead, they need a mix of highly analytical people with technological savvy, creativity, global know-how, adaptability, and great communication skills to collaboratively solve complex and rapidly changing issues.

Developing such skills is rarely achieved by spending more on training. Formal training programs are important, especially when employees lack key skills or knowledge. But even online courses that provide access to coursework 24 hours a day, 7 days a week can fall short when it comes to resolving complicated, time-sensitive issues.

A well-known MIT study found that people are *five times* more likely to ask a co-worker for information than to consult an intranet, database, or company computer system.[18] Other studies also suggest that "*who*" you know is increasingly more important than "*what*" you know.[19]

Rather than push more information onto employees through conventional training, it is more important that they "learn how to learn." The sales executive who must know the customer's business backwards and forwards, as well as his own, *and* those of his alliance partners can no longer be a deep specialist in a single product or service. It is more important that he knows *where* to go for information and *whom* to ask.

When people need to solve a problem, they tend to turn to others—not to their computers. Solving complex problems requires that critical talent focus on their relationships with others. Research suggests that people who cultivate broad and diverse networks are more successful than those who rely strictly on their inner circles.[20]

The best way to develop critical talent is through the collaborative resolution of real-life issues ("action learning"). A well-known study conducted over a decade by the highly respected Center for Creative Leadership finds that "stretch" assignments and daily interactions with others are far more important to the development of successful executives than the formal training they received.[21]

Not surprisingly, the hardships people endure provide the richest learning experiences of all. When asked to identify the key events that made a difference in how they manage today, only 3 percent of executives cited formal coursework. On the other hand, 12 percent pointed to business mistakes as their most potent learning experience. Another 12 percent cited a change in project scope as a key event in their development. Interactions with others also commanded high responses.[22]

In which situations do people learn most?
67% When working together with a colleague on a task. 22% When doing own research. 10% When a colleague explains something personally. 2% Through a manual or textbook.
Source: Lexis-Nexis.[23]

People learn the most in situations that stretch them—the "trial by fire" experiences that put them slightly outside of their comfort zones. They learn not by pondering a hypothetical problem, but by directly tackling real issues. As a senior Microsoft human resources executive has noted: "We have very limited educational and training opportunities for our managers. But I think that we have absolutely developed leaders. You get people having to move from managing ten people to managing 200 overnight. That kind of stretch in the job will either create growth or death. Fortunately, we have such great people that most of them have just grown by leaps and bounds."[24]

People also learn from those they trust: bosses, subordinates, peers, and mentors, both internal and external. At its heart, learning is social in nature. SAIC, a $6.7 billion employee-owned research and information systems development company, recognizes that people learn the most on-the-job and from each other. To ramp up learning before important initiatives, SAIC has formal processes that connect individuals and teams so that the inexperienced can learn from the experienced. These "peer assist programs" have become a natural way to approach complex assignments. Similarly, project managers at British Petroleum are required to request the help of peers before initiating large projects, such as drilling wells.[25] Classrooms, books, and e-learning are helpful when people know little and have time to learn from scratch. But when experience is accessible and high costs and time are at stake, "peer assists" can be a much more effective way to expose people to the knowledge and experience they need—fast.

Mentoring and coaching are also important to learning—especially when expectations are made clear and tied to explicit goals. Deutsche Bank's Global Partnership Network for Women (GPNW) employs "mentoring circles" to promote the productivity and networking of its growing population of female talent. Each circle comprises one to two mentors and four to five "mentees."[26] The approach gives employees greater diversity and exposure to the business than traditional one-on-one coaching. At Campbell Soup Co., CEO Douglas Conant measures managers on how well they coach and develop their staffs."[27] In this way, Conant acknowledges the crucial role that the *quality* of interactions has on the financial performance of the company.

Deploy

If people learn the most in jobs that stretch them, they perform best when they can actively discover and define the *role* that will tap their deepest passions and skills and the *conditions* required to succeed. For some, the key to feeling more committed is flexible work arrangements. Others love most aspects of their job but detest the 30 percent of it that causes them to look elsewhere. Still others are simply mismatched. That is, their performance is compromised because they have did not either the motivation or ability they need to succeed. Organizations cannot make everyone happy; in some situations, turnover is the price to be paid. However, voluntary turnover within critical segments of the workforce can put a company's strategies at risk.

At United Parcel Service (UPS), the people who drive the trucks and deliver packages are a critical talent segment. UPS pays great attention to selecting drivers, taking great pains to match their skills and interests to the job. Despite careful recruiting, though, UPS once suffered high turnover among drivers. The company found the reason was the tedious and exhausting task of loading trucks before delivering packages. When UPS shifted the task of loading to another group of workers, driver turnover dropped dramatically. Turnover in the loading jobs is 400 percent per year, but these positions have far less impact on the delivery process. They also require skills that are easy to fill with part-time students and temporary workers.[28]

SAS: Trust and Respect–Rather than Command and Control

Jim Goodnight, the chief executive officer of SAS Institute Inc., has long proclaimed that treating people right is good business. Few would argue his point. With revenues of $1.3 billion, the world's largest privately held software company boasts 3.5 million users, 90 percent market penetration of the *Fortune* 500, and 26 years of consistent revenue growth. In 2001 and 2002, when the economy forced many of its competitors to downsize, SAS increased its domestic workforce by 8.5 percent, enabling the Cary, N.C.–based company to post double-digit growth in 2003.[29]

SAS is often heralded for taking care of its people. Among the amenities and benefits offered to all employees are a free onsite health clinic, onsite child care, flexible scheduling, extensive recreational facilities, cultural programs, a dining hall with live piano music, an elder care referral service, unlimited sick days, and a masseuse to relieve strained necks and backs.

Such programs have long been held up as reasons that SAS's turnover is less than 5 percent in an industry where average churn exceeds 20 percent. Goodnight explains, "You can pay headhunters to replace the overworked, overstressed employees that leave your company every year, or you can invest that money in keeping your employees happy and productive. To me, it's a no-brainer."[30] Jeff Pfeffer, a professor at Stanford University, agrees. He estimates that retention of high-quality talent saves SAS US$60 million to $80 million annually.[31]

A large part of SAS's success can also be attributed to its dedication to the development, deployment, and connection of its key people. The company's philosophy is to invest in people for the long term and give them the experiences they need to grow. It is not unusual, for example, for employees to redeploy to new countries to grow the business globally. Giving people license to work on innovative projects is another big stimulator. Rather than monitoring and controlling its employees, SAS places a strong emphasis on intrinsic motivation—that is, helping people to find their niche and then coaching and mentoring them to perform to the best of their ability. Underlying this approach is a strong belief that trust and respect are the best motivators of all, says Frank Leistner, SAS's chief knowledge officer for Europe, Middle East, and Africa: "Hot-skills bonuses and other monetary perks don't work as effectively as giving people a cool opportunity. The experience of working at SAS is not just about the daycare facilities, but that people can make things happen. People stay on because they feel integrated and accepted."[32]

In a culture that encourages international travel and face-to-face meetings as a means to fuel connection, such comments aren't surprising. But true to SAS's roots, hard technology informs the soft stuff. For example, a key tool for project managers is a highly detailed skills database. The software helps SAS's managers analyze the gap between the skills they currently have in their departments for a business unit or project and the skills they will need in future. Dynamic models allow them to test different scenarios. By predicting their needs, they can set out to find and develop the best people to help them shift strategies. How do they find the best people? Not through software, but through connections. SAS employs dedicated "networkers" whose full-time job is to connect people and ideas. They are key players in the process, matching managers to the people and skills that they need, no matter where they reside in the firm.[33]

Deployment is about matching the correct candidate to a critical job or project. But it doesn't stop when people are assigned. Companies must continuously focus on their critical talent to ensure that their skills, interests, and capabilities evolve in line with strategic objectives. At times, this may mean re-evaluating the design of the job, as UPS did with its delivery staff. At others, it may mean redefining the conditions of the job through virtual arrangements and flexible schedules.

A Call for Greater Workforce Mobility

The traditional "career ladder" is shrinking as organizations are becoming flatter. Without vertical mobility, employees need lateral experiences that promise challenge and growth. To fulfill this need, firms must expand their definitions of advancement and offer diverse sets of career paths. This means providing opportunities across divisions, business units, geographies, and even professions—establishing a transparent and fluid internal job marketplace. By encouraging greater mobility, organizations inspire a more engaged workforce and promote greater strategic *flexibility.*

Deploying talent also means helping those who are mismatched in their jobs. By mismatched, we don't just mean lack of capability, although this is often the case. People are also mismatched when they have the skills, but not the burning interest. An example is the "quant jock"[34] at a large bank who excelled at crunching numbers, but whose heart was really in strategy. Such people unfortunately become typecast in their positions far too frequently, and it becomes difficult for them to break out of their roles without leaving the company. Similarly, people can be mismatched when they've accomplished their goals and wish to master something new.

It isn't surprising that most organizations hold people to the confines of their resumes. It is risky to hire or reassign people based on their potential, rather than their experience. But inviting talented people to explore their options is not as risky or costly as paying them when they're disengaged, or losing them altogether to the competition.

By and large, people are capable of doing many things. With the proper experiences, support, and connections, they are apt to gravitate to roles that unleash their passions. Indeed, some of the most successful business people were never educated or trained for the roles they mastered. The founder of the Lotus Development software company, Mitchell Kapor, had been a disk jockey and transcendental meditation teacher in his past careers. Ray Kroc sold milkshake machines to restaurants before he started to build the McDonald's empire in 1954 at age 52.[35] His modest sales roots wouldn't have predicted his later success as one of America's greatest entrepreneurs and CEOs. Advertising legend David Ogilvy was a chef in Paris, a farmer in Pennsylvania, and a member of the British Intelligence agency before making a mint in advertising. At age 38, he jumped into advertising with no credentials and $6,000 in the bank. Prior to running America Online, Steve Case was in charge of coming up with new pizza toppings for Pizza Hut.[36]

It is not unusual for people to try on different roles before they find the one (or two, or three) for which they are best suited. For every airline pilot or doctor who knows his or her passion at nine years old, there are likely more who are still trying to figure it out at 30. Indeed, interests and goals may shift over time. But by and large, people don't find the right fit until they "taste, touch, and feel" it.

INSEAD Professor Herminia Ibarra explains that finding one's career niche involves a process of experimentation. In her years of research, she has discovered that people often need to try several roles before they find their best fit. Self introspection is crucial, she argues, but cannot offer the insights provided to us by hands-on experience.[37]

Firms such as SAS and Microsoft go to great lengths to help their talent find the right niche—redeploying people each year, if necessary. Organizations that help valued employees redeploy typically win their commitment. If a mutually satisfactory solution can be struck, then they win it immediately. If an arrangement can't be struck, then they may win it in the future—even if a valued employee chooses to leave. Successful talent management includes strategies to stay engaged with alumni. Individuals granted latitude by their employers to explore new territory, often make their way back with renewed vigor and insights.

Connect

Few jobs are accomplished in isolation. Most require the backing, decision-making help, and knowledge of key individuals, both inside and outside an organization. As problems become more complex and collaboration more common, *who* you know is increasingly becoming more important than *what* you know. As a retail director at multinational ING Bank once remarked, "Our account managers have remarkable product expertise. But our clients' needs have changed. How do we cultivate generalists rather than specialists, and encourage our account managers to rely on *access* to experts, rather than *be* experts."[38] To increase performance in today's complex organizations, leaders must help key individuals build rich, diverse networks.

Southwest: The Power of Connection and Collaboration

Amidst industry turbulence and bankruptcies, Southwest Airlines continues to be heralded as "the most successful airline in history."[39] While competitors struggle to make money or avoid bankruptcy, Southwest surges ahead. In 2003, the airline's profits jumped 84 percent to $442 million over the $241 million of 2002. Since the new millennium began, Southwest has generated after-tax profits of nearly $2 billion, a number greater than the collective net profits of the entire airline industry in that period. This remarkable increase is not a story of overnight success—but one of three decades of sustained growth. Since its beginnings, Southwest has achieved steady 10 percent to 15 percent annual growth. More remarkably, the company has been profitable for 32 of its 33 years in business, under the consistent leadership of Chairman Herb Kelleher.[40]

Unlike other airlines, which bank on long-haul flights to fuel their margins, Southwest grew in dominance by mastering the less profitable short-haul market segment. The challenge of short-haul flights is that planes can spend more time on the ground than in the air, where they earn revenue. The only way to achieve profitability, then, is to turn around planes as fast as possible. No airline is as fast as Southwest. Its turnaround time averages 15-20 minutes. Sometimes it's as fast as five minutes.[41] As one flight attendant quipped, "Herb keeps telling us that we can't make money with the planes sitting on the ground."[42]

Achieving this kind of turnaround require's near-perfect synchronization among ground crew, flight attendants, pilots, maintenance, and the eight other functions required to get a plane off the ground. The recipe behind this synchronicity lies in the connections among these people, ones unique in an industry marked by divisiveness. Southwest pilots chip in to help clean the planes. Flight attendants, gate attendants, cleanup crew, and other personnel constantly communicate. The positive energy they generate is infectious. As one Southwest gate agent explained, "No one takes the job of another person for granted. The skycap is just as critical as the pilot. You can always count on the next guy standing there."[43] To gain empathy for another person's job, employees are encouraged to swap jobs through a "walk in your shoes" program.

This shared respect lies at the heart of Southwest's success.[44] The respect comes, in part, from the knowledge Southwest employees have about each other's jobs and is shaped by their shared goals to provide "outrageous" customer service (in the words of one employee) and to keep planes in the air.

Contd...

Contd...

Southwest's brand identity is clear to employees, and it helps shape their behavior. If Microsoft seeks "the best and the brightest," Southwest looks for people who take their jobs seriously, but put relationships ahead of their egos and know how to have fun.

As a magnet for talent, Southwest doesn't depend on tactics to "acquire" good people. The company lures thousands of candidates per position. Comments such as "I love to come to work every day," "We can be who we are," and "We love our customers" are pervasive throughout the company. Southwest gains such commitment by shunning layoffs, promoting from within, and developing people in good and bad times. By taking care of critical talent and stoking a highly collaborative culture, the airline demonstrates the power and profits achievable by investing in people.

People have always relied on informal networks to get their work done. Decades of research led by the University of Chicago and Stanford University validate the link between the strength and diversity of social networks and one's influence, or social capital.[45] Social capital determines one's ability to gain access to information, solve problems collaboratively, and achieve goals.

Work largely happens "off the organizational chart" through our informal networks. The glue that binds people together in these networks is *trust*.

It is often suggested that we learn 70 percent of what we know about our jobs through our informal networks. A wellknown study at Xerox found that the field technicians who fix copy machines learned the most when they gathered for coffee each morning – not when they consulted the manuals that had taken years to compile, but were largely ignored.[46] Research at MIT further confirms the importance of our social networks.[47] It found that engineers and researchers were five times more likely to turn to another person for information rather than to search an impersonal source such as a file or database. People with rich networks tend to solve problems faster, and with better results.

By rich networks, we don't mean that everyone needs to be connected with everyone else. People are likely to rebel against requests to attend more meetings or answer more e-mails. Instead, a targeted approach is required to connect people with the right people and knowledge. Rather than leave such connections to chance, organizations can do a lot to help individuals increase the quality of their interactions and knowledge flows. Encouraging "communities of practice," the self-organized groups that form around a common mission or interest, is one such means. Peer assist programs are another, as SAIC has found.

The *quality* of a person's informal networks also has a substantial impact on his performance. Rob Cross (University of Virginia) and Wayne Baker (University of Michigan) are making great strides to understand the characteristics of networks that lead to individual and organizational performance. In one study, they found that the "energy" we send to each other in our interactions is four times a greater predictor of performance as the information that we bring to the table.[48] We create positive energy when we listen carefully, respect others' needs and perspectives, and promptly answer questions. One only has to reflect on personal experience to know the impact of toxic interactions on our ability to perform.

Investments in social capital can bring richer returns than many technology investments.

This focus on networks and connections is one with which few organizations have deep experience. But emerging software is changing that picture. Social Network Analysis (SNA) tools are one of the hottest areas of investment for venture capitalists. We refer not to the software that drives dating Web sites, but to the technology that identifies the connections between people and their knowledge. By mapping such connections, leaders can gain important insights on how work really gets done in critical parts of the organization: who knows whom, who knows what, who trusts whom, who energizes others, and who creates bottlenecks. The tool is not meant to point fingers, but to create healthy flows of knowledge and relationships.

When properly used, Social Network Analysis can help leaders increase the success of an important merger, locate expertise for a crucial project, or strengthen executive team performance. It can reveal gaps in knowledge and highlight the differences in the personal networks of high and low performers. As such, it can be a powerful tool in the development and deployment of key individuals.

So What?

The Develop-Deploy-Connect model is interconnected and virtuous. An improvement in one area naturally leads to an improvement in another. For

> The Develop-Deploy-Connect model is interconnected and virtuous. An improvement in one area naturally leads to an improvement in another. Done right, a balanced strategy that integrates all three dimensions leads to increased capability, alignment, and commitment, which in *turn drives business results and performance.*

example, people develop better skills when they are deployed in stretch assignments and connected with others from whom they can learn and grow. Likewise, effective deployment occurs when people have the knowledge, skills, networks, and relationships they need to succeed. Finally, effective connection happens when people are deployed in work that engages their curiosity. In these circumstances, they are more likely to learn from and teach (i.e., develop) others.

Important benefits result from this virtuous circle. One is capability. When highly capable individuals work together, they build organizational capability. The second is the alignment that occurs when the right people are in the right jobs. A third result is commitment. People are more likely to master work that engages them, fosters their growth, and encourages productive relationships. When people feel the organization takes a keen interest in their interests, skills, and connections, they are far less tempted to look for challenges outside.

Going Forward: Taking the First Steps in Building Talent

So how can companies build this kind of cycle for generating top talent? The first step is defining exactly which jobs are critical. This is a central exercise, but it is not as straightforward as it might appear. It requires a clear vision of the range of current and future strategies that will drive organizational success. This doesn't mean banking on a single outlook, but may instead require alternative scenarios that acknowledge the uncertainty of business. It then requires a firm understanding of the talent supply and demand patterns outside and inside the organization. Energy suppliers such as ChevronTexaco and Shell are taking a hard look at their talent pipeline—especially in areas such as engineering, where the demand for qualified candidates will soon skyrocket due to retirement and a limited pool of graduates.

Within core business units, identifying critical workforce segments requires determining which jobs make or break organizational performance. Disney found

How do you Identify Your Critical Talent?

Critical talent are the people who create the value an organization needs to succeed. Answering the following four questions can help leaders to isolate these groups and individuals.

1. Which strategies, skills, and capabilities are crucial to your current and future success?
2. What emerging workforce trends (e.g., supply and demand of engineers) will impact your ability to deliver value?
3. Who supports your critical segments of talent within their network? Are these supporting people difficult to replace?
4. Within your critical workforce segments, who possesses the greatest current and future *potential?*

its park street sweepers were critical people because they were in touch with millions of customers every year.[49] The FedEx delivery person is another example.

Companies must also identify the skills that will drive future growth. SAS closely monitors turnover to precisely understand what skills are leaving. When combined with projections of skills needed for future projects, these data help the company plan the deployment and development of key individuals.

Once leaders identify their company's critical talent and skills, they must next match people, skills, and knowledge to company needs. Decisions to redeploy, develop, and stimulate connections evolve from this analysis. It is important that this need not be a top-down process. People are likely to underperform if they are deployed against their will. The same is true of the professional who is forced into a mentoring relationship as part of his development. The role of the organization is to communicate needs and create the support mechanisms (e.g., electronic job boards, coaching, and strategic networking events) that people need to grow in line with organizational goals. SAS, for example, creates development plans in individual departments—not in HR or at the top of the company. The strategy is communicated, but decisions are made on an individual basis. It's the responsibility of the line leader to be sure that individual and organizational goals are aligned.

As the competition for critical talent heats up, organizations must better understand the supply and demand of critical workforce segments. Energy companies that are highly dependent on geological and petroleum engineers must

> Decisions to develop, deploy, and connect cannot be mandated from the top. To work best, critical employees must initiate and drive their own paths to performance. The role of leaders is to communicate guidelines and strategies and to provide the tools that critical talent needs to succeed. Such an approach calls into question the efficacy of traditional, top-down driven *succession planning*.

anticipate and model shortages into their talent forecasts. A pharmaceutical giant such as Pfizer must monitor (and try to influence) the availability of researchers and clinicians as part of its talent strategy. SAS taps its Human Capital Management (HCM) system to gain insights on employee factors like turnover or age within its critical workforce segments. Such analyses help organizations understand the supply and demand of talent at the *professional*, or *job* level.

> Corporations are responding to the increasing demand for advanced training, an inadequate domestic talent pool, and the small representation of women and minorities among the upper ranks of education. For example, Pfizer has dedicated $2 million toward the creation of a three-year program aimed at increasing the graduation rate of PhDs. Only three-quarters of doctoral students complete their degrees—a proportion that could be improved with interventions such as improved *selection and mentoring.*[50]

A next layer of analysis involves determining the *skills* required to achieve important strategies. A complex software project, for example, may require a business unit to ramp up the quantity and quality of its programming skills. Many organizations are beginning to develop skills databases that provide an inventory of currently available skills. When properly designed, skills databases can be modeled to analyze the gap between what is currently available and what will be needed to execute shifts in strategy. Product managers at SAS, for example, employ skills databases to plan future projects. This helps them to plan the development and deployment of people—rather than wait to the last minute to arm people with the skills they will need to succeed. Such information can help fuel the growth of both individuals and business units. When used with internal demographic information, such as projected turnover and retirement, it can also help executives develop talent strategies at the enterprise level. As expected from a market leader, SAS is already on the way.

When a company manages critical talent in this manner, it must guard against unwittingly creating a culture of "haves" and "have-nots." A focus on critical talent and the people who support them doesn't mean other employees should be blocked out of the development process or kept in unsatisfying jobs. Managers must keep their eyes out for employees in less critical roles who possess the talent to succeed in critical roles. There are countless stories like the one of Southwest's chief operating officer, Colleen Barrett, who rose from being a legal secretary to a top position.

In the coming years, most companies will have no choice but to seriously rethink their approaches to talent strategies. But shifting demographics should not be the only reason. Improving the performance of critical employees directly improves organizational performance. Furthermore, focusing on critical talent is relatively new territory for most companies and, thus, offers a new way to compete. Compared to more popular investments in customer, technological, and financial strategies (which have been refined over decades), a well-designed talent strategy could truly differentiate an organization.

When a company's talent management process evolves in the manner described in this article, companies will be reluctant to go back to the stop-gap measures of recruiting and retention. Managers may be amazed by how often the talent they need resides right under their noses—or the noses of colleagues a continent away.

Rather than fight a futile "war for talent," leaders should look within for the critical skills and knowledge required to execute the company's most important jobs. By developing, deploying, and connecting these people the right way, leaders can raise their performance—and the performance of the entire organization—to a whole new level.

Acknowledgements

This study has benefited from the diligent help and wise insights of many people. Jeff Summer, National Director of HR, has been an unwavering sponsor, lending his intellectual and organizational support to transform the ideas into practice, both externally and internally. Jörg Schiele and Bill Chafetz, who head our Organization and People Performance practices in Europe and the United States, are also leading that campaign. Tina Witney has done a heroic job linking the concepts to an actionable framework. The study would not have been possible without the help of Deloitte Research interns Neeme Raud and Mara Rose who in a few months pulled together fodder for an entire series. Deloitte Research Global Director Ajit Kambil provides continuous sage advice, and Georgia Tech professor Luis Martins offered selfless thinking on the comprehensive talent model that has evolved from this piece. Frank Leistner offered generous insights on the unparalleled practices of SAS, and John Boudreau of the University of Southern California provided intellectual seeds from which the piece sprang forth. Other very helpful insights have been provided by Deloitte colleagues Sabri Challah, Randy DiBernardo, Mike Evangelides, Dick Kleinert, Sanjiv Kumar, Alice Kwan, Britton McMullian, Neena Newberry, Michelle Ruskin, Heide Schroeder, Stan Smith, Jim Wall, and Sarah Wooddy. Finally, I thank Bob Buday for his wise editorial guidance and Steve Barth for lending the title to the series.

(Robin Athey leads Deloitte's research on the people aspects of organizational performance. Her studies investigate the links between organizational knowledge, learning, leadership, collaboration, and performance. Her current series on Talent Management will be offered in five parts. She has recently conducted research on strategic account management and led a bi-annual Sales Executive Forum with partners from Columbia University and INSEAD. She has also produced studies and articles on diverse topics, such as knowledge and content management, e-learning, privacy, and the mobile enterprise, teaming with faculty from MIT and Harvard Business School. Ms. Athey has sat on councils at the Conference Board and Harvard, and served on the board of the UN Association, the civic branch of the United Nations. Prior to joining Deloitte Research, Ms. Athey spent ten years as a consultant with Kurt Salmon Associates and was VP Global Production with Cole-Haan, a subsidiary of Nike. She speaks Spanish fluently and has lived and worked in eight countries across Asia, Europe, Latin America, and the former Soviet Union. She holds a B.S. in Industrial and Systems Engineering from the University of Florida, an M.A. in International Economic Policy from Columbia University, and an advanced certificate in Organizational Development and HR Management from Columbia University and the University of Michigan. She can be reached at rathey@deloitte.com).

Endnotes

1 Conversation with Pfizer, September 2004.

2 John W Boudreau and Peter M Ramstad, "Talentship and the Evolution of Human Resource Management: From Professional Practices To Strategic Talent Decision Science," University of Southern California, Center for Effective Organizations Working Paper #G04-6, 2004.

3 Boris Groysberg, Ahshish Nanda, and Nitin Nohria, "The Risky Business of Hiring Stars," *Harvard Business Review*, May 2004.

4 Successful companies have higher average returns on assets. Source: "CEO Challenge 2004," The Conference Board, August 2004.

5 "Before It's Too Late,"National Commission on Mathematics and Science Teaching for the 21st Century, US Department of Education, 2000.

6 Boudreau and Ramstad, supra, n.2.

7 Ibid. See *http://www.hcbridge.com.*

8 Eurostat, HRI Fortnight Report, May 12, 2004.

9 "The Next Society," *The Economist*, Nov 1, 2001. *http://www.economist.com/surveys/* displaystory.cfm?story_id=770819.

10 "Keeping America Competitive: How a Talent Shortage Threatens US Manufacturing," National Association of Manufacturers, The Manufacturing Institute and Deloitte & Touche, 2003.

11 "Vaunted German Engineers Face Competition from China", *The Wall Street Journal*, July 15, 2004.

12 Inc.com 25th Anniversary issue. *http://www.inc.com/magazine/20040401/* 25goodnight.html.

13 Jay Greene and Greg Forster, "Public High School Graduation and College Readiness Rates in the United States," Manhattan Institute for Policy Research, Sept. 2003. *http:// www.manhattaninstitute. org/html/ewp_03.htm.*

14 The Gallup Organization. *www.gallup.com.*

15 Ibid.

16 In the US, companies spend $1,415 on average in recruiting costs for every $10,000 of new-employee compensation. But the median training expense per full-time worker in 2000 was $288. In companies of more than 5,000 people, it was only $109.

17 "HR Executive Review: Implementing the New Employment Compact," The Conference Board, 1997.

18 Tom Allen, *Managing the Flow of Technology*, Cambridge, MA, MIT Press, 1977.

19 Rob Cross, *The Hidden Power of Social Networks*, Harvard Business School Press.

20 This is a core tenet of social network theory.

21 *www.ccl.org.* Results of the original CCL research are summarized in Morgan McCall, Michael Lombardo, and Ann Morrison, *The* Lessons of Experience: How Successful Executives Develop on the *Job*, Free Press, 1988.

22 Christina A Douglas, "Key Events and Lessons for Managers in a Diverse Workforce," Center for Creative Leadership, 2003.

23 "LexisNexis Deutschland, GmbH, Ergebnisse der Wissensmanagement Studie 2004," March 2004, *http://www.lexisnexis.de/downloads/040305praesentation.pdf.*

24 "Microsoft's Vega Project: Developing People and Products," Harvard Business School case study, 1999.

25 Chris Collison and Geoff Parcell, "Learning to Fly: Practical Lessons from One of the World's Leading Knowledge Companies", Oxford: Capstone Publishing, 2001. A very helpful overview of peer assists can also be found on the Web site of the National Electronic Library for Health in the UK: *http://www.nelh.nhs.uk/knowledge_management/km2/peer_assists_toolkit.asp.*

26 Interviews with Caroline Israel and Denise Montana, Deutsche Bank, July 2004 and January 2005.

27 This quotation came from Denise Morrison, president of global sales and chief customer officer at Campbell, in an August 17, 2004, *Wall Street Journal* article by Carol Hymowitz, "Unlike Politicians, Business Executives Seek Profit, Not Votes," Page B1.

28 Peter Cappelli, "A Market-Driven Approach to Employee Retention," *Harvard Business Review*, February 2000.

29 Inc.com 25th Anniversary issue. *http://www.inc.com/magazine/20040401/25goodnight.html* and SAS website *http://www.sas.com/news/feature/16feb04/softbusiness.html.*

30 "CEO takes HR to Primetime – Between the Lines – Jim Goodnight, SAS," Workforce, December 2002, summarized at: *http://www.findarticles.com/p/articles/mi_m0FXS/is_13_81/ai_95120706.*

31 Ibid.

32 Interview with Frank Leistner, SAS, August 2004.

33 Ibid.

34 A "quant jock" is someone with superior quantitative skills.

35 From the corporate history section of McDonald's Web site: *http://www.mcdonalds.com/corp/about/mcd_history_pg1.html.*

36 Kara Swisher, *Aol.com,* Times Business, 1998, p. 27.

37 Herminia Ibarra, "How to Stay Stuck in the Wrong Career," *Harvard Business Review*, December 2002.

38 Interview with Phillipe Wallez, Retail Director, ING Bank, 2003.

39 Katrina Brooker, "The Chairman of the Board Looks Back," *Fortune*, May 28, 2001.

40 Jody Hoffer Gittell, *The Southwest Airlines Way*, McGraw-Hill, 2003.

41 "Southwest Airlines (B): Using Human Resources for Competitive Advantage," Stanford Graduate School of Business, 1995.

42 Gittell, supra, n.37.

43 Ibid.

44 Ibid.

45 Among the pioneers in Social Capital and Social Network theory are Ron Burt (University of Chicago) and Mark Granovetter (Stanford University).

46 Julian Orr, "Talking About Machines: An Ethnography of a Modern Job", Cornell University Press, 1996.

47 Research by Tom Allen of MIT summarized in Rob Cross, "The Hidden Power of Social Networks: Understanding How Work Really Gets Done in Organizations", Harvard Business School Press, 2004, p. 11.

48 Conversation with Rob Cross, University of Virginia (discussing research done with Wayne Baker, University of Michigan). Also see Rob Cross, Wayne Baker and Andrew Parker "What Creates Energy in Organizations?" *MIT Sloan Management Review*, Summer 2003, Vol. 44, No. 4, p. 51-56.

49 Boudreau and Ramstad, supra n.2.

50 Council of Graduate Schools, Ph D Completion Project, *http://www.phdcompletion.org*.

Section II

Issues

5

Poaching: The Best Talent Worldwide

Tools and Approaches Ranging from Aggressive to Passive

John Sullivan

Poaching talent is not a new approach, but has been deployed around the world for ages, particularly in the US and Eastern Europe. Poaching talent is the practice of proactively targeting and hiring top talent away from competitor or top firm with the intention of securing skills or capabilities faster, mitigating high-level talent losses due to attrition, damaging competitor's ability to achieve strategic objectives. The war for talent is expanding and those with the most to lose need to understand the tools and approaches used by the competition. This article discusses the three dominant poaching strategies. It further discusses the six categories that power the "attract them with honey" strategy—Employment branding, Employee referrals, Event recruiting, Magnet hiring, Boomerang hiring and Internet.

Few topics in the field of recruiting evoke such strong opinions as the subject of poaching talent, but it is a topic that must be explored further. In the United States, it is clear that a number of corporate recruiters shy away from poaching

Source: www.ere.net, 2005. The article was reprinted with permission from © ERE Media (www.ere.net).

talent on the grounds that it is unethical to approach and offer possible employment to someone who is already gainfully employed by another organization, such as a direct competitor, despite the fact that the target employee could always just ignore the recruiter's efforts or opt out at any stage in the process.

Given that firms in the United States are typically the most aggressive recruiting organizations, having pillaged other countries for top talent in information technology, healthcare, and the sciences for years, you might assume that the dominant perceptions around poaching talent in the Unites States are similar to those of recruiters abroad. If you did do that, you'd be wrong!

US Perceptions Exist in a Vacuum

Two weeks ago, I spoke at ERE's first European conference, to a crowd of recruiters representing some of the Europe's most recognized companies and a handful of US companies with a strong global footprint. I opted to speak on what I consider the most aggressive recruiting tactic available to corporate recruiters: targeted talent poaching.

Prior to arriving in Brussels, Belgium, I prepared for a negative reaction, based on previous experiences with this topic in the US. But to my surprise, the reaction wasn't negative. In fact, one member of the audience spoke up and indicated that poaching had become part for the course, a comment that drew affirmation from the rest of the audience. This caught me by surprise, only because over the years I have worked with a number of European firms, and when compared to firms headquartered elsewhere, their hesitation to adopt aggressive approaches was by far the most resolute I've experienced anywhere in the world.

Reflecting on that experience, I realized that it wasn't out of line with other global experiences I've had this year. Throughout 2005, I touched down in eleven countries, mostly in Southeast Asia and Central and Eastern Europe. The perceptions around poaching encountered in Europe could be seen in Australia and New Zealand, where the shortage of skilled talent has threatened the survival of dominant industries. One banking organization was so aggressive that it approached the spouses of targeted candidates, while their respective partners were at work to recruit the spouse as a decision influencer.

It seems as though the dominant position the US has enjoyed for years in the political/economic landscape has perhaps made our recruiting organizations complacent. As migration to the global economy causes rapid wage inflation in underdeveloped nations such as India, China, and Eastern Europe alongside steady wage deflation in hyper-developed nations like the US and Great Britain, it is clear that such complacency may tip the scales in favor of the developing nations as the war for talent escalates.

A Primer on Poaching

Poaching talent is the practice of proactively targeting and hiring top talent away from a competitor or top firm, with the specific intention of:

- Securing skills or capabilities faster than if you were to attempt to develop talent internally through training and development efforts.
- Securing expanded capacity (i.e., more bodies) that will require less ramp up time.
- Mitigating high-level talent losses due to attrition.
- Damaging your competitors' ability to achieve their strategic objectives.

The approach is not new and has been deployed around the world for ages, particularly in sports. Take a World Cup soccer (football) team for example. Can you think of a single team that is made up entirely of players from the country that team represents? The truth is that when winning matters, the best teams seek out the best talent wherever it resides, be it their backyard or a tiny undeveloped country nestled between two warring nations.

An Unstoppable Global Trend

The migration to a truly global economy is impacting every nation large and small in both positive and negative ways. One of the most apparent impacts is that it has increased demand for labor in nations that once supplied a surplus to developing nations, causing dramatic increases in local wages, in turn making it more difficult to recruit talent abroad. In addition, the rampant growth of offshore outsourcing has imbued developing nations with disposable income, making possible their investment into higher value work.

Combined, these two external forces are complicating the pillage model that for so many years have filled hospitals with nurses and hardware/software firms with engineers. It has also turned the tables, such that developing nations must now devise ways to steal talent back from hyper-developed nations, i.e., poach!

Aggressive firms in such nations are following the leaders, they are:

- Putting work where the talent resides.
- Subcontracting outsource contracts for low value activities to other developing nations.
- Opening offices in locations that compete directly with their clients.
- Offering very lucrative compensation packages for key players who return or are willing to relocate to a developing nation.

In short, the war for talent is no longer a local war, but rather a global one that will drive the evolution and practice of talent poaching.

Three Dominant Poaching Strategies

Poaching activities largely fall into one of three categories:

Direct sourcing: Firms use new data-mining techniques and tools, combined with age-old recruiter phone techniques, to mine the organizational structure, employee identities, and employee performance indicators of talent and product competitors. This competitive intelligence is later used to determine whom specifically should be targeted for poaching. All work is carried out internally.

Third-party poaching: This strategy relies on using a vendor or series of vendors to identify everything, that ranges from which firms to target, to what individuals to go after based on your strategic objectives. (It is also by far the most common way organizations that find poaching unethical actually practice it themselves. In their minds, poaching is perceived as unethical only if you do it yourself.)

Attract them with "honey": The third strategy is likely the one that few organizations would associate with poaching, what we call the "attract them with honey" strategy. This approach utilizes six different channels to drive candidates to your organization from other specific organizations, much like product firms steer you to their products in grocery stores.

All three strategies have the same impact in the long run, but offer firms a varied level of "ethical exposure," timeline, and cost. The three strategies outlined above are rank ordered, in terms of their time to productivity and cost, from least expensive with quickest impact to most expensive with slowest impact.

Because the ethical concerns over poaching are so great in the United States, the remainder of this article will focus on the channels that power the "attract them with honey" strategy.

The "Honey" Strategy: Six Primary Channels

The "honey" strategy is powered by a number of channels that drive candidates into your recruiting process. While the list of actual channels is long, most of them fall into six categories:

- Employment branding.
- Employee referrals.
- Event recruiting.
- Magnet hiring.
- Boomerang hiring.
- Internet.

Each of these channels is outlined below.

The Employment Branding Channel

Many firms that have made an attempt to manage their employer brand do so with no particular goals other than to develop either "Best Place to Work" or "Employer of Choice" status (note that both of those terms are registered trademarks!). Such efforts are, for lack of a better word, lame.

Employment branding is not an art, but rather a science. It focuses on identifying which employer attributes and characteristics are needed to recruit a highly defined target audience, aligning organizational structure and management practices with those attributes where possible, and communicating both directly and indirectly with the target audience to position the organization as a leading firm providing those attributes.

Employer branding relies on:

- External recognition as a leader in providing specific employer attributes, such as a value on diversity, innovation, or talent development.
- Consistent messaging that continuously communicates who and what the firm is and what value it provides to prospective employees.
- A story inventory that provides specific examples of how management programs and practices deliver value to employees.
- A specific and differentiated theme (slogan) that competitors cannot easily mimic or assert.
- Recognition for functional excellence.
- Lots of lots of press coverage in very specific publications that reach into the targeted audience.

The Employee Referral Channel

Just as most firms approach employment branding with no specific goal or outcome in mind, they often develop employee referral programs that meander and produce mediocre results at best. A targeted employee referral program, on the other hand, utilizes the employee population to do all of the competitive intelligence mining that enables targeted poaching, with an added benefit—It gets employees to utilize their personal networks to initiate the recruiting process.

A targeted poaching effort that utilizes the employee referral channel relies on:

Active referrals: An approach that goes to employees with a specific set of questions that prime them to remember who they know in specific roles, organizations, etc.

Top performer referral prioritization: An approach that acts on all referrals coming in from proven top performers before acting on those from other employees.

Reference referrals: An approach that contacts references of past hires that proved to be top performers and asks who else they know.

Stakeholder referrals: An approach that leverages non employees who have a vested interest in the success of the company to generate referrals, such as consultants, suppliers, stock holders, etc.

The Events Channel

Nearly every organization that recruits will attend at least one event a year, be it a recruiting event, an industry trade show, or a vendor exposition. But few select events to participate in based on their probability of attracting employees from specific competitors.

Utilizing events as a poaching channel relies on:

- Identifying and participating in specific industry trade shows or association events that have a proven attraction to employees of targeted competitors.
- Hosting onsite seminars and certification courses that are attractive to the competition.
- Participating in non-industry/non-professional events that attract a target audience, such as a beer and wine or arts festival.

The Magnet Hire Channel

The magnet hire channel is quite possibly the easiest one to understand. It simply relies on polling top performers to identify the most respected or most visible professional who they would be interested in working with, and then working to hire that person in hopes that they would attract others to your organization.

The Boomerang Channel

At some point of time, nearly every employee decides to make a change and severs an employment relationship. The boomerang channel is used in poaching by identifying former employees that are currently employed by a competitor and developing specific strategies to lure them back—which brings the added benefit of lots of competitive intelligence about organizational structure and management practices, but not trade secrets or product information!

The Internet Channel

The final major channel that is used to power the "honey" approach to poaching is the Internet channel. Unlike job posting and data mining, these approaches use the Internet to develop resources that employees of competing organizations are drawn to.

Examples include:
Hosted information resource sites: These sites provide valuable information that is useful to the target audience in their current role. For instance, a hospital organization might launch an e-newsletter for nurses that provides summaries of the latest breakthrough and techniques.

Moderated professional forums: These tools enable professionals from a multitude of organizations to share information and discuss issues in a safe environment, free from advertisers and spammers.

Conclusion

The battle lines in the war for talent are expanding, and those with the most to lose need to understand that aggressive tools and approaches will be used by the competitors. There is no place for complacency on the battlefield, which causes unnecessary death. Developing firms in developing countries are desperate for talent, and they have no reservations about poaching your best people.

The evolution of poaching has begun, and there is no turning back. While the honey strategy will work in the short term, it is expensive and takes time. Eventually recruiters will have to learn to accept the role they play in their organizations' future and get past what concerns they may have with direct poaching.

(Dr. John Sullivan (JohnS@sfsu.edu) is a well-known thought leader in HR. He is a frequent speaker and advisor to Fortune 500 and Silicon Valley firms. Formerly the chief talent officer for Agilent Technologies (the 43,000-employee HP spin-off), he is now a professor of management at San Francisco State University. Dr. Sullivan is also the editor of VP of HR, an e-newsletter providing "out of the box" solutions for senior HR managers.)

6

Meritocracy: Responding to the Myth

Mike Hyter

This article is an experience of the author of the interactions with senior level executives about their organizations' human resource practices. He says that what he keeps hearing consistently is that their organizations are "true" meritocracies where the "gifted" rise to the top as a result of a fair process. The irony is that women and professionals of color in those same companies often tell me that the environment is far from fair to them. They also feel that the developmental opportunities and promotions are not based on merit but are reserved for those who play the game and special treatment is given to those few at the expense of the others.

In my consulting practice, I spend a great deal of time talking with senior level executives about their organization's human resource practices. One theme I hear consistently is that their organizations are "true" meritocracies where the "gifted" rise to the top as a result of a fair process. The irony is that women and professionals of color in those same companies often tell me that the environment is far from fair to them. They feel that developmental opportunities and promotions are not based on merit, but are reserved for those who play the game; special treatment is given to a few at the expense of others.

Source: http://www.emeraldinsight.com/10.1108/10775730410494224. Handbook of Business Strategy, Volume 5, Issue 1, Page: 41-44, 2004.

This contradiction in perceptions caused me to ask two questions: "do most companies truly have a meritocracy?" and even more fundamentally: "is it in the best interests of an organization to strive for a system of meritocracy?" I would argue that the answer to both questions is "no." In most companies, despite the best of intentions and the diligent efforts of dedicated managers and HR professionals, our system of assessing and rewarding talent is flawed—it is neither fair nor accurate. Furthermore, I believe it is not in the best interests of an organization to attempt to correct the flaws. Rather, we need to replace our current system of meritocracy with another approach—a system of inclusion based on the assumption that almost every employee is talented enough to contribute to our business objectives and that our role as managers is to nurture and develop the talents of all our employees, not only the "talented few."

Why this emphasis on developing all employees? In today's marketplace, people represent the only compelling competitive advantage for companies. Products can be duplicated, technology is constantly advancing, and access to raw products is virtually the same across the board. Quality and service—both people-based—are the only differentiators that companies can use to promote themselves. Furthermore, the largest expenditure a company has is payroll and related expenses, yet we manage human beings as fixed assets rather than the appreciable assets that they are. We are often content to rely on the talents and contributions of the 10-15 percent of our employees who are seen as the "go-to" folks, while ignoring the potential of the large majority.

The key to maximum return on these "appreciable assets" is development to a high standard for all employees, regardless of differences. A workforce that is becoming more and more diverse makes this understanding critical going forward in the twenty-first century. And for those who assume that a fair and equitable process of developing employees exists in your organization, given the above reality of human assets as the key advantage, you can't afford to be wrong.

The Myth of Meritocracy

I realize that the viewpoint that most organizations do not truly have a meritocracy, and furthermore shouldn't strive to have one, flies in the face of widely respected HR policies and practices, including those of the largest and most successful corporations in the world. So why do I think that our belief in meritocracy is a myth?

To answer that question, we have to start by examining the assumptions that underlie our current system of meritocracy:

- Some people have extraordinary talent; some (perhaps even most) don't.
- It is possible to make an accurate assessment of who has this talent and who doesn't.
- Once we've made this assessment, the organization is best served by focusing attention and support on helping these few, particularly valuable, individuals to succeed.

These underlying assumptions give rise to the phenomenon of the "go-to" employee. "Go-to" employees:

- Are enthusiastic about taking on new challenges.
- Take initiative and are innovative towards solving problems.
- Consistently exceed expectations with a focus on business objectives.

Their propensity for getting things done and their obvious display of talent make them the individuals managers rely on for most, if not all, of the important work of the business. As a result, our "go-to" people have significantly more opportunities to work on high visibility projects, more support for risk-taking, more managerial coaching—more of almost all the opportunities and management interactions that support increased development and business savvy.

So an upward cycle gets put into place. "Go-to" employees display talent and then are rewarded with the key assignments which further development. They become more attractive to other executives who find new opportunities for them in their areas. With all of this development and exposure, it is no surprise that these are the people who advance in organizations.

What is important to note here is that the very process of selecting those with talent and distributing key assignments to them accelerates the development of talent in those who are chosen. And it's why I hold that our system of meritocracy is flawed. The process doesn't just impartially reward talent; it creates talent in some and not in others—and leaves as much as 90 percent of our workforce disconnected, underdeveloped, and/or under-utilized.

Diversity in a Meritocracy

What we often see is that the default for selecting "go-to" folks is to tap those who are a lot like us—who resemble us in areas such as work style, interests, gender, or race. I believe it is a normal human response to entrust the most critical work of the business to folks with whom we feel most comfortable. After all, it takes more effort to interact effectively with someone who is different from us in some significant way. It takes more skill to have a difficult discussion about needed areas of improvement with someone with whom you are less comfortable. We need to acknowledge this reaction and we need to stop feeling guilty about it.

However, we also need to recognize the cost. Diversity is a given, and we are at a competitive disadvantage, if we fail to maximize the richness of a pool of employees who could bring new perspectives and innovative solutions. We need to develop an approach that eliminates the obstacles that are getting in the way of the development of all people and to create processes that encourage the full utilization of everyone towards business objectives.

The Alternative: A System of Inclusion

Instead of a system of meritocracy, we need a system of inclusion. Inclusion is a set of management practices, corporate culture, and interpersonal relationships that support the full utilization of a diverse workforce at all levels. How do companies make this change from a "some have it, some don't" environment of a meritocracy to an environment of inclusion? I believe there are three key elements:

1. Believe that most people are capable of high levels of performance.
2. Position everyone for growth and development.
3. Coach performance based on clearly-defined standards.

Believe that Most People are Capable of High Levels of Performance

The key to unleashing the unlimited talent that exists in an organization is directly connected to the belief that "most people are capable of high levels of performance."

When managers believe that most people have enough raw ability to make substantive contributions to the organization—from whatever position they occupy, no matter what their ethnicity or gender, tenure or previous experience—they cultivate that potential by stretching all employees toward achieving clearly defined outcomes.

Believing in the capacity of most people to grow and develop starts with a recognition of the factors beyond innate ability that contribute to any individual's development. Development is a by-product of two elements: the level of confidence an individual brings to a situation, and the degree of effective effort expended by a person. If two people have equal ability, and one is highly motivated to work hard at a task, and the other is not, what do you think will occur regarding long-term performance and development? It is my belief that differences in effort and the seriousness with which one approaches a task have a far more significant impact on development outcomes than the "raw firepower" with which one is born. When managers believe that every person has sufficient innate ability to be successful, they are free to focus their attention on building confidence and shaping effective effort for everyone—not on sorting and selecting the "cream of the crop."

Position Everyone for Growth and Development

The most critical aspect of building confidence and shaping effort is in what I call a person's position. By that I do not mean the person's job title, but the nature of the individual's assignments and the quality of the support he or she receives.

All employees in the organization need to understand how their responsibilities are connected to meeting the business objectives. They need to feel that it is their job to learn about the business and improve it. They need to have assignments that promote the growth of their analytical and operational skills—whether it's figuring out how to file more efficiently or penetrate a new market. The key element here is that every good Position (with a capital "P") challenges the individual in some way and requires the person to learn new skills in order to be successful.

Not only does such positioning benefit the bottom line, it also impacts on the person's "disposition." When someone is supported and given opportunities to learn, a level of confidence, determination, and commitment emerges that enables these individuals to take advantage of the opportunities for growth—they start to look more like those "go-to" employees!

Coach Performance Based on Clearly-Defined Standards

The first step in coaching all our employees to become "go-to" people is to clearly articulate the standards. Although most managers believe they do a good job of this, my observation is that too often we base our judgments of satisfactory performance on the "way we've always done it" or "how I like to see things done." Or, in trying to accommodate differences we change the standards and expectations, rather than allow for variation in how individuals meet the standards. Taking the time to think and communicate clear expectations is key to ensuring that employees focus their effort on what is important to the business.

Once individuals clearly understand the level of performance that is required, the next step is to provide feedback about how they've met the standard and how they haven't. When we operate with a belief that most people can hit the standard, data that suggest someone has fallen short lose their sting. The information is not an indictment of the individual's worth or indication of his or her future potential; it is only feedback about how to improve.

The last step is to support employees to develop a strategy for improvement. Focus on incremental, positive changes based on the standards and your understanding of the individual's current strengths and weaknesses.

Inclusion is the Key

The ability to maximize the contributions of every person at every level within an organization is the key to ensuring a competitive advantage. The organization that does this will always have the advantage over those that don't. We can't assume that, based on our good intentions, all managers are equipped to provide this level of developmental support for their people just because it is the right thing to do. The capability to provide strong developmental support for everyone, regardless of who they are, is a learnable skill. The investment made to provide this capability among the leadership within an organization provides the basis for consistently exceeding standards.

It is important to create an environment where everyone in your organization (management and non-management) subscribes to a way of thinking that supports the development of all. Make sure that all of your policies and management practices are in place to reinforce that belief.

Your bottom line will be glad you did.

(Mike Hyter is as president and CEO of Novations/J.Howard & Associates (www.jhoward.com). Michael Hyter is responsible for the management and strategic direction of the company. He serves on the board of the Efficacy Institute, a not-for-profit affiliate of Novations/J.Howard & Associates, which provides consulting services to public school systems and community-based organizations. He is also a member of the Executive Leadership Council, a network and leadership forum for African-American executives, and a member of the Board of Trustees for The Wang Center for the Performing Arts in Boston.)

7

Workforce Ageing: The Challenges for 21st Century Management

Margaret Patrickson and Rob Ranzijn

Population ageing has given rise to a host of issues, including the pressures placed on workforce management. At the same time as the proportion of younger workers entering the workforce is declining in all developed societies, the largest age cohort, the baby boomers, is fast approaching retirement age. Governments are urging older workers to delay retirement, yet the rapidly changing nature of work and the explosion of knowledge and systems for its storage, manipulation and distribution mean that both employers and employees are faced with continual requirements for skill maintenance and development. This paper considers the dilemmas facing employers as they strive to resolve competing demands from government to keep people working, challenges emanating from new skill demands in consequence of technological advances and resolution of the strengthening demand of many workers to exit when they choose. The paper brings together two streams of research—retirement decisions on the one hand and the pressures placed on employers by changing global and community expectations on the other—to argue that

Source: International Journal of Organisational Behaviour, Volume 10 (4), 729-739.

balancing these competing demands is possible, but will require changes in the conditions under which employment for older workers is both offered and maintained.

Introduction

Population ageing, that has become a feature of the majority of developed economies over the last two decades, has socio-economic implications for the distribution of work and incomes (OECD 2002) and is predicted to have massive implications for the Australian workforce until at least around 2040 (Productivity Commission 2004). Low birth rates, coupled with increasing longevity in all developed countries, mean that a shrinking proportion of the population in the paid workforce now has to support an expanding proportion of those without work. Many of those not working are mature aged individuals who have either been unsuccessful in finding work, prefer to participate in a reduced capacity, or have chosen to exit the workforce permanently. In response to this situation, the government in Australia is urging its older citizens to continue working for as long as possible (Costello 2004). This generates a paradox where policy is directed toward encouragement of workforce participation beyond the traditional (for most of the 20th century) retiring age of 65, whilst many older individuals, especially those over 55, are either being denied the opportunity to continue working by employers unwilling to hire or retain them (Ranzijn 2004), or else in many cases are voluntarily choosing to cease their employment before they reach sixty-five. As a broad generalisation, government is asking older workers to keep working and directing employers to retain older workers, but many employers either don't want them or are unwilling to explore alternative conditions under which their employment might be of benefit. Similarly, many older workers indicate they would prefer to retire, and seem equally unwilling to explore alternative conditions where they could continue to work, perhaps in a reduced capacity.

This paper addresses the challenges this paradox poses for management. How do employers resolve this dilemma, which is compounded by yet other factors? Recent technological advances have significantly altered the skills required for job performance, individuals are more aware of their work choices and more likely want to exercise them in favour of reduced participation, should the option be available, government penalties and subsidies impact on individual preferences, and community attitudes, and expectations are divided about the value older employees can bring to their employment. This paper discusses the potential impact of these factors and explores the strategies, policies and practices that managers need to implement to best capitalise on these shifting movements in government policy, contemporary work demands, and individual preferences.

Government Policies

Currently, governments throughout the developed world are concerned about the impact of population ageing on the sustainability of their workforces, and are particularly concerned that, in the near future, after the Baby Boomers retire, there will be insufficient workers paying taxes to support social security and health care at its current levels, let alone potential increased demand for services (De Valk 2003; Engardio & Matlack 2005; Spiezia 2002). A number of strategies are being considered and, in Australia, some have already been enacted as Commonwealth Government policy (Costello 2004; Guest & McDonald 2002).

Recent Initiatives

Encouraging women to have more babies (Costello, 2004), or encouraging more skilled migration (Spiezia 2002) has been touted, but neither seems able to make much impact in the short term, since almost all developed countries are trying to do the same and, since it is fast becoming a 'seller's market,' the skilled workers are likely to go where they perceive they will receive the best deal, which is primarily in the United States and Europe (CSIRO 2002). Moreover, demand for labour in the immigrants' home countries will also be rising (Engardio & Matlack 2005) so many immigrants are likely to return.

Another strategy is to try to increase the productivity of the shrinking workforce, but given that most organisations have been restructuring, improving their technological base, and in many cases, downsizing for two decades, most workforces could not get any leaner, and given the increasing concerns about work stress (Halbesleben & Buckley 2004) and the need for work/life balance (De Cieri, Holmes, Abbott & Pettit 2005), it is doubtful whether productivity could be increased much further.

It seems the only viable route for Australia and most other developed countries over the next few decades may be to increase mature-aged workforce participation (Access Economics 2001). At present, the workforce participation rate for those over 65 is extremely low, around 4% (Australian Bureau of Statistics [ABS] 2005), and the vast majority of these are in high-demand highly skilled or professional occupations.

Present Government Policy

Present government policy towards assisting older individuals to continue working consists of a carrot-and-stick approach, supplemented by public education. The stick consists of blatant attempts at coercion, public statements by leading politicians along the lines of 'if you're thinking of retiring, forget it' and 'you've got to work as long as you physically can' (Legge 2003).

The carrot is, of course, financial. In recent years the Commonwealth Government has introduced increased individual pension entitlements to those who work beyond 65 once they do enter full retirement. In this way an older individual remains a taxpayer, rather than a transfer payment recipient, for a few more years. However, this practice is predicated on the option to continue working being open, and realistically this may be available to only a relatively small number of people. The second set of policies is directed towards employers. These include statements about the benefits older workers can offer, public recognition of employers who employ older staff, and subsidies for employing older workers. Yet, with a few isolated exceptions—primarily large organisations—these initiatives are having little, if any, effect. Many employers seem unconvinced that older workers are better than younger ones and financial incentives may be acting to reinforce a perception that there must be a problem with older workers otherwise an employer would not need to be paid to employ them. Given that ABS (Australian Bureau of Statistics 2005) statistics continue to record low workforce participation for full time older employees, there is a need for a new approach in which human resource managers have a crucial role.

Older Workers in the New World of Work

The Rise of the Knowledge Worker

Increasingly in the last ten years there has been a growing recognition that, regardless of the kind of industry, much, if not most, of an organisation's profit-making potential and effectiveness resides in its store of intellectual capital (Carson, Ranzijn, Winefield & Marsden 2004; Pelz-Sharpe & Harris-Jones 2005). Intellectual capital has been defined in numerous ways (Nafulko, Hairston & Brooks 2004), but there is common agreement that it includes such things as occupational competencies, firm-specific knowledge, creativity and innovativeness (Carson *et al.*, 2004). Furthermore, because of the extremely rapid changes in the nature of work, it is essential for an organisation to be able to rapidly adapt to changing external circumstances and internal task requirements. In particular, it seems desirable to separate knowledge type workers from routine workers (Vickerstaff, Cox & Keen 2003; Yeatts, Folts & Knapp 2000).

Those employed in knowledge occupations are more likely to improve competency with increasing age, possibly until 70 years of age or even more, whereas those in low knowledge occupations may not face such challenges and thus their competency in their specific job may deteriorate as they age. It has been argued that older workers should be poised to take advantage of this growth in demand for knowledge work, given that intellectual capacity rarely shows any sign of decline prior to seventy years and this is one area where experience can be of benefit (Patrickson 2004).

The Need for Innovation

However, the 'knowledge economy' (Allee 1998) is also characterised by the need for innovation, and new ideas and innovative behaviour are more commonly associated with youth, not experience (Laing, Palivos & Wang 2003). Though older workers are valued for their task- and organisation-specific abilities, as long as they have adapted to changing technology and work practices, they can quickly be regarded as 'has-beens' (MacDonald & Weisbach 2004). This illustrates another paradox, a schizophrenic attitude on the part of many managers: lip-service is paid to the 'virtues' of older workers, but in reality these 'virtues' (e.g., stability, experience, reliability) are liabilities if what is required are adaptability, new ideas, and flexibility (Ranzijn 2004). Unfortunately for older workers, they are seen to have less of these more desirable attributes. These negative stereotypes are erroneous, since increasing evidence shows that older workers are just as adaptable, flexible and innovative as younger ones, yet stereotypes influence perceptions, and perceptions influence behaviour. Hence, there is a need for managers to inform themselves about up-to-date reliable evidence, otherwise they may not be getting the most out of their older employees. This point will be taken up again later.

Pressures on Managers

Managers are in a particularly difficult situation when it comes to older workers. On the whole, they like and value their older workers, think they do a great job and would like to keep them on (Ranzijn 2004). However, they also have responsibility for maintaining the productivity and effectiveness of their organisations. Beliefs that older workers are less suited to the demands of the modern workplace underlie much of the discrimination against older workers, especially with regard to hiring a new employee. Though many employers believe their current older employees are productive, a potential new older employee is an unknown quantity, and if deep-down they think that new ideas and new skills are required, younger employees are seen as a better investment.

In summary, although most managers value their older employees, they are also under pressure to maintain productivity and profitability. It seems to be that innovativeness and entrepreneurship—traits that are valued in today's economic activity—are more likely to be assessed as being associated with youth (de Vos, Buyens & Schalk 2005). Though stereotypes that older workers do not fit into this new frame are erroneous, nevertheless they continue to influence many managers.

Expectations of Older Workers

Attitudes of older workers toward continuing to work have shown significant swings over the last three decades and now appear geared toward accepting early retirement if offered (O'Brien 2002). Certainly, there is now an increased level of awareness, or at least a perception, among older workers that they may have a choice about whether to remain working in their present employment, switch to an alternative job—either full time or part time—or alternatively cease working entirely. Choices are a consequence of health, financial position and motivation to work (Patrickson 2001). Those with good health, and those who feel they need the money are the most likely to stay. Those whose skills are in short supply are most unlikely to have the opportunity to stay.

One crucial factor in any retirement decision is money. Interviews with older Australians still working in their late 50s and early 60s would indicate that a number are seriously concerned that retiring too soon may jeopardise their future financial position (Ranzijn, Patrickson, Carson & Le Sueur 2004) and this is confirmed in overseas research (Timmermann 2005).

Older workers are receiving mixed messages that they are finding difficult to resolve (Ranzijn 2004). Government seems to want them (Costello 2004), but employers don't (*HR Focus* 2005). These mixed expectations need to be juggled against their own personal preferences to either continue working full time, continue working part time, or ceasing to be part of the workforce altogether. Financial considerations, employment opportunities, life expectancy, alternative activities, and the desire to contribute all will play a part in their preference. Options offered by employers will either enable or inhibit the degree to which these preferences are realised. Managers have the opportunity and, we would argue, the responsibility to initiate discussions with their older employees to consider employment options they may not have thought of themselves, which may have the effect of prolonging their productive working lives to the benefit of the organisation, as well as the employees. The next section addresses this issue.

Employment Options Available to Older Workers

Indications are that though employers are becoming more aware of the potential impact of workforce ageing, few have policies in place to deal with it, generally preferring to deal with each case individually (Anderson 2004; Vickerstaff & Cox 2005; Willet 2005). Many have their freedom to manoeuvre restricted to offering staff variations of remaining or going, rather than exploring more creative ways to retain and utilise their people. To some employers, the age issue is not nearly as serious as the looming future talent shortage they need to address if they hope to remain competitive (Rappaport, Bancroft & Okum 2003). Few see these issues as interactive. Options currently available to address talent shortage include part time jobs, and short term contract opportunities. Vulnerable groups such as older workers, unskilled workers, and inexperienced workers have had to settle for such options.

To date, however, there is little recognition that the older workforce should not be treated as a cohesive whole, but would benefit from being separated into those who can offer an important contribution, those who can maintain existing productivity, and those whose skills are waning, may need re-education or maybe retirement. Data collected in 1999 (Ranzijn, Carson & Winefield 2004) indicate that a number of managers then thought that it would be illegal to have policies specifically directed at older workers because of anti-discrimination legislation. More recently the issue of illegality seems to have disappeared and the emphasis is gradually changing towards selecting some older workers for retention in some capacity (Brooke 2003; Chiu, Chan, Snape & Redman 2001).

Yet this can only happen if there are agreed, independent and objective criteria on which to base such judgments. This will necessitate judgments based on knowledge of the characteristics needed to perform each job and measurement systems in place that deliver reliable and valid measures of capacity and potential. The present focus of performance appraisal is on achievement and individual commitment (Beam 2001; Patrickson & Hartmann 2001; Sparks, Faragher & Cooper 2001). Yet any criteria to assess potential must include measures of capacity if they are to have credibility. There is little evidence of widespread adoption of this aspect of performance appraisal (Hanley & Nguyen 2005), or that employers are cognisant of the need to develop different policies for different groups of older employees.

Developing HRM Strategies for Older Workers

Given that the present context facing managers is one of scarcity of talent at all organisational levels, accompanied by continual pressure for performance in an increasingly competitive environment, recognition and separation of the talented has become critical, whatever be the workers' age. Practices that identify talent early become vital, as does flexibility in being able to respond to individual needs. What does this mean for older workers? It seems likely that talented older individuals will always be able to find work that is congenial and be in a better position to dictate the terms of employment, and consequently organisations need to identify these high performing people, find out their work and retirement expectations and needs, and develop individualised programs to meet these needs, otherwise they may retire or move elsewhere.

Be Proactive, Not Reactive

It is essential for employers to get away from thinking of older workers as a homogeneous group. Organisations need to collect information on each of their older workers to find out what their intentions, expectations and aspirations are, and to identify the range of employment options that they could possibly put in place. Managers need to initiate discussions with their individual older workers to explore different options and possible new roles.

Diversity of occupational experience is a crucial consideration. There are vital and pertinent differences, in terms of constant updating of skills, adapting to change, and needing to be creative, between, for example, older scientists, engineers, carpenters, bus drivers, and production workers (Holtmann, Ullmann, Fronstin & Longino 1994). Therefore, the first consideration for managing an older worker is the nature of the task. For some tasks an older worker may be more productive than a younger one.

Once identified, talented older workers should be retained, even in a reduced working capacity, and the challenge is to reach agreement on an employment option suitable for all parties. The higher skilled have a broader variety of alternatives and are in a better position to dictate terms. For the less talented there are four basic options: to adapt features of the workplace; to retrain or update skills in the existing task; to change the task; or to manage out of the organisation. None of these options is simple.

Adapting the Workplace

Adapting the workplace or work procedures may or may not be possible. Older people commonly have hearing difficulties and may be somewhat slower to grasp instructions or understand what is being asked (Haight 2003). It may, therefore, be a simple matter of speaking more loudly, more slowly, or taking more time to explain what is required, perhaps going through the required tasks in a one-on-one, step-by-step, process. Ergonomic adaptations may be required (Griffiths 1999) if there are mobility or strength issues. Attention could also be given to other environmental factors, such as loud noises or music, or even a work culture in which the older person may feel uncomfortable.

Retraining the Older Worker

The extent to which an older worker can be retrained is a controversial topic (Fuller & Unwin 2005). Evidence indicates that older people can learn new skills, even if they take longer to learn them, and different training methods may be optimal for different age-groups because of differences in preferred learning styles. For instance, classroom-type instruction may be more suitable for older people, whereas younger ones may prefer to use web-based resources.

An important consideration is whether the benefit of investing in training older workers outweighs the cost in time, money and other resources. Research indicates that older workers tend to be offered training at a much lower rate than younger ones (Cully, Vandenheuvel, Curtain & Wooden 2000; Wrenn & Maurer 2004). Employers' beliefs that the investment in training older workers will not be recouped during their remaining time with the organisation constitute another myth (Ranzijn 2004). In fact, evidence shows that older workers, even those in their 50s, are likely to stay with the organisation longer than younger people, who are being socialised to change jobs every three years or so (Spiezia 2002).

Reassignment to a New Job

The older employee may wish to remain within the organisation but perform a different role, possibly a completely different one, possibly to work on time-limited projects. There is emerging evidence (Moyers & Coleman 2004) to show that many older workers have achieved all that they want to in their careers and are not particularly interested in further advancement or climbing up the corporate ladder. Anecdotal evidence shows that people can work into very advanced ages, even into their 90s in some cases (Hoffman 2000), as long as the work is interesting and under circumstances within their control. A sideways move to another role, even a downshifting in terms of money and status, may be quite attractive if it represents a combination of a new (but not too difficult) challenge, an interesting task, and reduced responsibility.

Transition to Full Retirement

The final option, easing the transition from the workplace by exploring forms of staged retirement, has received the most consideration so far. There is increasing acknowledgment that external factors, such as caring needs and other responsibilities can impact productivity, and working hours and conditions for many employees are increasingly being modified on an individual basis to reflect this. Platman (2003) reports data indicating that this option has become increasingly attractive to employers in the UK. Levinson (2000) reports a similar trend in the United States. Australian data (Patrickson & Ranzijn 2004), by contrast, would suggest that until recently few employers have considered options beyond the transition to full retirement. Though there is some evidence that they are beginning to do so (Vickerstaff & Cox 2005), such actions represent only a minority of employers. The overwhelming majority, though they appear favourably disposed to the concept, still appear to feel that the practicalities of individually designing employment options are simply too difficult.

What is Being Done and What Needs to be Done?

The key point here is that despite twenty years' of awareness of continuous population ageing, few integrated options are actively being addressed in Australia. There is recognition of the problem from government, but such recognition is prompted more by a need to reduce future pension liabilities for the older non-working population than by any desire to promote a better life for older Australians or to investigate alternative employment options. There is a gradually increasing acknowledgement by employers that workforce ageing will soon require them to develop and implement appropriate policies to manage the situation and a swing has occurred toward offering more part time and short term contract employment opportunities. There is, as yet, little recognition of the need to develop management practices specifically for older workers. Measures need to be developed and implemented that will separate older workers into categories for retention, retraining, redeployment or separation. Policy and practice concerning older workers has been fragmented, piecemeal and reactive. Policy and practice need to become much more evidence-based, rather than relying on simplistic slogans about the virtues of older workers on the one hand, and erroneous negative stereotypes on the other.

Conclusion

An ageing workforce raises questions about productivity and sustainability in a competitive, increasingly global environment which is constantly changing and requiring rapid adaptability, creativity and innovation. Though a range of emerging options are available to manage an ageing workforce, including modifying work practices, sideways and downwards shifting, upskilling and retraining, and easing the transition to extend productive working life, there is little evidence that there has been any wide scale adoption of options other than premature separation into early retirement. Such practices are becoming unacceptable and unsustainable, especially if the baby boomers start to exit the workforce in large numbers. Managers have the opportunity and responsibility to take measures to prolong the working lives of their older employees. The need to develop new HRM practices for older workers is already urgent and will soon become critical if organisations wish to survive.

(Margaret Patrickson (email: Margaret.Patrickson@unisa.edu.au) is Associate Professor in Human Resource Management at the International Graduate School of Business, University of South Australia. Though her research interests have been concentrated on older workers she has also published in the management of change and diversity.

Rob Ranzijn (email: rob.ranzijin@unisa.edu.au) is the Program Director, School of Psychology, University of South Australia. He completed his PhD in psychology in 1998 on the topic of successful ageing. His main research areas since then have been in the productive contributions that older adults make to society, the impact of mature aged unemployment, and factors in discrimination against older workers. He is also researching the role of older people, both as consumers and producers, in environmental and social sustainability.)

References

Access Economics 2001, *The Tax Base and an Ageing Australia,* Canberra, ACT, *<www.accesseconomics.com.au>*.

Allee V 1998, 'Creating Value in the Knowledge Economy', *HR Monthly*, April, 12-17.

Anderson, S 2004, 'Time to Tackle the Challenge', *Personnel Today*, October, 63-68, Australian Bureau of Statistics 2005, *Labour Force Report*, 6202.0, <*www.abs.gov.au*>.

Beam W 2001, 'Information Literacy: Requirements of the 21st Century Workplace', *Journal of Instruction Delivery Systems*, 15, 14-16.

Brooke L 2003, 'Human Resource Costs and Benefits of Maintaining a Mature-Age Workforce', *International Journal of Manpower*, 24, 260-285.

Carson E, Ranzijn R, Winefield AH & Marsden H 2004, 'Intellectual Capital: Mapping Employee and Work Group Attributes', *Journal of Intellectual Capital*, 5, 443-463.

Chiu W, Chan A, Snape E & Redman T 2001, 'Age Stereotypes and Discriminatory Attitudes Towards Older Workers: An East-West Comparison', *Human Relations*, 54, 629-662.

Costello P 2004, Budget Speech 2004-05, Canberra, ACT, Commonwealth of Australia.

CSIRO 2002. 'Future Dilemmas: Options to 2005 for Australia's Population, Technology and Environment'. October, Report to the Department of Immigration and Multi-Cultural Affairs, Canberra ACT.

Cully M, Vandenheuvel A, Curtain R & Wooden M 2000, 'Participation in, and Barriers to, Training: The Experience of Older Adults', *Australasian Journal on Ageing*, 19, 172-179.

De Cieri H, Holmes B, Abbott J & Pettit T 2005, 'Achievements and Challenges for Work/Life Balance Strategies in Australian Organizations', *International Journal of Human Resource Management*, 16, 90-104.

De Valk P 2003, 'Ageing Workforce Issue Now a Matter of Extreme Urgency', *Personnel Today*, June, 20-22.

De Vos A, Buyens D & Schalk R 2005, 'Making Sense of the New Employment Relationship: Psychological Contract-Related Information Seeking and the Role of Work Values and Focus of Control', *International Journal of Selection and Assessment*, 13, 41-52.

Engardio P & Matlack C 2005, 'Global Aging', *BusinessWeek Online*, January 31.

Fuller A & Unwin L 2005, 'Older and Wiser?: Workplace Learning from the Perspective of Experienced Employees', *International Journal of Lifelong Education*, 24, 21-40.

Griffiths A 1999, 'Work Design and Management—The Older Worker', *Experimental Aging Research*, 25, 411-421.

Guest D 2004, 'The Psychology of the Employment Relationship: An Analysis Based on the Psychological Contract', *Applied Psychology: An International Review*, 53, 541-556.

Guest R & McDonald I 2002, 'Population Ageing and the Projections of Government Outlay in Australia', *The Australian Economic Review*, 33.

Haight J 2003, 'Human Error and the Challenges of an Aging Workforce', *Professional Safety*, 48, 18-25.

Halbesleben J & Buckley M 2004, 'Burnout in Organizational Life', *Journal of Management*, 30, 859-880.

Hanley G & Nguyen L 2005, 'Right on the Money: What do Australian Unions think of Performance—Related Pay?', *Employee Relations*, 27, 141-160.

Hoffman R 2000, 'Working Past 90', *Fortune*, 142.

Holtmann A, Ullmann S, Fronstin P & Longino, C 1994, 'The Early Retirement Plans of Men and Women: An Empirical Application', *Applied Economics*, 591-602.

HR Focus 2005, 'More Workplace Stress and Conflicts for Older Workers', *HR Focus*, 82, 8-16.

Laing D; Palivos T & Wang P 2003, 'The Economics of "New Blood"', *Journal of Economic Theory*, 112, 106-156.

Legge K 2003, 'All Work, No Play', *The Australian*, March 18, 13.

Levinson H 2000, 'Approaching Retirement as a Flexibility Phase', *Academy of Management Executive*, 14, 84-96.

MacDonald G & Weisbach MS 2004, 'The Economics of Has-Beens', *Journal of Political Economy*, 112, S289-S310.

Moyers P & Coleman S 2004, 'Adaptation of the Older Worker to Occupational Challenges', *Work*, 22, 71-79.

Nafukho F, Hairston N & Brooks K 2004, 'Human Capital Theory: Implications for Human Resource Development', *Human Resource Development International*, 7, 545-557.

O'Brien A 2002, 'Retire Early', *Money*, July, 28-32.

OECD 2002, 'Maintaining Prosperity in an Ageing Society', OECD Policy Brief, *<http://www1.oecd.org/publications/Pol brief/1999/0007eng.pdf>*.

Patrickson M 2001, 'Older Workers: Factors Influencing their Workforce Attachment and Disengagement', unpublished PhD thesis, University of South Australia.

Patrickson M 2004, 'Human Resource Management and the Ageing Workforce', in R Wiesner & B Millett (eds.), *Human Resource Management: Challenges and Future Directions*, Wiley, Brisbane, Australia, pp. 33-43.

Patrickson M & Hartmann L 2001, 'Human Resource Management in Australia: Prospects for the Twenty First Century', *International Journal of Manpower*, 22, 198-206.

Patrickson M & Ranzijn R 2004, 'Bounded Choices in Work and Retirement in Australia', *Employee Relations*, 26, 422-432.

Platman K 2003, 'The Self-Designed Career in Later Life', *Aging and Society*, 23, 281-303.

Pelz-Sharpe A & Harris-Jones C 2005, 'Knowledge Management: Past and Future', *KM World*, 14, 8-11.

Productivity Commission 2004, 'Economic Implications of an Ageing Australia', Draft Research Report, Productivity Commission, Canberra, ACT.

Rappaport A, Bancroft E & Okum L 2003, 'The Ageing Workforce Raises New Talent Management Issues for Employers', *Journal of Organisational Excellence*, 23, 55-67.

Ranzijn R 2004, 'Role Ambiguity: Older Workers in the Demographic Transition', *Ageing International*, 29, 281-308.

Ranzijn R, Carson E & Winefield A 2004, 'Barriers to Mature Aged Re-Employment: Perceptions about Desirable Work-related Attributes Held by Job Seekers and Employers', *International Journal of Organisational Behaviour*, 8, 559-570.

Ranzijn R, Patrickson M, Carson E & Le Sueur E 2004, 'Independence and Self-Provision in Old Age: How Realistic are These Goals?', *Australasian Journal on Ageing*, 23, 120-124.

Sparks K, Faragher B & Cooper C 2001, 'Well-being and Occupational Health in the 21st Century Workplace', *Journal of Occupational and Organizational Psychology*, 74, 489-510.

Spiezia V 2002, 'The Greying Population: A Wasted Human Capital or Just a Social Liability?', *International Labour Review*, 141, 71-+.

Timmermann S 2005, 'Looking into the Crystal Ball and Seeing Gray: Predictions for Financial Services', *Journal of Financial Service Professionals*, 59, 24-29.

Vickerstaff S, Cox J & Keen L 2003, *Social Policy and Administration*, 37, 271-288.

Vickerstaff S & Cox J 2005, 'Retirement and Risk: The Individualisation of Retirement Experiences?', *Sociological Review*, 53, 77-96.

Willet M 2005, 'Early Retirement and Phased Retirement', *Benefits and Compensation Digest*, 42, 31-36.

Wrenn K & Maurer T 2004, 'Beliefs About Older Workers' Learning and Development Behavior in Relation to Beliefs About Malleability of Skills, Age-Related Decline, and Control', *Journal of Applied Social Psychology*, 34, 223- 243.

Yeatts D, Folts W & Knapp J 2000, 'Older Worker's Adaptation to a Changing Workplace: Employment Issues for the 21st century', *Educational Gerontology*, 26, 565- 583.

8

BOOK REVIEW

Mismanagement of Talent: Employability and Jobs in the Knowledge Economy

N Janardhan Rao

As the world becomes a 'global village', governments worldwide face the challenge of enhancing the employability of its workforce. For this, the governments must make efforts to expand access to higher education and dismantle barriers to talent regardless of social circumstances, to meet the demands of the new economy. In this context, the book examines what determines the outcome of the workforce when a degree loses its badge of distinction.

People are born with talent and everywhere it is in chains. Fail to develop the talents of any one person, we fail Britain. Talent is 21st century wealth.

– Tony Blair

Source: The Icfai Journal of Knowledge Management, June 2005. This is the review of the book, "The Mismanagement of Talent – Employability and Jobs in the Knowledge Economy" by Phillip Brown and Anthony Hesketh and published by Oxford University Press.

The Promise

The knowledge economy is a world of smart people, smart jobs, doing smart things for smart money. These jobs are increasingly open to all rather than a few. Unlike in the old reality, knowledge economy conveys an image of enlightened employers actively seeking to diversify the talent pool, reflected in their approach to identifying, hiring and retaining outstanding talent. The economy represents a historic solution to the struggle for wealth creation based on the brains rather than the brawn of the workforce. It signifies a turning point in the evolutionary transformation from industrial information-rich, Knowledge-Based Economies (KBEs). At this juncture, a university degree is not enough to make one employable as credentials do no more than permit entry into the competition for tough-entry jobs rather than entry into the winner's enclosure.

The book examines this promise. First it examines the assumption about education, work and labor market in a 'knowledge' economy. It further probes into issues like: Does KBE lead to a significant increase in the demand for highly educated knowledge workers? Is the problem of employability one of the developing appropriate attitudes and skills or does it reflect a mismatch between the aspirations of university graduates and labor market realities? Can the expansion of higher education and policies aimed at increasing social diversity overcome enduring inequalities in the allocation of jobs and life chances? Second, how are companies redefining the employability skills of the future knowledge worker? Do employers believe that there is an expanding talent pool or a more intensive "war for talent"? What makes a successful manager or future leader and how do companies seek to attract and select them? Third, how do individuals understand, manage and experience the competition for a livelihood?

By addressing answers to the above questions, the book offers invaluable insights into the production, reproduction and reshaping of social advantage and disadvantage; social inclusion and exclusion are two sides of the coin. Accordingly, the focus of the book is not only restricted to the issue of who wins in the competition for tough-entry jobs, but also considers why the job market is structured in the way that it is. The key argument in this book is that employability policies are flawed because they ignore the realities of 'positional conflict' in the competition for a livelihood, especially as the rise of mass higher education has arguably done little to increase the employability of students for tough-entry jobs.

The New Competition

> *There is a lot of fuzzy thinking about the Knowledge Economy, globalization and international competition and all the rest of it and that needs to be examined very carefully because we could be going for a large picture and miss out on the specifics that really count.*
>
> – A Policy Maker

The authors observe that in the 18th century such qualifications were not foremost on Adam Smith's mind, given that the division of labor condemned most workers to jobs that made them as stupid and ignorant as it is possible for a human creature to become. However, with the dawn of the 21st century, things were looking more optimistic as new technologies were believed to accelerate the demand for a skilled workforce. Getting the right people, with the right knowledge, into the right jobs, is seen as essential for business success. However, access to tough-entry jobs not only depends on one's qualifications, knowledge, and social skills, but also on how one stands compared to other job seekers. The competitive advantage of leading edge companies in the KBE no longer are made, monitored, distributed, and sold by vast armies of blue-collar and white-collar employees, but on technological innovation, applied knowledge and the intellectual capital of a highly skilled workforce. Accordingly, one of the most powerful social groups created by the knowledge economy are so-called 'knowledge workers'—mobile, skilled, affluent, independent, hard-working, ambitious, environmentally conscious people who can trade on their skill, expertise and intellectual capital. These knowledge workers will be highly mobile.

The High Skills, High Wage Economy: In the KBE, organizational success depends on the utility of talent rather than alienated labor. Self-development is fit from the transformation of work if people are willing to grasp the opportunities that are now available. The demand for knowledge workers is growing rapidly. Unlike the old economy, there are no certainties in the KBE, only constant recapitulations of dominant generic themes, such as teamwork, creativity, leadership and innovation to specific domains. The principal justification for the advent of the KBE lies in the shift from an unskilled or low skilled economy to one based on high skills and high wages.

As the change requires technical skills and social skills, university graduates are expected to demonstrate a willingness to learn and reflect on learning, as well as develop self-promotional and career management skills. Knowledge workers cannot assume that there are jobs 'out there' waiting for them. They must take responsibility for their own employability. The authors say, after all, no democratic government can be responsible for making people learn or to be enterprising. Individual achievement must remain the basis for educational and job selection, equalizing the competition for a livelihood is no longer the essence of social justice as it is global competition rather than a domestic competition for jobs.

The War for Talent

As in ancient times, talent has become the coin of the realm. Companies that multiply their human talents will prosper. Companies that don't will struggle.

This chapter focuses on how organizations understand managerial talent and leadership potential. Current thinking about the knowledge economy, global economic competition and organizational change, and the view that these changes are putting more pressure on organizations to attract, develop, and retain truly talented people. On the other hand, knowledge has become more important than money, land, or machines. The value of human capital has never been greater, given the increasing value of intangible assets such as proprietary networks, brands, intellectual capital, and capital. It is important to acquire great talent, since the differential value created by most knowledge workers is enormous.

Organizations today need managers who can respond to these challenges through enterprise, creativity, and leadership. Excellent talent management has become a crucial source of competitive advantage. Companies that do a better job of attracting, developing and retaining their talent will gain more than their performance dramatically.

According to the authors, despite the rhetoric of organizational change and recruitment for diversity, companies have maintained an elitist view of managerial employability. They further observe that the move to a mass system of higher education has not been mirrored within major organizations, where most have maintained a system of elite, fast-track recruitment. This is because they do not see a wealth of talent that could lead them to rethink the way they organize their businesses, think about leadership or manage their human resources. Many organizations appear to be locked into a Darwinian 'War for Talent' (WfT), which makes it appear that no amount of higher education would significantly increase the supply of employable people.

The WfT presents a view of economic competition and corporate efficiency based on the assertion that human resources are a decisive facet of competitive advantage, and that there are significant differences in the contributions of members of workforce that are reflected in their remuneration. The authors argue that WfT is not the result of the poor quality of university education.

Talent is often viewed as the sum of a person's abilities, his or her intrinsic gifts, skills, knowledge, experience, intelligence, judgement, attitude, character and drive. It also includes his or her ability to learn and grow. However, the authors define talent as a code for the most effective leaders and managers at all levels, who can help drive a company's performance.

The Science of Gut Feeling

What counts cannot always be counted, and what can be counted does not always count.

– Albert Einstein

Jobs in the 21st century are far different from the jobs undertaken by our parents or even ourselves a decade ago because the stakes in managerial labor markets in the new knowledge economy are high. People no longer want to be managed, but led. Consequently, companies are not just looking for managers, but for leaders. People have to be more than intelligent or well qualified; they need to be innovative and creative problem-solvers. For best talent, companies are adopting a vast array of methods and techniques to ensure accuracy, cost effectiveness and, more importantly, the objectivity of the process of recruitment. However, the authors suggest that the process establishing a candidate's employability is not simply triggered by the observable capabilities of individuals ticked off against the

Management of Talent	
The Old Reality	**The New Reality**
People need companies.	Companies need people.
Machines, capital and geography are the competitive advantage.	Talented people are the competitive advantage.
Better talent makes some difference.	Better talent makes a huge difference.
Jobs are scarce.	Talented people are scarce.
Employees are loyal and jobs are secure.	People are mobile and their commitment is short-term.
People accept the standard package they are offered.	People demand much more.

employer's list of required competencies, but through the outcome of negotiation—tacit as well as overt—between candidates and selectors at recruitment events. They further say that candidates often do not play by the rules laid down by the recruitment industry, but opt instead to manipulate inherent inconsistencies to their own advantage.

Players and Purists

The people who do well in this new world are not necessarily those who were viewed as 'well qualified' in the traditional world of jobs.

If people invest in university education, there are managerial and professional jobs waiting for them. At the same time individuals are expected to take responsibility for their own employability and to see their careers as a portfolio of jobs rather than a job for life. The authors say that they are encouraged to develop their employability through greater attention to personal skills and self-promotion alongside their academic studies, as employers are looking for people, who exhibit drive, self-reliance and charisma.

In the process of finding well-paid and rewarding jobs to capture differences in the way job seekers understood and managed their employability, the authors identified two ideal types of people—players and purists. The players understood employability as a positional game. There was recognition of other well-qualified competitors looking for the same jobs; this led them to market themselves in ways that conformed to the requirements of employers in order to win a competitive advantage. They understood the task of learning to be competent at being competent. Alternatively, the purists viewed employability as winning a competitive advantage in a meritocratic race, where differences in individual achievement reflected innate capabilities, effort and ambition. Work was viewed as an expression of the self. The authors suggest that as companies rely on managerial and professional talent they have developed competency-base l recruitment techniques that enable them to identify objectively, the best person for the job irrespective of social background, gender, or personal contacts.

Picking Winners

This chapter draws evidence to expose the realities of how assessors try to identify the star performers of the future. The authors' research on this aspect reveals a more complex picture than commonly assumed, as there are genuine attempts by assessors to neutralize the impact of social class, gender and ethnicity.

Despite a high level of professional integrity, the organizational contexts in which recruitment decisions are made militate against cultural diversity. Consequently, even the best efforts of recruitment staff can do little to overcome the problem of cloning. Overall, in the process of acquiring best talent, many companies have yet to fully grasp the full implications of the mass higher education, or in some cases, the requirements of knowledge-based productivity.

The Wealth of Talent

According to the authors, the knowledge economy points in two directions—the WfT or the liberation of talent. The WfT focuses on the limited pool of outstanding talent that becomes even more important as companies compete on innovation, knowledge and ideas. It assumes that organizations are driven by a small set of leaders that stand above the rest of the workforce. It also supports the view that leaders should be identified and developed at an early stage.

The liberation of talent begins with a different view of the knowledge economy. It recognizes that the problems of intelligence and knowledge have changed. The major problem today is not about a limited pool of innate talent, but rather is how to utilize the capabilities of the workforce.

The authors observe that the liberation of talent begins with a different view of the knowledge economy. The problems of intelligence and knowledge have changed. It calls for new ways of approaching the management of talent that reflects the fact that in the coming decade, around half of all those entering the job market in many developed economies will be university graduates of one form or another.

The Great Training Robbery

In this chapter, the authors highlight the limitations of current government policies and the inherent contradictions associated with the duality of employability. They argue that the policy focus on raising employability skills is flawed, because it fails to understand the realities of the knowledge economy and the positional conflict that it engenders. According to the authors, this has profound implications for the way equality of opportunity has been reduced to little more than equality of access, which ignores the reproduction of unequal life chances and lifestyles.

The authors opine that the manner in which the book raises issues of inefficiency and justice in the knowledge economy does not solve, but brings it into sharp relief. Most importantly, they believe that it calls for a national debate as the knowledge dividend associated with a university education may be declining at precisely the time that students and their parents are being encouraged to see education as a private investment rather than a public good.

In the end, the authors observe that the rapid expansion of education is having a profound impact on the employability of highly qualified labor, but not in the way that people anticipate. Rather than being recruited into high skilled jobs, many potential knowledge workers are finding themselves in a competitive scramble for managerial and professional jobs that will leave many of them disappointed. The authors predict that this will not only lead to underemployment, where university graduates are in jobs that make little use of their formal training, but to unfulfilled personal and social expectations.

(Philip Brown is Professor in the School of Social Sciences, Cardiff University. Anthony Hesketh is Lecturer at Lancaster University Management School.)

(N Janardhan Rao, Consulting Editor, The Icfai Journal of Knowledge Management.)

Section III

Impact on Industries

9

Employee Attrition in the IT/BPO Sector in India: Cost and Consequences

Sagar Chakraverty

There was a heavy exodus of employees from one organisation to another especially in the information technology (IT) – business process outsourcing (BPO) sectors in India and the biggest challenge for the HR managers was to retain employees. The battle for head hunting had become fierce and the organisations adopted all possible means to recruit the available talent pool. The rampant practice of poaching and bulk recruitment with lucrative offers, were important catalysts to accelerate the high attrition rates. The mushrooming placement consultancies and job websites had played a big role as catalysts too. Formulation of an amicable retention strategy was a good option but, there was no clear cut formula to devise the strategy. A particular strategy could work for a few organisations and could fail for others. Therefore, was the employee supposed to shoulder the entire blame for attrition? In the years to come, it will be really interesting to see how the answer to this question will evolve.

Sandip Sharma (Sandy as pseudo name) was a BPO employee earning over Rs.3 lac (US$6651) per annum. Termed as a 'satisfactory employee' as per the HR Managers, he never fell short of the level of performance expected of him and guided his team members effectively. The pay package and perks that he got was one of the best in the industry.

Suddenly, Sandip resigned. In the exit interview that followed he cited no complaints. The reason for quitting his current job was another organization that had offered him better package and opportunities. Sandip was just one of many such cases.

There was a heavy exodus of employees from one organization to another especially in the IT/BPO sectors and the biggest challenge for the HR managers was to retain employees.

India was arguably the world leader in the offshore outsourcing market. In this sector, client confidence was high and there were huge expectations from the industry. There was high optimism about the growth in the years ahead but, there were challenges too. Many MNCs had opened their bases in India but the global vendors blaming high attrition rate in India, started to set up offshore development bases in economically advantageous countries and this challenged India's position in the IT/BPO business.

About the Sector

The Indian IT-ITES industry was broadly categorised into IT services & software, ITES-BPO and Hardware segments. The software plus services along with ITES-BPO continued to remain the key contributors to IT-ITES export revenues (approximately IT share: 67.8% and BPO share: 28.4% in FY 2004-05). The growth in the Indian BPO sector had been a major factor in boosting the Indian IT industry and the spirit of entrepreneurship. After a sharp increase in revenues, the industry was set for the next level of success and stability. The focus was on consolidation, change management and operational excellence for securing global leadership[1].

IT services included project oriented services, IT outsourcing, support and training and R&D services. IT software products included product development, design and development of embedded systems and sales of packaged/proprietary software. Customer care and support services were the main revenue earners within the ITES-BPO export market. The global financial services remained the largest user of Indían ITES-BPO services, followed by telecom, healthcare and airline segments. Customer analytics[2] and CRM[3], legal transcription support, Knowledge Process Outsourcing and Financial Process Outsourcing (FPO) emerged as new, high-potential service lines for ITES-BPO companies. India's revenue from outsourcing was $17.2 billion in the fiscal year ended March 2005. A further growth of at least 30% in the F.Y. 2005-06 was predicted.

India had positioned itself well as a major knowledge and hi-tech destination. New areas where significant progress was made included network management, IT infrastructure management and the managed services. The country could boast of providing these services to several of the Fortune 500 companies, ranging from very high-tech enterprises like AMD[4], to 'mass-market' companies like Reebok, whose lifeline depended on IT and networking infrastructure.

In F.Y.2004-05, the BPO industry had a growth rate of 45% and continued its dream run. The popularity of the segment resulted in several high profile mergers and acquisitions. As the total number of people working in IT and ITES went up by 17%, it was also the biggest employment generator in the country. It was estimated that by the year 2008, total employees in this sector would grow up to 11,00,000.[5]

There were over 400 companies operating within the Indian ITES-BPO space, including captive units[6] (of both MNCs and Indian companies) and third-party service providers. Captive units continued to dominate the segment, accounting for over 65% of the value of work off-shored to the country. While the independent/third-party ITES-BPO vendors outnumbered the captive units, the scale of work undertaken by captive units were significantly higher.

India's technology hub, Bangalore, had experienced a 20% growth to 90 billion rupees (US$2.05 billion) in its software and back-office outsourcing exports in the April-September 2005 half-year period. Many of the world's largest technology companies, including Microsoft, Intel, Oracle and Google, had their offices in Bangalore. Another 57 foreign companies had opened offices in the city and had invested a total of 9.2 billion rupees ($209 million) by September 2005 (when the figures were calculated)[7]. It was expected that full year (2005) revenues to be at least $8.7 billion, or 30% higher than last year's (2004) figure of $6.7 billion.

The MNC Effect

With the expected growth in outsourcing, multinational companies (MNCs) rushed into India to stake a claim to the IT outsourcing market. While a large number of companies were outsourcing their software development to Indian companies, others had established a presence in India and participated actively in the software export game. They came to India, set up branches and hired local manpower aggressively. They hired the best and the brightest. This tempted the employees of other Indian companies to look for job changes as the MNCs offered better pay package. The outcome was large scale job attrition.

The three MNCs, IBM[8], Cognizant Technology[9] and Accenture[10], added over 15,000 people in India in the year 2004. Companies like Microsoft[11], Oracle Corporation[12], Electronic Data Systems[13], Computer Sciences Corporation[14], Cisco Systems[15], Intel[16], Xansa[17], SAP[18], Cap Gemini[19] and Deloitte[20] had cumulatively recruited over 20,000 people in India in the year 2004 and had announced plans of hiring an equal number, in the near future. The big Indian software giants like Wipro[21] and Infosys[22] also added thousands of employees. In contrast, 10 Indian mid-tier[23] IT companies like Patni Computers[24], NUT[25], Mastek, i-flex[26], Polaris[27], CMC[28], Tata Infotech[29], Mahindra British Telecom[30], Birlasoft[31] and MPhasis BFL had cumulatively added less than 10,000 people.

An analyst at a Chennai-based IT firm said, *"Multinationals are stealing the thunder from Indian companies. History always repeats itself. It happened to the fast moving consumer goods, financial services, automobile and pharmaceutical industries. We are now seeing a replay of it in IT services."*

Vivek Paul, Vice Chairman, Wipro Ltd., concurred, *"Foreign companies will end up hiring more Indians than Indian companies will, not because they are US or foreign based service companies but because of US companies setting shop in India. This will be a very fast growing area."*

N Lakshmi Narayanan, president and CEO at Cognizant Technology, who conceded that attrition rates would go up, believed that the battles would be fought on college campuses around the nation. He said, *"Hiring by multinationals will have more of a trickle-up effect rather than a trickle-down effect. This will lead to small companies losing people to the mid-tier ones and the mid-tier ones losing people to the larger ones. In turn, this will see more and more of the small and medium companies going to campuses for hiring."* As he pointed out that the level of employee attrition depended on the growth of an industry—the higher the growth, the higher the average attrition and employees would shift to those companies that had higher growth because those companies would offere them better growth opportunities.

Amidst the head hunting battle played by the biggies, there was a subtle apprehension amongst the mid-tier companies. They feared to be hit with a double blow — they would neither be able to hire from the best campuses nor would they be able to retain existing employees. The smaller IT companies were aware of this emerging situation and were doing their best to combat it through better brand building. Ashok Soota, CMD of the Bangalore-based $50 million MindTree Consulting said, *"We are conscious of this but as a company we have invested in creating a good brand. We have had absolutely no problem in attracting talent so far and the fact that recent 'best employer' surveys have put us in the top league is proof of that."* MindTree itself planned to hire about 1,000 people at its newly-opened Hyderabad centre next year (2006).[32]

Exhibit I: A Model Calculation

If a company had 100 people doing a certain job and was paid 25,000 with a turnover or attrition was at 10%, the replacement cost was estimated around 80% of salary – and this was on the conservative side. The cost of attrition was: (Total staff x attrition rate %) x (annual salary x 80%).100 staff at 10% attrition means 10 people leave and are replaced each year.

1. A replacement cost of 80% of a salary of 25,000 means the cost of each replacement is 20,000.
2. The cost of turnover is therefore 10 x 20,000 or 200,000 a year.
3. The cost to the overall salary bill is 8%.

Saving 8% of salary costs would be a considerable achievement for the HR manager.

Source: www.bpoindia.org Author: Sanjeev Sharma.

The Impact of Attrition

Analysts believed that the level of turnover could exceed a company's capability to handle it and could force a strategic crisis—schedule slips, quality degradation, business process breakdown and delivery delays. This would lead to increased recovery costs such as recruiting, rehiring, and retraining, and sometimes reacquiring customers (Annexures I & II). In fact, a new employee typically was a cost to the company until he or she reached a threshold of productivity. In higher level technical and management positions this could exceed up to 6 months. The cost calculation (Exhibit I) elucidated the impact in an effective way to comprehend the consequences of attrition from purely financial angle.

As per the HR center of Boston Works[33], for any organization's success, Vital Intangibles (Vis) played a crucial role, which were in the form of informal relationships – favors from vendors or other business contacts that can be called in as needed. Vis were hard to identify and were even harder to retrieve. Undocumented work styles, tricks, tips and the knack that came from experience in multiple roles within the organization made up as a collection of Vis. Many companies took the steps to protect trade secrets, intellectual property, copyrights and patents, but no steps were taken to control loss of intangible assets, which were no less critical to an organization, and their loss was no less damaging. Vis were rarely formalized or disseminated throughout an organization. Rarer still were they captured nor documented. Critical customer relationships carefully nurtured over the course of several years were at risk when the employees walked out. Most companies had done nothing to ensure the safeguarding or documentation of those assets.

The Employers Concern

Despite the optimism about future growth, India's booming offshoring business faced the twin challenges of a shortage of skilled labor and rising wages. Annual salary raises of 10%-15% or more were the norm in India's US$17.2 billion-a-year outsourcing industry for the bulk of workforce whose category and compensation package as depicted in Exhibit II. But despite rising pay, outsourcing firms faced an annual attrition rate of up to 30% (average) in their Indian labour force, compared with 10% in Eastern Europe, 13% in Philippines, 15% in China,

Exhibit II: Average Salary in BPO Industry (2005)

- Customer Service Representatives (CSRs): Rs.8,000 – Rs.15,000 per month.
- Team Leaders: Rs.17,000 – Rs.26,000 per month.
- Managers: Rs.3 lacs – Rs.5.5 lacs per annum.
- Training Heads: Rs.8 lacs – Rs.12 lacs per annum.
- Training Managers: Rs.5 lacs – Rs:8 lacs per annum.
- Trainers: Rs.2 lacs – Rs.5 lacs per annum.

Source: www.bpoindia.org 2005.

18% in Malaysia and 19% in Singapore according to industry experts. CEOs and HR heads of most BPO companies were losing their sleep over the high rates of attrition—50% per annum in the case of some companies—in the industry. In the year 2004, 60,000 of the 171,000 BPO employees changed jobs, costing the industry approximately Rs.300 crore ($66.5 million) in recruitment and training.

Reports cited by Gartner[34] India said that the India was likely to lose its market share in offshore BPO, from 80% (2005) to about 55% by 2007 and that India's share would be cut away by a number of countries that would together account for about 45% of the offshore BPO market by 2007.

The alarm bells had already started ringing because the cost of running BPO centres was increasing with the policy of raising average compensation levels by 10-15% every year. Analysts feared that it could negate the Indian BPO sector's biggest advantage in the global market—its low costs.

According to Debashish Das, President, Human Resources & Training, Keane Worldzen, who pointed out *"the concentration of the BPO industry in specific BPO 'hot spots' within Indian cities like Gurgaon, Bangalore, and Mumbai, has resulted in many companies targeting the same resource pool, leading to wage inflation and a high rate of employee attrition."* He added *"being able to identify the resource pool, recruit them, train them, and lastly, being able to manage their aspirations is one of the major challenges for 2005."*

Rohit Kapoor, President and CFO of EXL Services, a leading third-party service provider, said companies would move towards Tier 2 and Tier 3 cities, which were formerly outside the realm of business geography for most BPO companies. Exhibit III showed the expanse of IT/BPO industries all over India.

"High turnover, rising wages and a shortage of suitable talent in India's most popular offshoring destinations are proving to be bottlenecks," said Diana Farrell, director of the McKinsey Global Institute[35], a research group based in San Francisco. *"Employee churn is now one of the biggest challenges for the Indian outsourcing industry,"* said Nandan M Nilekani, Chief Executive of Infosys Technologies. He added *"Talent acquisition, transformation and management are critical anchors for the growth of the industry,"* (Infosys had 46,196 employees as of September 2005).

In low-skilled back office jobs like call center services, the problem of attrition was even more acute. Once trained, employees often moved from one company to another. Some outsourcing companies in that field reported a complete turnover of employees in the span of a year. There were sometimes trivial reasons for which employees left as mentioned by Saurav Adhikari, VP, corporate strategy at HCL[36]

Exhibit III: Expanse of IT/BPO Sector

IT/BPO Landscape of key Indian cities

City	Focus	Prominent Firms
Delhi (including Gurgaon and Noida)	Call centres, transaction processing, chip design, software	GE, American Express, STMicro electronics, Wipro Spectramind, Convergys, Daksh, ExL
Mumbai	Financial research, back office, software	TCS, MphasiS, i-flex, Morgan Stanley, Citigroup
Bangalore	Chip design, software, bioinformatics, call centres, IT consulting, tax processing	Infosys, Wipro, Intel, IBM, SAP, SAS, Dell, Tisco, TI, Motorola, HP, Oracle, Yahoo, AOL, E&Y, Accenture
Hyderabad	Software, back office, product design	HSBC, Satyam, Microsoft
Chennai	Software, transaction processing, animation	Cognizant, World Bank, Standard Chartered, Polaris, EDS, Pentamedia
Kolkata	Consulting, software	PwC, IBM, ITC Infotech, TCS
Pune	Call centres, chip design, embedded software	MsourcE, C-DAC, Persistent Systems, Zensar

Source: www.bpoindia.org

Outline Map of India

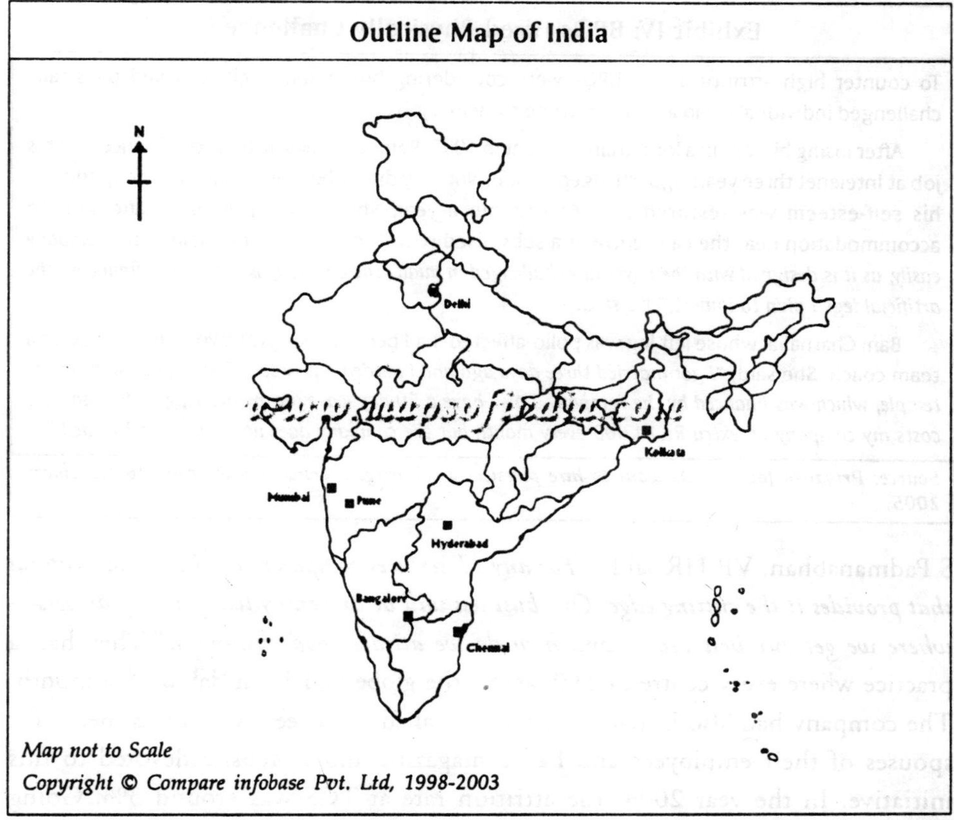

Map not to Scale

Technologies, based in New Delhi *"...Employees could leave because the chicken curry at the place next door is better or the girlfriend has moved to another company."*[37]

At times, companies did not even realize that an employee had quit. *'Wo resignation...employees actually disappear. It takes about three days to realize that an employee has quit,"* said R. Elango, VP (HR and training), MsourcE.[38]

The Initiatives for Retention

Companies were bent on adopting all possible means and measures to check the rate of attrition. They experimented with innovative strategies to counter the mass exodus of employees. Some organizations even hired physically handicapped people as narrated in Exhibit IV. TCS[39] one of the top most IT company in India, constantly reviewed its people centric policies to control attrition. As

Exhibit IV: BPOs Hired Physically Challenged

To counter high attrition rates, BPOs were considering hiring senior citizens and physically challenged individuals who are not as prone to switch jobs.

After losing his legs in a local train accident in 1993, Ramesh Shukla lost his confidence. But his job at Intelenet three years ago, changed his life. Not only did he become financially independent, his self-esteem was restored too. And within a year, Shukla was promoted and offered accommodation near the call centre at a subsidised rent. *"I can access all sections of the company easily, as it is designed with the physically challenged in mind. The company is also partly financing the artificial legs I plan to import,"* he said.

Bani Charnalia, whose left leg was polio-affected, had been working for two years with 3G as a team coach. She said, *"I got married three days ago and I needed a new set of calipers to wear in the temple, which was financed by the company. I also have a 50-day leave for my marriage. My transport costs my company an extra Rs.14,000 every month but the company does not mind. I feel valued."*

Source: Priyanka Jain, BPOs want to hire physically challenged, www.mid-day.com, 16 November 2005.

S Padmanabhan, VP-HR said , *"For any IT services company, it is its human capital that provides it the cutting edge. Our business will be driven by two primary drivers—where we get our best people and how do we attract good customers."* They had a practice where every centre of TCS across the globe had a fun-day once a month. The company had also initiated a program called 'Maitree', which was meant for spouses of their employees and had a magazine and a website devoted to this initiative. In the year 2004, the attrition rate at TCS was around 3%. Going forward, TCS expected attrition levels to settle between 6-8% per annum.[40]

Another company, Convergys Corp.,[41] which offered services in 40 countries, was considered to be a global leader in providing outsourcing services to help the companies to manage functions like billing, payrolls, benefits and pensions. Ironically, while the company became a global leader in providing "employee care" for other companies, its own workers felt slighted. Rampant attrition was dragging down profits and hampering its growth.

The attrition problem began in the year 1999, following Convergys' successful initial public offering. In that first year, sales from its software and services grew 70% percent, to $1.8 billion, while its workforce almost doubled, to 35,000 employees. Turnover became so significant that Convergys had to recruit 50,000 employees just to maintain that staffing level.

Convergys used an analytical approach to determine what programs would keep employees around. It applied a sophisticated analytical technique, often used in consumer marketing, to determine what programs would keep employees happy and make them stick around. This was where Convergys borrowed a technique from consumer marketing: "conjoint analysis." The company quizzed employees through such means as surveys and focus groups. It analyzed data to determine what types of rewards would have the biggest impact on attrition. It was then able to predict how many more employees would stay if, they were guaranteed that 75% of their requests for specific paid days off would be granted as opposed to just 50% of those requests. With such precise information, Convergys could weigh the value of its retention initiatives.

The rewards that generated the greatest retention were not always the ones that required the greatest investment. Instead of receiving raises once a year, for example, employees wanted half of their money every six months—and would stay longer. As a result, Convergys discovered that attrition couldn't be fixed by a one-size-fits-all approach, but required a complex blend of initiatives, including scheduling, tuition aid and recognition. Employee Engagement Teams were established in each of its 57 customer contact centers to customize the initiatives to meet the local needs.

"A conjoint analysis program like that was very complex and required a lot of time, effort and investment," said Rich Utecht, the company's Director of human resources. *"To use it, you need a situation that promises a big payoff."* As a result, attrition was reduced by 57,813 jobs over four years, avoiding at least $57 million in recruiting and training costs. For its success at retaining employees and slashing costs, Convergys was the 2005 winner of the *Optimas Award*[42] for Financial Impact.

According to the magazine *Businessworld*[43], Noida based BPO company EXL Service.com offered accommodation to its employees in a bid to control attrition. EXL, had a policy to hire at least 70% of its workforce from outside the National Capital Region (NCR) because of its experience that, of the 250-275 employees it hired every month, those from non-NCR areas were twice as likely to stay on with the company than the ones from the NCR region. Consequently, it had set up recruitment offices in Chandigarh, Lucknow and Kolkata. In addition to accommodation, EXL also paid for water and electricity bills. If the employee left, he had to vacate the apartment.

Sierra Atlantic[44], an outsourcing company that specialized in writing business software, based in Hyderabad, did something unusual. It invited employees at its Hyderabad office to bring their spouses along to the office. There, counselors offered sessions on better relationships, good parenting and work-home balance. Sierra Atlantic's "Bring Your Spouse to Work" and "Bring Your Parents to Work" programs were among the new benefits and strategies that outsourcing companies in India were using to retain their employees in an increasingly competitive market for skilled English speakers. It also adopted retention strategies like allowing crucial employees to change jobs across departments. The company offered top performers bonuses and flexibility in work arrangements. As a result, it had cut attrition from 22% (2004) to 16% in 2005.

Shiv Nadar, the Chief Executive, HCL Technologies said the company followed an 'employee-first' philosophy. A few months ago, HCL's President, Vineet Nayar, flew to HCL offices across India to shake hands with 10,000 of the company's employees. To celebrate having reached a revenue milestone, the company threw a party for more than 900 employees at a nightclub in the New Delhi suburbs that was billed as the country's biggest dance floor party. The company's employee strength was 26,000.

Apart from this, companies preferred to keep a larger bench—often 100-strong. Daksh eServices, GTL, EXL, MsourcE were keeping a bench ready to replace workers as and when they leave. Efforts were also made to form HR clubs. These clubs worked like knowledge clusters, with a tacit agreement against poaching. About 14 firms had joined together to form a club in Hyderabad. Bangalore and Mumbai had their own clubs. Various other initiatives adopted by some of the companies included in the Exhibit V.

The Employees' Perspective

Analysts believed that in the process of elucidation of the plight of the companies facing high rates of attrition, it was important to see the other side of the coin too and take a note of the employees' perspective behind attrition. They felt that pay

Exhibit V: Innovative Retention Measures

Chennai-based OfficeTiger (8% annual attrition) used career growth to retain employees. Here employees could look forward to becoming a financial analyst or a research professional or anything they were interested in, rather than just a call-answering specialist. CEO Joseph Sigelman said, *"The large degree oj judgement required in our work makes it more meaningful."*

Global Tele-Systems (GTL) started employee parent-company interaction (similar to parents-teacher meetings in schools) to convey the criticality of the employees' work. GTL also had an association of 4,000 people who left the company. Their efforts to build up ex-employee relation produced positive results. It claimed that in the last quarter, 200 of its former employees returned to the company. Company brought down the attrition from 60% to 36%.

WiproSpectramind offered the MBA course of the Pune-based Symbiosis Institute to its employees. At least 180 employees had taken up this course. The catch was, if you left the company, you had to leave the course. ICICI OneSource planned to finance part-time MBA courses that one-year-old employees could take up. Career counselling and planning career paths also helped to retain the employees.

Other measures included performance bonuses. Global Vantedge employees walked home with Rs. 25,000 – Rs.41,000 (in August 2005). This amount included performance bonus for the month. Daksh, an IBM subsidiary, gave out bonuses of up to Rs. 4,000 every month to almost 85% of its 4,000-strong workforce.

Source: Businessworld, 25 August 2005.

package was the only superficial and easily observable reason, but digging deeper into the matter could expose and answer the question—*Was salary the only driving force behind the attrition*'.

According to Barbara J Kreisman, Insights Denver, a part of global learning and development organization 'Insights'[45], when managers or supervisors were asked why good people left, most responded by saying, "it's all about money" or, they said, the employee "received a better offer." When viewed from the employees' perspective, a 'healthy' organization was one in which people were generally satisfied with the quality of their work life. On most days, they felt good about going to work. They felt empowered to help shape decisions that affected them, they had the resources and skills to satisfy customer needs and they were generally confident in the abilities of the leadership team. The manager, who had most influence on employee's work life, had a big role to play. People could leave if they did not like their manager; even when they were well paid, received recognition and had a chance to learn and grow (Annexure III).

Exhibit VI: Probable Reasons for Attrition	
The CEO Refresher – Investing in Your Employees: Research based on Barbara J Kreisman, PhD with Insights Denver showed following reasons—	
1. Employee/manager relationship 2. Job contents – Inability to use core skills 3. Not able to impact the organization's goals, mission 4. Frequent reorganizations; lack of control over career 5. Inability to "grow and develop"	6. Employee/organization values mismatch 7. Lack of resources to do the job 8. Unclear expectations 9. Lack of flexibility; no 'work-life balance' 10. Salary/benefits
Harvard Business Review research:	**California Strategic HR Partnership (CSHRP) Results**
1. Job content 2. Level of responsibility 3. Company culture 4. Caliber of Colleagues 5. Salary	1. Low growth potential 2. Lack of challenge 3. Lack of autonomy 4. Not enough money 5. Work environment issues

Kreisman[46] said that it was very important to know that the reasons cited by the employees (Exhibit VI) were often not mentioned in most attrition studies published by individual organizations. Additionally, the above reasons did not match with the data frequently obtained during an employee's exit interview, when asked about the reasons for departing. The rationale behind the discrepancy was that 'exit interviews' were frequently conducted by the departing employee's manager or Human Resource Manager, hindering their honest responses. Typically, employees were hesitant to tell the 'company representatives' the truth about their decision to leave for fear of 'burning bridges' or 'getting a bad reference'. A post exit interview could have helped to bring out the exact reasons for employees departure (Annexure IV). An attempt to reflect the difference in opinion about attrition between today's employees and the HR manager was highlighted in Annexure V which elucidate the employees' psychology.

A Way Forward

The battle for head hunting had become fierce and the organizations adopted all possible means to recruit from the available talent pool. The rampant practice of poaching and bulk recruitment with lucrative offers were important catalysts to accelerate the high attrition rates. The mushrooming placement consultancies and job websites played a big role as catalyst too. Formulation of amicable retention strategy was a good option but, there was no clear-cut formula to devise the strategy. A particular strategy could work for few organizations and could fail for others.

Therefore, was the employee supposed to shoulder the entire blame for attrition? In the years to come, it would be seen how the answer to this question would evolve. But, till that time... no one could deny that the ideal dream for any HR manager would be an organization where employees liked their jobs, liked their peers, worked hard for their employers, satisfied with their salary, had ample chances for advancement, and flexible schedules so that they could attend to personal or family needs whenever necessary. Those employees served the organization for a long period too.

But it was an Utopian idea. After the reverie, the HR managers had to wake up to reality - the real bad world where employees, incessantly left, either because they wanted more money, disliked the working conditions, wanted a change, wanted to learn more or wanted to grow faster, or.. .the list was endless.

As per Mark S Putnam,[47] Advisor, Business Ethics, hunger for success could be defined as, *"An overwhelming desire to have more of something such as money, power, prosperity and designation."* He felt most people did not struggle with overwhelming desire to sit atop a pile of money; they simply wanted to have a better life, drive a nicer car, have a better furnished house, better quality of education for their children, and lesser financial stress.

So...neither did Sandip Sharma elucidate the exact reasons of his resignation nor did the thousands of Sandip Sharmas who resigned regularly gave any clear picture behind their resignations. The need of the day was an in-depth analysis to dig deeper to find the crux of the problem and consequently to evolve company-specific strategies to create a win-win situation for both the employer and the employees.

Could the companies too just overlook the problem of attrition like the quotation, "... *for men may come and men may go but I go on forever*[48]*?*

(Sagar Chakraverty was a Team Leader at Icfai Centre for Business Research Center, Bangalore.)

ANNEXURE I

Monetary Loss due to Attrition Costs Due to a Person Leaving

1. Calculate the cost of the person(s) who fills in while the position is vacant. Calculate the cost of lost productivity at a minimum of 50% of the person's compensation and benefits cost for each week the position is vacant, even if there are people performing the work. Calculate the lost productivity at 100% if the position is completely vacant for any period of time.
2. Calculate the cost of conducting an exit interview to include the time of the person conducting the interview, the time of the person leaving, the administrative costs of stopping payroll, benefit deductions, benefit enrollments.
3. Calculate the cost of the manager who has to understand what work remains, and how to cover that work until a replacement is found.
4. Calculate the cost of training your company has invested in this employee who is leaving.
5. Calculate the impact on departmental productivity because the person is leaving. Who will pick up the work, whose work will suffer, what departmental deadlines will not be met or delivered late.
6. Calculate the cost of lost knowledge, skills and contacts that the person who is leaving is taking with them out of your door. Use a formula of 50% of the person's annual salary for one year of service, increasing each year of service by 10%.
7. Subtract the cost of the person who is leaving for the amount of time the position is vacant.

Recruitment Costs

1. The cost of advertisements; agency costs; employee referral costs; internet posting costs.

2. The cost of the internal recruiter's time to understand the position requirements, develop and implement a sourcing strategy, review candidates backgrounds, prepare for interviews, conduct interviews, prepare candidate assessments, conduct reference checks, make the employment offer and notify unsuccessful candidates. This can range from a minimum of 30 hours to over 100 hours per position.

3. Calculate the cost of the various candidate pre-employment tests to help assess a candidates' skills, abilities, aptitude, attitude, values and behaviors.

Training Costs

1. Calculate the cost of orientation in terms of the new person's salary and the cost of the person who conducts the orientation. Also include the cost of orientation materials.

2. Calculate the cost of departmental training as the actual development and delivery cost plus the cost of the salary of the new employee. Note that the cost will be significantly higher for some positions such as sales representatives and call center agents who require 4-6 weeks or more of classroom training.

3. Calculate the cost of the person(s) who conduct the training.

4. Calculate the cost of various training materials needed including company or product manuals, computer or other technology equipment used in the delivery of training.

Lost Productivity Costs

As the new employee is learning the new job, the company policies and practices, etc., they are not fully productive. Use the following guidelines to calculate the cost of this lost productivity:

1. Upon completion of whatever training is provided, the employee is contributing at a 25% productivity level for the first 2-4 weeks. The cost therefore is 75% of the new employees full salary during that time period.

2. During weeks 5-12, the employee is contributing at a 50% productivity level. The cost is therefore 50% of full salary during that time period.

3. During weeks 13-20, the employee is contributing at a 75% productivity level. The cost is therefore 25% of full salary during that time period.
4. Calculate the cost of mistakes the new employee makes during this elongated indoctrination period.

New Hire Costs

1. Calculate the cost of bring the new person on board including the cost to put the person on the payroll, establish computer and security passwords and identification cards, telephone hookups, cost of establishing email accounts, or leasing other equipment such as cell phones, automobiles.
2. Calculate the cost of a manager's time spent developing trust and building confidence in the new employee's work.

Lost Sales Costs

1. Calculate the revenue per employee by dividing total company revenue by the average number of employees in a given year. Whether an employee contributes directly or indirectly to the generation of revenue, their purpose is to provide some defined set of responsibilities that are necessary to the generation of revenue. Calculate the lost revenue by multiplying the number of weeks the position is vacant by the average weekly revenue per employee.

Example: If a company has 100 people doing a certain job and gets paid 25,000 and that turnover or attrition is running at 10%. The replacement cost estimate around 80% of salary as a truer rule of thumb—and this will be on the conservative side.

The cost of attrition is: (Total staff x attrition rate %) x (annual salary x 80%).

100 staff at 10% attrition means 10 people leave and are replaced each year.

- A replacement cost of 80% of a salary of 25,000 means the cost of each replacement is 20,000.
- The cost of turnover is therefore 10 x 20,000 or 200,000 a year.
- The oncost to the overall salary bill is 8%.

(Saving 8% of salary costs would be a considerable achievement for the HR manager).

Source: www.bpoindia.org Author: Sanjeev Sharma.

ANNEXURE II

Cost of Turnover

A. Sample Calculations

- Start with the assumption that losing a "Hi-Per's" (High Performing Employees) is three times as bad as losing a "Lo-Per" (Low Performer).
- Split your range of the "normal" performance appraisal scores your employees normally receive into three divisions (Top 25%, Middle 50%, and Bottom 25%). For example, performance appraisal scores of 90-100 are in the top 25%; 70-89 middle 50%; and below 70 in the bottom 25%.
- Now assuming that losing a top performer is three times worse than losing a bottom performer do this calculation.

  TP = Top Performer; MP = Middle Performer; BP = Bottom Performer.

Example 1:

A. 1 Middle Performer plus 3 Bottom Performers left.

1 – Top Performers

PA Score = PA =100

Weighting Factor = WF = 1.5

Number Who Left = NWL = 0

TP Total Score = PA x WF x NWL

NWL = 60 x 0.5 x 3

TP Total Score = 100 x 1.5 x 0

2 – Middle Performers

PA Score = PA = 80

Weighting Factor = WF = 1.0

Number Who Left = NWL = 1

MP Total Score = PA x WF x NWL = 80 x 1.0 x 1

3 – Bottom Performers

PA Score = PA = 60

Weighting Factor = WF = 0.5

Number Who Left = NWL = 3

BP Total Score = PA x WF x

TP Total Score = 0

MP Total Score = 80

BP Total Score = 90

Total Example 1 = TP + MP + BP = 0 + 80 + 90 = 170

(High numbers are bad; 3 Lo-Per Employees out of a total of four who left)

Example 2:

B. 3 Top Performers plus 1 Middle Performer left.

1 – Top Performers

PA Score = PA = 100 Weighting Factor = WF = 1.5

Number Who Left = NWL = 3

TP Total Score = PA xWFx NWL = 100x1.5x3

NWL =60x0.5x0

TP Total Score = 450

2 – Middle Performers

PA Score = PA = 80 Weighting Factor = WF =1.0

Number Who Left = MPWL = 1

MP Total Score = PA x MPWF x NWL

MP Total Score = 80 x 1.0 x 1= 80

3 – Bottom Performers

PA Score = PA = 60 Weighting Factor = WF = 0.5

Number Who Left = NWL = 0 BP Total Score = PA x WF x

BP Total Score = 0

Total Example 2 = 450 + 80 + 0 = 530

(High numbers are bad; 3 Hi-Per Employees out of a total of four who left).

The results are calculated monthly and compared to previous months and years.

In this example where 4 employees left in both cases the score when 3 Hi-Per's left was 530 compared to 170 when 3 Lo-Per's left. The point difference differentiates the difference between Performance Turnover and the traditional turnover calculation (where the score would have been 320).

Hi-Per turnover = 530 Lo-Per turnover = 170 Traditional calculation = 320 (Where a high number is bad).

Source: www.drjohnsullivan.com By Dr. John Sullivan, Head and Professor of Human Resource Management College of Business, San Francisco State University.

ANNEXURE III

Model Format

Employee Retention Survey and Response Percentiles					
* Please put a tick mark as per your suitable rating					
Statement	«Less true			More true»	
	1	2	3	4	5
1 I work for a great company					
2 This company has a clear mission and positive values					
3 My job is exciting					
4 I need the benefits					
5 My efforts are appreciated					
6 I control how my work is accomplished					
7 Work life and home life is easily balanced					
8 My job matches what I do best					
9 The people I work with are very professional					
10 My co-workers are wonderful					
11 I really like my boss					
12 I live pay cheque to pay cheque					
13 There is room for growth					
14 What I do is important to the company					
15 The commute is easy					
16 My compensation is fair and reflects my efforts					
17 The fringe benefits are more than adequate					
18 I cannot earn this much elsewhere					
19 My job is secure					
20 The atmosphere is relaxed					
21 I will be with this company for next three years					
Source: Report on employee retention, Prof.J. Vaghel, St. Josheps College, New York.					

ANNEXURE IV

Post-Exit Interviews (More useful than exit interviews)

Expect to find a significant difference in the answers you get from post-exit interviews/questionnaires (as opposed to traditional exit interviews) because:

- Individuals are less emotional 6 months later. They have had time to reflect and compare "us" to their new situation. And they no longer have the need for a "good" reference from their manager "restricting" their answers.

Note: Have a process in place for using the results of the survey to improve the way we manage. If you just put the answers in the employee file or if management does not actually act on the results...stop the process.

Don't be surprised if the answers you get differ significantly from your traditional exit interviews! Expect the top reasons for leaving to be:

- Poor management and Lack of challenge/excitement!

Most do. Also, don't be surprised that you are already aware of who the "bad" managers are and...that top management will be resistant to do anything.

Alternatives or Supplements to Post-Exit Interviews Include

- ***Why employees stay? survey,*** where you ask current employees the reasons they like (or stay in) their current job.
- ***Barriers to your productivity*** (and frustrating things that could easily be changed) survey where you try to identify things that prevent employees from being the most productive.

Send them a paper survey within 3 to 12 months of a voluntary termination (Attach a $5 bill to the questionnaire to reimburse them for their time. It will probably double your response rate). Pre-test the questionnaire so you are sure it can be done in 15 minutes or less. Include a stamped return envelop (if possible, include a mini-pencil).

Suggest Questions Related to:

1. What were the positive things about your job/manager/the company that caused you to STAY as long as you did with us?
2. Are there any aspects in your CURRENT job/manager/the company that are superior to what we offered?
3. What were the 3 biggest BARRIERS to productivity in the last 6 months with us?
4. Can you help us improve the way we manage/do business by telling us what were the significant "triggers" or REASONS that made you to decide to leave our firm.

Can you let us know the TOP 5 significant reasons for leaving us: (1 = most important reason, 2 = next most important, etc., up to 5 reasons, in descending order of importance).

- Working conditions.
- Co-workers/team.
- Actions by my manager.
- Lack of action by my manager.
- Actions by top management.
- Lack of action by top management.
- Compensation issues.
- Benefits issues.
- Reasons unrelated to my job.
- Lack of challenge/job growth.
- Lack of promotional opportunities.
- Insufficient training.
- Inadequate equipment/tools/support.

- Poor communications (mostly from______).
- Lack of job security.
- Not appreciated/lack of recognition by my manager.
- Issues related to our product, customers or firm performance.
- An offer I couldn't refuse.
- Other, please specify _____
- Other, please specify _____
- Other, please specify _____

Are there any other comments or suggestions that you can offer that might help us IMPROVE the way we manage/operate?

____

____

5. Would you consider returning to our company at any time in the near future? Give them a choice of returning the questionnaire anonymously or giving their name. Give them a choice of listing their current job and company or keeping their job/company confidential.

Send them a follow up questionnaire if you don't get a response within 30 days.

Source: www.drjohnsullivan.com By Dr. John Sullivan, Head and Professor of Human Resource Management College of Business, San Francisco State University.

ANNEXURE V

The Employees' Psychology

Analysts said, in work environments, money was typically viewed as a powerful indirect motivation, whereas job satisfaction and a pleasant social environment were more direct motivations.

Psychologist Hara Estroff Marano[49] said that people wanted to feel that they were making a difference, especially when it came to the jobs they do. When employees were aware that their work made a difference to others—even in small ways—their job satisfaction would rise and so would their productivity. Below excerpt elucidated the thought process of an employee in this context.

An Example of an Employee's Thoughts

The excerpt given below portrayed the thought process of Sudha Sen, an employee of an IT company.

She said, "History says that one particular industry plays major role in giving momentum to the economy and cause boom, for India it is the IT/ITES sector. The ground rule for this sector is to evolve continuously, because the latest technology today gets obsolete tomorrow. People have to constantly upgrade as per market needs and so also the companies. Would it be really wise that owing to loyalty one should stick to a company, which neither can upgrade itself nor it can provide its people with latest technology to work with and in turn improve their intellectual capital? Employees not only seek for good salary but also seek for good opportunity to learn. 'Loyalty' always pays; but, we need to find out the appropriate place to implement it. If an employee invested his loyalty in a company which is not capable enough to give me right push at the right time then it would be an unwise decision to remain loyal to that company... Can we be fully productive and efficient if we are not happy (in this case you may take happiness equals mental peace) from inside? Can we do proper justice to our work if we do not intend to do it from heart? Can we progress in our life without showing results? And above all can we stay in a place for almost 50% of each day without being happy?

She added, "Currently there is a phase of boom for India, it is sensible to grab opportunities that a boom phase has to offer... 'make hay while the sun shines'. When the economy is moving at a faster pace then one has to speed up to keep him/her moving. We know that this is not going to last forever. We will reach to a saturation point and then things will slow down... 'Long years of service' itself has changed its meaning. In the current scenario, 5 years of continuous service would be called as a long or at least a decent. However, 15 years ago, long service meant 15 years or so. So the term itself is very flexible. Now-a-days if a person doesn't change a job in every 2-4 years or

Contd...

Contd...
even at least get a new offer then something some where is wrong. This shows the current mental attitude of today's youth (20-35) of India. *If attrition were so very unacceptable then companies should have taken the step to stop it by not accepting the candidates in bulks. But, they didn't... they take in bulks as the requirement is huge. So people leave in bulks too.* In today's world there has to be win-win situation for both employee and employer."
Source: www.o3.indiatimes.com/IT blogs

Ganesh Chella, CEO of Totus Consulting[50], a strategic HR Consulting firm, had presented and alternate view to the desire factor of employees. According to him, all human achievement had been the result of dreams and deep desires. In fact, desires were the well-springs of human motivation. He believed that one needs to become "deserving" before "desiring". The point was that there were some who desired and deserved and some who desired but did not deserve. This relationship between desiring and deserving is what he called "the D factor".

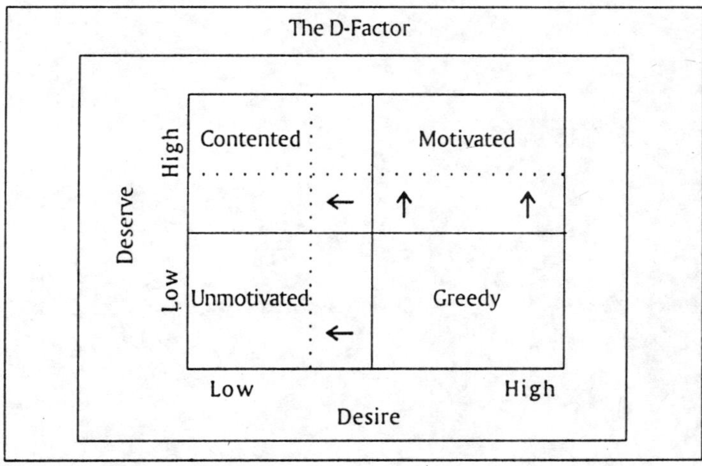

Ganesh Chella asked a question—*"do today's employees, in particular, and youth, in general, more desire than deserving and why?"* He added, *"When any average senior professional or HR manager was asked, they will tell with a sense of despair that today's young employees certainly "desire" more than they "deserve". The demands made by young employees, their career aspirations, the frequent job changes, the rampant cases of falsification of employee records, would all be seen as symptoms of today's young*

employees desiring beyond deserving. The excessive pursuit of money and material ends, the media celebration of "the richest", "the highest paid" and "youngest millionaires" and so on, only fuel the desire of today's youth well before they deserve, they will maintain."

According to Chella, the term "deserve" was used to describe the state where the individual had the competence and abilities and was therefore, "worthy of or "merits" rewards. The term "desire" was used to describe the urge, the "craving" and the "hankering" for rewards and material gains. In fact, he saw 'four types of employees'—the unmotivated, the contented, the motivated, and the greedy. He thought that (with relevance to India), the fact that the large numbers being added to the workforce at disproportionately high salaries with few skills and fewer role models to emulate, most would soon fall into the last type. Therefore according to him, it would be fair to conclude that the answer to the question seemed a categorical "yes".

Source: Compiled by the author.

Endnotes

1 Source: NASSCOM's India ITES-BPO Strategy Summit, 7-8 June 2005, Bangalore.

2 Customer analytics comprised of all programming that analyzes data about an enterprise's customers and presented it so that better and quicker business decisions can be made. Customer analytics was a form of online analytical processing (OLAP) and might employ data mining.

3 Customer Relationship Management.

4 Advanced Micro Devices.

5 Source: INDUSTRY OVERVIEW: Home Alone, No More, *www.dqindia.com*

6 Captive units were subsidiaries of large IT companies. Those centers operated for servicing their own clients and not third party clients.

7 As indicated by B. V. Naidu, director of the federal government body Software Technology Parks of India. Source: S. Srinivasan, Bangalore Outsourcing Revenue Increases, AP, 09/28/05.

8 International Business Machines (IBM) was the world's top provider of computer products and services. Among the leaders in almost every market in which it competed, the company made mainframes and servers, storage systems, and peripherals. Its service arm was the largest in the world, and IBM was also one of the largest providers of both software (ranking #2, behind Microsoft) and semiconductors.

9 CTS provided application maintenance services, data warehousing, software development and integration, and reengineering services for legacy systems, primarily to medium-sized and large businesses. The majority of its sales were to customers in North America, including IMS Health, First Data, and ACNielsen. Most of the company's software development centers and employees were located in India, with others in the US. CTS served clients in industries including financial services, health care, retail, and manufacturing.

10 The world's largest management and technology consulting firm, Accenture offered its multinational clientele business and technology consulting services as well as outsourced technology services across 17 industry groups. Its service areas included enterprise integration, human resources, strategic planning, and supply chain management. It had performed work for such global heavyweights as British Airways, Microsoft, and T-Mobile. The company, which was domiciled in Bermuda but headquartered in New York City, had more than 100 offices in about 50 countries.

11 The world's No.1 software company provided a variety of products and services, including its Windows operating systems and Office software suite. The company had expanded into markets such as video game consoles, interactive television, and Internet access.

12 The enterprise software giant provided a range of tools for managing business data, supporting business operations, and facilitating collaboration and application development. Companies used Oracle's database management software to store and access data across numerous platforms. The company also offered business applications for data warehousing, customer relationship management, and supply chain management.

13 Electronic Data Systems (EDS) pioneered the computer outsourcing business, and was the largest independent systems management and services firm in the US. EDS delivered such services as systems integration, network and systems operations, data center management, application development, and outsourcing. It served customers in a number of different industries, including health care, manufacturing, and transportation; EDS was also one of the largest federal government contractors.

14 With core capabilities in the areas of IT outsourcing, systems integration and consulting, CSC's business expertise spanned a range of industries, solutions and geographies. Hundreds of government agencies and more than one-third of the Global Fortune 500 depended on CSC for their success.

15 The company's products were routers and switches; Cisco's switch line included equipment based on Ethernet, Gigabit Ethernet, and ATM technologies. Other products included remote access servers, IP telephony equipment used to transmit data and voice communications over the same network, optical networking components, and network service and security systems. It sold its products primarily to large enterprises and telecommunications service providers.

16 Intel was the foremost semiconductor maker in the world. Intel remained famous for its superior execution in all parts of its business, and showed no signs of falling from its lofty perch, atop the chip industry. Though best known for its Pentium and Celeron microprocessors—about four-fifths of new PCs had them—Intel also made flash memories embedded semiconductors for the communications and industrial equipment markets.

17 "The company provided information technology (IT) services, developing systems that managed such functions as accounting, billing, customer services, online banking, purchasing, and sales. Xansa also provided IT outsourcing. Specializing in large-scale projects, Xansa worked with companies in the banking, government, retail, telecommunications, and utility industries primarily in Europe.

18 SAP *(Systemanalyse und Programmentwicklung)* by five former IBM employees in Mannheim, Germany. The acronym was later changed to mean *Systeme, Anwendungen und Produkte in der Datenverarbeitung* ("Systems, Applications and Products in Data Processing").

19 Capgemini was one of the world's leading providers of systems integration and consulting services, with operations in more than 30 countries. It offered enterprise systems development

and implementation, as well as analysis and consulting services to help businesses to choose the technology best suited to their needs. It also offered a range of business process outsourcing (BPO) services in such functional areas as customer relationship management (CRM), finanace, human resources, and supply chain management. Capgemini also provided traditional management consulting services.

20 Deloitte offered traditional audit and fiscal-oversight services to a multinational clientele. It also provided human resources and tax consulting services, as well as services to governments and international lending agencies working in emerging markets. (China and India are important markets.)

21 Wipro commenced operations as an agro-based industry and later diversified in Information Technology, Finance, Insurance, Banking, Manufacturing, Healthcare, Retail, Utilities, Telecom, Datacom. Wipro was a global provider of software services to Fortune 500 companies.

22 Infosys Technologies Ltd (Infosys) was incorporated on July 2,1981 and was the first Indian company to be listed on American Stock Exchange. Infosys is one of India's leading information technologies (IT) services companies. It was mainly engaged in custom software development,maintenance,re-engineering services,e-commerce and internet consulting as well as dedicated offshore software development centres for certain clients. The company had its Headquarters in Bangalore and had 17 offshore development faciltites located throughout India.

23 Tier II companies were called mid-tier. Indian Tier I included Tata Consultancy Services (TCS), Infosys Technologies Ltd and Wipro Ltd that had already entered the billion-dollar league over the last couple of years.

24 Patni Computer Systems Ltd. (Patni) was one of the leading global providers of Information Technology services and business solutions. Over 11,000 professionals service clients across diverse industries, from 23 sales offices across the Americas, Europe and Asia-Pacific, and multiple offshore development centers across 8 cities in India. They had serviced more than 200 companies of the Fortune 1000 companies, for over two decades.

25 NET Technologies was a global IT and Business Process Management Services provider, with a footprint that spanned 14 countries across the world. It had been working with global corporations in the USA, Europe, Japan, Asia Pacific and India for over two decades. NET Technologies focused on well-defined industry verticals of Finance, Transport, Retail and Manufacturing for its IT Solutions business.

26 i-flex solutions was a world leader in providing IT solutions to the financial services industry, with more than 600 customers in over 120 countries. Its range of products, custom solutions

and consulting services enabled financial institutions to cut costs, to respond rapidly to market needs, to enhance customer service levels and to mitigate risk.

27 Polaris Software Lab Ltd was one of India's leading institutions contributing to the knowledge economy of the global financial services marketplace. It had headquarters in Chennai (India). Polaris ranked 9th in the top 20 list of Indian Software companies in 2005.

28 Computer Maintenance Corporation Private Limited.

29 Established in 1977, Tata Infotech was one of India's leading IT companies specialized in the areas of systems integration, hardware manufacturing and IT education. With a focus on global systems integration, the company provided customers with innovative offerings that brought together hardware, software, solutions and services, worldwide. The company offered seamless on-site as well as offshore software services through its SEI CMM Level 5 assessed delivery centres. Tata Infotech had executed over 5,000 projects worldwide for clients across 50 countries.

30 Tech Mahindra Limited (formerly known as Mahindra-British Telecom Limited) was the global leader in providing end-to-end IT services and solutions to the Telecom industry. Over 9500 professionals service clients across various telecom segments, from multiple offshore development centers across 7 cities in India and UK and 12 sales offices across Americas, Europe and Asia-Pacific.

31 Birlasoft was the global technology services division of the CK Birla Group, one of India's premier commercial and industrial houses, with strategic equity participation by GE Capital. Birlasoft offered IT services worldwide from development centers in India and Australia. Birlasoft had 2,800+ technical employees and a large number of clients among Fortune 1000 companies.

32 Source: *www.inhome.rediff.com,* Facing a multinational onslaught, Sanjay K Pillai, January 12, 2005.

33 BostonWorks was a division of the Boston Globe, New England's largest daily newspaper and a wholly-owned subsidiary of the New York Times Company. BostonWorks was the largest and most popular recruitment agency dedicated to the Boston market.www.bostonwork.com

34 Gartner was an information and technology research and advisory firm with over 10,000 clients. Gartner's businesses consisted of Research, Consulting, Measurement, Events and News.

35 The McKinsey Global Institute, a think-tank founded within McKinsey & Company in 1990, offered original research, analysis, and recommendations on critical economic issues—from outsourcing to competitiveness—facing businesses and governments worldwide.

36 Hindustan Computers Ltd (HCL) was a global technology and software services company offering a suite of services targetted at technology vendors, software product companies and organizations.

37 Source: *Business Times*, 14 Nov 2005

38 Source: Shelly Singh, Keep them from straying, *www.businessworldindia.com*

39 Tata Consultancy Services (TCS) was the world-leading information technology consulting, services, and business process outsourcing organization that envisioned and pioneered the adoption of the flexible global business practices that enabled companies to operate more efficiently and produce more value. TCS had achieved this by creating and perfecting the global deployment and delivery of high quality, high value services and products in IT. TCS was not only the largest IT services company in India. It provided comprehensive range of services, one of the best track records of executing large end-to-end mission-critical projects, long-term client relationships, very extensive global footprint, strong Indian presence, R&D capabilities, one of lowest employee attrition levels, strong brand and, of course, strong management.

40 Harshad Oke and Ganesh Ramamoorthy, Pushing boundaries, *www.tata.com*

41 Convergys was one of the world's leading providers of business process outsourcing (BPO) services, such as billing, human resources administration, and customer care. Its Employee Care unit offered outsourcing of benefits and payroll operations, staffing, and training. Its Customer Care division, the largest teleservices business in the US, provided both inbound and outbound call handling for sales, marketing, and support through more than 60 call centers. Convergys also offered bill processing services and provisioning software to telecommunication companies through its Information Management Group.

42 Since 1991, the *Optimas Awards* had been given by *Workforce Management* to recognize workforce-management initiatives that achieved business results for the a source of ideas, direction and inspiration for workforce management professionals. The awards celebrated the winners' success at solving some of the biggest business challenges of our time. The ten categories of the award are: Competitive Advantage, Financial Impact, Global Outlook, Innovation, Managing Change, Partnership, Ethical Practice, Service, Vision, and General Excellence.

43 India's No. 1 Business Magazine in-circulation.

44 The company provided custom software development and other information technology (IT) services from its development center in Hyderabad, India, and from offices in Indonesia, Malaysia, Singapore, the UK, and the US. Offerings include systems integration, network

design, consulting, training, and support. Sierra Atlantic's customers came from fields such as financial services, telecommunications, health care, manufacturing, and transportation.

45 Based in Dundee, Scotland, the organization- founded in 1988 had presence in over 30 countries and boasted of a suite of materials available in over 25 languages. It had working partnership with some of the most successful companies in the world. Their offering included personality profiles, competency diagnostics, e-learning programmes and facilitator-led learning. They also provided expert advice on a range of people development issues including personal effectiveness, team dynamics, culture analysis and transformational leadership, *www.insights.com*

46 Barbara J. Kreisman, Ph.D. from the University of Texas at Austin. Barbara consulted primarily in the areas of individual, team and organizational effectiveness. She was a skilled coach and facilitator and had over 25 years of experience in OD/HR-related specialties. She was highly regarded as an expert in areas of employee motivation, career management and strategic Human Resource planning.

47 Mark S. Putnam was the founder and President of Character Training Inc. and the author of the Business Ethics Advisor. He's an ethics expert who had worked with big and small companies to develop ethics training programs. He had authored *Ethics for a Modern Workforce, Ethics for Success,* and *Generations at Work* programs.

48 The line taken from the poem, The Brook by Lord Tennyson, 1887.

49 Hara Estroff Marano, Editor-at-Large *of Psychology Today,* had been writing about psychological issues for more than twenty years. She lived in Brooklyn, New York.

50 Totus consulting was a strategic Human Resources Consulting firm that partnered with organisations to design and implement HR solutions that met their business needs. Using expertise in conceptualizing, designing and implementing end-to-end HR solutions in a variety of business contexts, Totus helped organisations in harnessing their potential and managing their growth. Founded in June 2000, Totus had completed 75 client engagements for over 50 clients across several industry verticals. Totus makes significant investment in Thought Leadership through its research and publications. Totus had also developed world-class tools, templates and methodologies that helped in addressing its clients' business challenges. Totus had a team of seven consultants with collective industry experience of over 75 years. Three of them were Principal Consultants having extensive work experience with leading organisations like IBM, Citibank, RPG, TVS and Whirlpool.

References

1. Gaurie Mishra, Bipin Chandran & Nistula Hebbar, "BPO Blues: Attrition Goes Down as Hiring Slows", *www.rediff.com,* November 02, 2005.
2. Sanjeev Sharma, "BPO Industry—A report," *www.bpoindia.org,* August 2004.
3. Shelley Singh, "Keeping 'em from Straying," *www.businessworldindia.com.*
4. "Combating High Attrition," *www.expresscomputeronline.com,* 27 December 2004.
5. Saritha Rai, "Outsourcers in India Fight for Skilled Labor," *The New York Times,* December 3, 2005.
6. Rajneesh De, "Call Center Maladies, BPO Employee Survey," *www.dqindia.com* November 8, 2004.
7. Venkatachari Jagannathan, "HR Managers to Face Tough Days," *www.domain-b.com*
8. T Radhakrishna, "People-Centric Policies," *www.domain-b.com*
9. Flexi fixing, *www.financialexpress.com,* February 2, 2005.
10. Chandraprakash Loonker, "Managing Attrition Through Corporate Alumni," *www.expresscomputeronline.com,* November 7, 2005.
11. *www.bavendamresearch.com*
12. "India's Outsourcing Firms Struggle to Retain Staff," *Business Times* -14 Nov 2005.
13. Arti Sharma, "Temporary High," *www.business-standard.com,* 2 December 2005.
14. Scott P Schulz, with James W Armitage, Nancy A Brooks, and Matthew C Carlen, The perfect storm: The Coming Tidal Wave of Employee Attrition, Part 1, *bostonworks.boston.com,* 12 April 2004.
15. "India 2005: Facing the Challenges of Labor Shortage and Rising Wages," *Outsourcing Journal,* - Jan, 2005, *www.vcustomer.com*
16. S Srinivasan, Bangalore Outsourcing Revenue Increases, Associated Press, 28 September 2005.
17. Joe Mullich, Attackin Attrition in Convergys, *www.workforce.com,* March 2005.
18. Harshad Oke and Ganesh Ramamoorthy, "Pushing boundaries," *www.tata.com*
19. John Sullivan, Head and Professor of Human Resource Management College of Business, San Francisco State University, *www.drjohnsullivan.com*

10

The Indian Aviation Scenario – Shortage of Skilled Human Resources

E Naveen Kumar

Flying as a pilot is one of the most exciting and challenging career fields successfully accomplished only by a chosen few. The emergence of almost half a dozen private air carriers had resulted in huge demand for the trained commercial pilots, a trend being witnessed since 1993, when private airlines started entering the industry. The shortage has, however magnified after the launch of the country's first low-cost carrier—Air Deccan in August 2003, and its success brought in a number of other low-cost airlines such as King Fisher, GoAir, IndiGo and SpiceJet. The enduring growth of the existing airlines is further contributing to the problem. This article discusses the various perspectives on the shortage of the crucial human resources in aviation, viz., pilots and airhostesses and the need for more training establishments in the airlines industry.

Introduction

With the advent of more private carriers in the aviation industry, Indian aviation is witnessing unprecedented growth. The emergence of private players such as

King Fisher, SpiceJet, GoAir, Paramount, IndiGo, Air Sahara (taken over by Jet) and Jet Airways has marked a boom in the aviation industry. In the current scenario, inefficiency and insufficiency of infrastructure coupled with the shortage of pilots and airhostesses threaten to derail the plans of a dozen-odd new airlines waiting in the wing.

Major Segments in Aviation

The airline industry is classified into six major segments: Majors, flag-carriers, cargo airlines, independents, Low Cost Carriers (LCCs), regional, and leisure. The majors are airlines which have annual revenues in excess of $2 billion; flag-carriers are the national airlines; regional are the niche airlines limited to certain geographical parts; LCCs are the new breed airlines operating point to point with lower costs; and leisure are the charter operators. According to the recent analysis by IATA, it is revealed that Low Cost-Carriers had an operating margin of 28% in 2005.

Entry of Low-Cost Carriers

The "no frills" LCC business model was based on the hypothesis that there is a large segment of customers who prefer reduced fares, as they did not need all the service frills the major network carriers were offering. These travelers only needed an economical, prompt, secure and timely service between two cities. LCCs like Air Deccan offered just this.

In 2005, India was the third fastest growing domestic aviation market in the world after China and Japan. Air Deccan was the first low budget airline entering the market in August 2003 and it created a major impact in the industry and this model was then pursued by other private carriers such as Kingfisher, SpiceJet and Go Air. In the current year of frenetic action, almost half a dozen new low cost carriers such as IndiGo, magic Air, East West, Indus, Premier and Star Air are waiting to take wing. It was Air Deccan, the pioneer in budget airlines, which played a significant role in transforming the Indian aviation industry. Air Deccan acted as a catalyst in opening the skies to middle-class Indians offering fares as low as $11.

Exhibit I: Indian Skies – A Fare to Remember

(Normal one-way fare in Rs)

Routes	Jet Airways	Indian Airlines	Air Deccan	Rail II AC	Rail I AC
Bangalore-Hyderabad	4,700	4,705	2,375	1,211	2,286
Mumbai-Goa	3,405	3,410	2,135	1,232	2,345
Chennai-Bangalore	3,235	2,905	1,755	747	1,402

Cost Structure of a full-service airline (in India)

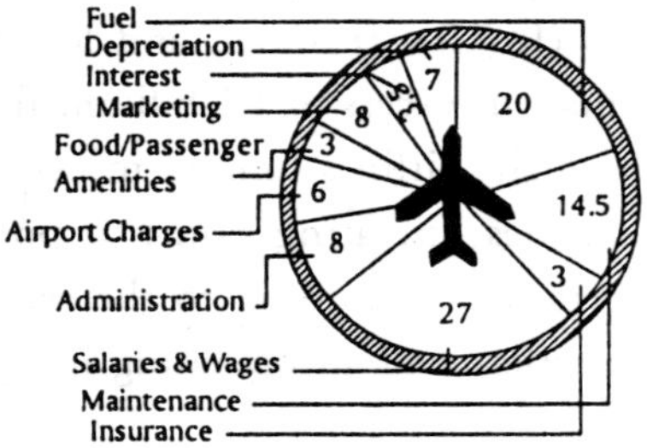

Cost structure of a low-cost airline (in India)

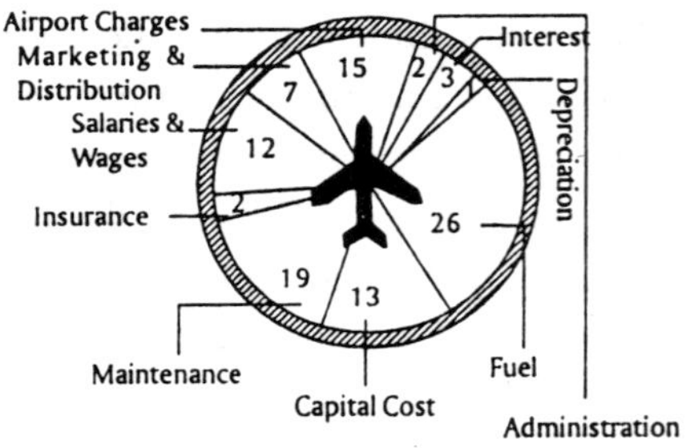

Source: Businessworld, July 2004.

The comparative cost structures of a full service airline versus low cost airline is given in Exhibit I. As can be seen, staff costs for a low cost airline is just 12% whereas it is slightly more than a quarter of the costs (27%) in the case of a full service airline.

The economical discounted fares offered by these low cost airlines created a whole new segment of customers, who hitherto found air travel too expensive. Despite these low cost carriers flocking the aviation arena, now the big question is insufficiency of infrastructure coupled with the shortage of pilots, air hostesses and technical ground staff.

Synergy between the Private Players – Sharing of Resources

The emergence of a monolith airline following the acquisition of Air Sahara by Jet Airways worth $500 million has opened the spectre of higher air tariffs, or even predatory pricing, which could eventually kill the other low cost carriers, thus, emerging as a dominant market player in the aviation market. The issues affecting these new and upcoming airlines relate primarily to parking bays, flight routes, time-slots for take-off and landing and mainly the shortage of pilots, which would ultimately hit their revenues.

While Jet-Sahara combine would account for nearly half the domestic traffic, it is followed by Indian public sector with about 29 per cent of market share. These two entities together control over 80 per cent parking bays while Sahara has another valuable asset—over 200 qualified pilots who will now go to Jet along with a large cabin crew and ground staff.

In an increasingly competitive sector, private airlines have come together to share engineering resources, equipment, technical manpower and training requirements, for downsizing the costs of operations. Air Deccan has tied up with Jet Airways to explore operational synergies in various areas like ticketing, transfers to Jet's international flights, ground handling and engineering. This development assumes significance in the backdrop of Jet's $500 million acquisition of Air Sahara and reports of other airlines teaming up to take on Jet. The four-member league of Kingfisher, GoAir, IndiGo, and Air Deccan have concurred on several issues: these airlines would transfer passengers of other flights on a flat fare in case of flight disruptions or overbooking. They have also decided to avoid conflicting departure timings between the city pairs being served and agreed on interlining so as to provide a wider network choice to passengers. They would also share simulators for training and ground support equipment at all common stations provided at a common charge and establish a common compensation package for all licensed expatriates. Most significantly, the carriers had agreed not to poach licensed manpower from each other subject to sharing of technical manpower and training instructors.

Various Issues in Human Resource Shortage

Flying as a Pilot is one of the most exciting and challenging career fields successfully accomplished only by a chosen few. According to the International Air Transport Association, 65% of the world's airline Pilots will retire during the next decade creating an estimated requirement of over 2,00,000 Pilots to fill the positions by the turn of this century across the globe. The emergence of almost half-a-dozen private air carriers in India has resulted in huge demand for the trained commercial pilots, a trend being witnessed since 1993, when private airlines (Jet Airways) started entering the industry. The shortage has, however magnified after the launch of the country's first Low-Cost Carrier—Air Deccan in August 2003, and its accomplishment brought in a number of other low-cost airlines such as King Fisher, GoAir, IndiGo, and Spice Jet. The enduring growth of the existing airlines is further contributing to the problem.

Currently, there is a demand for 1,650 pilots (assuming 1:10 requirement of aircraft to pilots) against a supply of just 1,200. The shortage of 450 pilots results in around five per cent aircraft being stranded at any given time. The yawning gap between the demand and supply is all set to widen with more than half a dozen airlines still waiting to enter the industry. In the next five years, need for additional pilots is projected at 3,500 which is a huge requirement considering the present annual supply of just 100 pilots a year graduating from 39 flying schools of the country.

The shortage of pilots has also contributed to a lofty salary to pilots, thus affecting the bottomline of the airlines. A captain of a commercial airlines can command a monthly salary of anywhere between Rs.4,00,000 and Rs.4,50,000 compared to only Rs.25,000 to Rs.40,000 by his counterparts in the Indian Air Force. The commercial pilots stand apart in terms of international comparisons, too. In 2000, our pilots were found to be the highest paid (in real terms per unit of output) amongst the 17 selected airlines of the world.

This distinction, however, does not augur well for a poor country like India; where just 15 million passengers travel by air every year, out of a population of over 1 billion. In comparison, Malaysia has 13 million annual air passengers with a population of 22 million.

The Minister for Civil Aviation stated that in a bid to overcome the dearth of pilots in the face of heightened aviation activity in the country, the Directorate General of Civil Aviation (DGCA) is considering rising the retirement age for professional pilots to beyond 61 years, especially for commanders. The DGCA's move to raise the retirement age of pilots would result in adding over 100 trained pilots. There is a shortage of between 150 and 180 pilots in the two public sector carriers, Air-India and Indian Airlines. The new as well as old private carriers have employed large number of foreign pilots as commanders to overcome the shortage. In India, the Commercial Pilots License is granted after 250 hours of flying, whereas the international standard is only 200 hours.

According to Mr. Rono Dutta, President of Air Sahara, "All airlines in the country are growing due to surging air passenger traffic. Also, there is terrible shortage of skilled manpower. It will be good to evolve a mechanism, which is in everybody's interest." Capt. G R Gopinath, Managing Director of Low-Cost Carrier Air Deccan added, "Nobody wants a situation where 20 pilots leave overnight. Sometime ago, we had to cancel flights and ground planes due to mass exodus. There should be a code of conduct in which employees wanting to switch jobs give notice of three or six months."

However certain precautionary measures have been taken by the government to curb the shortage of pilots. The government recently made mandatory for pilots to give six months notice period before quitting any airline. It has been decided by the government that "any act on the part of pilots, including resignation from the airlines without a minimum notice period of six months, which may result in last minute cancellation of flights and harassment to passengers, would be treated as an act against the public interest," a Civil Aviation Requirement (CAR) issued by the Directorate General of Civil Aviation (DGCA) said. However, the notice period "may be reduced if the airline employing them provided a 'No Objection Certificate' and accepted their resignation earlier than six months. Pilots, therefore, are required to give a 'Notice Period' of at least six months to their employer, indicating their intention to leave the job and shall not refuse to undertake the flight duties assigned to them," it added.

The CAR comes in the wake of a large number of pilots quitting public sector carriers to join private carriers. DGCA warned that the non-fulfillment of the fresh CAR condition could attract penalties mentioned in the Aircraft Rules about debarring pilots permanently or temporarily from holding any license or rating.

The national carrier, Air India also had decided to revise the salary structure for the pilots of Air-India Express making it at par with the other airlines in the country, in the wake of mass resignation of its pilots. According to industry sources, a domestic airline pilot earns Rs.40,000-80,000 per month while foreign airlines pay much more, going up to Rs.1.5 lakh per month and even higher than that. With the hike, Air India is hoping that those pilots who have resigned may eventually not leave Air-India Express.

Aviation Training Scenario

It is estimated that currently there are about 1,200 trained commercial pilots in the country flying 165 jets, which does not meet the growing requirement of the sector. With several private airlines expanding operations, pilots and engineers are switching jobs due to substantial hike in salaries. This is despite the government recently raising the retirement age limit of pilots by a year, from the existing 60 years.

At present, there are about 31 flying clubs in India for pilots in which only about seven are actively operational namely Ludhiana, Patiala, Karnal, Hisar, Indore, Bombay and Delhi and six training academies for Air Hostesses, of which Air Hostesses Academy and Frankfinn Management Consultants, New Delhi are only reportedly active. Indira Gandhi Rashtriya Uran Academy (IGRUA) is the premier institute for flying training in India under the Ministry of Civil Aviation, which was set up in 1986 as an autonomous body to bring about a quantum improvement in the standards of flying and ground training leading to issue of commercial pilot licenses to the trainees. The Academy is equipped with the most modern and sophisticated single engine trainer TB-20 aircraft (13 Nos.) and twin-engine King Air Turbo prop aircraft (2 Nos.), up-to-date audio visual training aids including computer based training systems, centrally air-conditioned classrooms, flight simulators besides having its own airfield with 5600 ft. runway, night flying facilities and dedicated Air Traffic Control and airspace.

Encumbered with the acute shortage of pilots, civil aviation ministry had decided to invest Rs.3.6 billion to set up a new flying institute, Aerospace Academy in Coimbatore and upgradation of IGRUA. The Airports Authority of India (AAI) had also explored the possibility of a joint venture for a new pilot training institution by extending a consortium of 49% equity to a consortium of domestic and international and $14 million had been invested for the academy to upgrade the existing infrastructure and to accommodate more candidates for the revised curriculum which will churn out an additional 20 pilots every year.

Similarly the Central Training Establishment of the Indian Airlines at Hyderabad has emerged as a premier establishment in the South Asian Region for training pilots. It has simulators for different types of aircraft, which enable personnel to experience live flying conditions within the centre.

Prospects for Indian Pilots

As there is a huge demand for commercial trained pilots, the compensation for them also has gone up manifold. The first step to get into this lucrative career is to acquire a Student Pilots License (SPL which can be obtained from a flying club in India after a test of air regulations, aviation meteorology and navigation. The minimum age requirement is 16 years and one can join right after your school degree having studied Physics, Chemistry and Mathematics in the secondary grade. The next step is to get a Private Pilots License (PPL). During this time, one is introduced to flying trainer aircraft, at first with an instructor and later single. A PPL has to have 60 hours of flying experience. A Commercial Pilots License (CPL) requires 190 hours of flying. Examinations are held on a continuous basis and one has to keep clearing them to become a full-fledged pilot. Training on a Cessna is about Rs.700 an hour including fuel and training. The CPL is more expensive, which may cost Rs.1500 an hour. Training also incurs huge costs: A commercial pilot's license costs upwards of Rs.5 lakh. Private flying schools and foreign flying schools may charge Rs.15 lakh or above. To start early, it is advisable to go for a commercial pilots' license straightaway.

To join the Indira Gandhi Rashtriya Uran Academy at Rae Bareilly (IGRUA), one should have a PPL with 60 hours of flying. After the initial license, one will have to get an airline endorsement, which means training on large aircraft like the Boeing 737. The cost of training on such aircraft can work out to Rs.50,000 per hour. Indian Airlines will bear this cost if one joins them but they would require the person to sign a seven-year financial bond. Private airlines charge up to Rs.6 lakh for an endorsement, and the cost of training abroad is about Rs.15 lakh, if not higher.

Training in State of the Art CAT IIIB Systems

Another crisis that these private airlines face during winter is that they do not have trained pilots to operate the flights during foggy conditions. The recent chaos in Delhi and Mumbai made evident in which flights were delayed or cancelled due to heavy fog. The Civil Aviation Ministry later stated that all the airlines who do not train their pilots to operate in CAT IIIB (Instrument Landing Category IIIB) conditions would not be permitted from next winter. Category IIIB landing system means a landing followed by a precision using the Instrument Landing System with: a decision height lower than 50 feet or no decision height and a runway visual range less than 200 meters but not less than 75 meters. The Director General of Civil Aviation stated that "The training of pilots to fly in foggy conditions is not a one time thing. They have to go back for training every six months. Besides, if the airline has the infrastructure to train them in-house, then the cost of training will come down". He also said that "Many airlines do not train their pilots to lands in very foggy conditions as the training is expensive and is not considered cost effective."

Bottlenecks in Pilots Shortage

- Most of the existing flying schools are financially unviable, operating with poor infrastructure and on a limited scale due to which they lose their trainers to the better paid airlines.
- The largest and prime flying school of the country—IGRUA generates only 40 pilots a year, compared to 1,000 pilots passing out from the CTC Aviation Group of the UK.
- The financial support and the job assurance needed to motivate the flying trainees are absent in India.
- Since the pilot training is an expensive course, even after obtaining CPL there is no job assurance as the market conditions are highly volatile.
- Most of the flying schools do not have simulators and, hence, it is left to the airlines to train the pilots for a specific aircraft.
- Currently, the DGCA takes around three months to clear the appointment of a foreign pilot and the contract is valid for just three months.

Suggestions to Overcome the Bottlenecks

- The governments have to revitalize the flying schools by restricting their numbers to around 10 and providing them with lucrative tax concessions (on buying of aircraft, simulators, land, aviation turbine fuel and so on) and other incentives necessary at the take-off stage.
- Provision of some subsidy may also be considered by generating revenue through imposing a cess on the earnings of the airlines.
- Flying schools should work in close co-ordination with banks and airlines which would help the trainees to meet the financial requirements of the training and also increase their chances of getting jobs with airlines.
- Airline sponsorship should be particularly stimulated as it not only helps the trainees but also the airlines by bargaining a lower salary in lieu of financial support and the job assurance.
- Efforts should be made to equip the flying schools with simulators, enabling them to produce aircraft-specific pilots.
- A prompt processing and a contract of a year in the appointments of foreign pilots would enormously help in solving the shortage problem.

Prospects for Cabin Crew and Technical Staff

About 40,000 vacancies are expected in the next three to four years, just for cabin crew jobs. The Air Hostesses Academy and Frankfinn Management Consultants, New Delhi are the only two institutes, which seem to be active in providing training for these positions. There are no standardized courses offered by universities in India and hence most of the airlines recruit seeing the abilities and the presentableness of the candidates and groom them in house. Similarly with expansion in infrastructure and in the number of airlines operating in India, there are plans for establishing new Maintenance, Repair and Overhaul (MRO) bases in the country. This is bound to push up the demand for technical staff especially the aircraft maintenance engineers.

Conclusion

The aviation scenario in India is currently in the throes of a boom. New airlines are waiting in their wings to fly, while the existing ones have ambitious plans to fly more routes. In the absence of proper and sufficient training facilities, it is but natural that there would be a tremendous shortage of talent. Even though the government has restricted one of the major indicators of pilot shortage—poaching, it still has miles to go before it addresses the problem in its totality. The government, on a priority basis, should lay emphasis on improving the training infrastructure in the country to overcome the shortage of skilled human resources.

(E Naveen Kumar is Research Associate at Icfai Business School Research Center, Chennai and he can be reached at enkumaribs@rediffmail.com).

11

HR Issues in Advertising Agencies in India

Shalini Govindan

The advertising industry is facing a talent crunch and is unable to attract good creative talent. Considering the high attrition rates and the stressful work environment, the human resource personnel are stepping in and trying to address the problems plaguing the advertising industry. The reasons for the constant job-hopping and the HR initiatives taken by agencies like JWT, Lowe and Ogilvy Mather to curb the insecure feeling prevailing among the professionals are discussed.

The *'naya ghar, naya gaadi'* of Asian Paints, *Thanda matlab Coca-Cola* of Coke, the pug following the little boy of Hutch, the Fevicol ad, the *Lalitaji* of Surf ad, the *Hamaara Bajaj* ad, are some of the campaigns that viewers reminisce and advertisers discuss for their ability to wade through several other advertisements and leave a mark on the customer's psyche. "Consumers are getting harder to influence as commercial clutter invades their lives," says a recent report by Deutsche Bank. These top-of-the mind recall campaigns have managed to give the brands an enduring and indelible image. According to Pranesh Misra, president and COO of Lowe, advertising is no less than story telling, it requires a great deal of understanding of the customer's behavior or attitude to inspire any change.

Source: The article earlier appeared in the book "Advertising Agencies – Trends and Cases" edited by V Parthasarathy.

Spare a thought for those who racked their brains to arrive at such stimulating campaigns. These creative men get into the shoes of viewers, read their minds and arrive at ideas formulating strategies that invoke interest in the product or service being advertised.

The advertising agency is primarily involved in planning and creating ads for its clients. The creative men rip apart the product or the client's brief to get new perspectives. The agency conducts market research to understand the product, brand, the consumer, the consumer's relationship with the brand, customer preferences, etc. The specifics are discussed with the client and the agency is entrusted with the task of crafting an ad that would contribute towards building the desired brand images. Ogilvy Mather, the most famous advertising man in the world postulates that, advertising is a part of long-term investment in the personality of the brand.

Agency Bandwagon

Advertising agency, part of the knowledge based industry, thrives on human capital. People are considered as a valuable asset. The agency personnel perform functions that fall into five categories—account management, creative, media, research and support services and administration. The account management team liaises with the client and works closely with them trying to understand their need and expectation from the agency. Account planners focus on brand's communication strategy based on consumer insights and also synthesizes all kinds of research relevant to clients' businesses. The creative department, which forms the hub of an ad agency, creates the actual ads. It is headed by the creative director who interprets and develops creative approaches that align with the client's communication strategy. The creative team includes the art director and the copywriter. While the copywriter is responsible for verbal content of the ad, the art director has the responsibility for the ads' visual appeal; both with the common goal of creating an appealing memorable ad. The common thread that connects the ad personnel across various departments is their communication skills, creativity, good people skills,and problem solving ability. The success of a campaign is a result of the combined effort of all ad personnel. The agency creatives and the clients feel that the cues to judge a good campaign include the message/creativity, the ad budget, market research, media planning and client-agency relationship.

Ad Agency's Predicament

One of the imperative problems plaguing the ad industry is the dearth of talented professionals. Advertising is the business of ideas. The agencies witness constant job-hopping, and increased departure of high profile personnel from one agency to another. The reasons for switching could vary from anything like a new challenging opportunity or inability to move to the top, the desire to earn more, a more congenial work environment or a stimulating work assignment.

The industry has been witnessing a series of mergers in the past few years. In the wake of these consolidations, there are only a few positions at the top slot. While the number of contenders for the top slot are more, the mantle is finally handed over to only one of them creating distrust among the rest and compelling them to look for other greener pastures. The agencies as an answer to this chalk out succession plans based on the performance, merit, leadership potential, etc. But unexpected moves by the prime players can throw these plans awry. According to Sam Balsara, chairman and managing director, Madison Communications, "Succession plans can go haywire because even senior people quit at the drop of a hat."[1] The flip side of it is when other contenders in the race find a mismatch between their career plan and the company's succession plans.

Advertising agency, which is seen as one of the veterans of the knowledge industry, has not been fortunate in attracting good talent unlike its late entrants like the software industry and the financial services, which are able to lure good talent. Knowledge management has gained critical importance in the advertising industry due to the ongoing poaching and talent crunch. The attrition rate in the industry is a high 20-28 percent.[2] The 15% commission system is seen as one of the culprits for this. With the ad agency being bifurcated into creative and media buying divisions, the margins have shrunk. Agencies are resorting to undercutting and are willing to work for margins as low as 0.5%. The squeeze in margins has resulted in the lower pay

---

1 N Shatrujeet, "Managing Agency Succession Walking the Tightrope", *www.agencyfaqs.com*

2 Shubha Madhukar, "Why is Media Buying Stagnating?", *www.domain-b.com*

packets for the junior and middle level personnel and thus dampening their creative efforts. Moreover, the compensation system is based on the media spend rather than on the qualitative aspect of the service provided. The agencies feel that commission system where the remuneration is based on media spend, does not consider the efforts of the ad personnel in producing great commercials. So according to the ad agency, it is pointless to have talented employees whose work will not be rewarded.

Also, the ad agency personnel, with an intention to get the best talent and the top accounts resort to poaching by offering massive salaries or golden handcuffs to prospective hoppers. But Ranjan Kapur, executive chairman, Ogilvy & Mather, feels otherwise. According to him "Poaching will continue. It is good for the industry because the blood has to circulate, the talent must circulate so that the whole industry grows. It should not be sole repository of one or two agencies".[3]

Another reason for unrest in the agency is the job content in the entry level for freshers, which involves taking care of the operations of the brand for two to three years. Experts feel that while it is vital to impart training on the operational aspects of creating an ad, to get him do the same job for three years would impede his growth and mean a huge waste of his talents. "There is a need to create a new layer consisting of employees with lesser educational qualifications to take care of only the operations of the brand so that the more qualified new recruits learn the operations during their training period, and after the training period supervise these operations along with being involved in brand management jobs. This system will alleviate the problems of the existing system where young, intelligent kids from good management institutes have to act as glorified courier boys, and never get to use their brain power until they reach the middle management of an agency" says Biju Joseph Dominic, senior brand services director, Lowe Lintas & Partners, Mumbai.[4] Also it takes a long time for the middle level manager to graduate to senior positions.

---

[3] Ranjan Kapur, executive chairman, Ogilvy & Mather, *www.exchange4media.com*

[4] Biju Joseph Dominic , "Face It: No One's Willing to Work for Ad Agencies Anymore", *www.etstrategicmarketing.com*

The Way Out: The HR Pitch

The HR personnel in any organization embarks on the task of creating a congenial atmosphere for its employees, innovating programs and policies that will on the one hand sustain the interest of its employees and on the other hand help move towards the greater goal of achieving their business objectives. To retain their best talent and protect them from the prying eyes of poachers, is one of the biggest challenges that the HR executives face, considering the high attrition rates prevalent in the industry. The task gets more daunting when it comes to managing the non-conformist creative professionals. The ad agencies' HR has to perpetuate a culture where new fangled ideas and creativity are constantly encouraged. "Handling temperamental and highly-strung creative staff and keeping them motivated is a very delicate issue. Admittedly, there is a fair amount of non-compliance and tantrum throwing, but the trick to deal with this is to respond rather than react to them," adds Sujaya Banerjee, vice president, Corporate—HRD & Personnel at Lowe.[5]

J Walter Thompson, which claims to be the number one agency in India is known to create the most effective ads. The agency of late has taken some initiatives to step up its creative work. Patrick Pitcher, area director, Asia-Pacific South, believes that India has a huge talent base and to capitalize on this, JWT conducts workshops in which creative people from India and China, crack ideas that can be used in both the markets. An initiative called the 'Young Tigers,' is in which young talents from Asia Pacific region are selected and training in creativity is imparted. With the intention to create a common platform to share ideas, the employees in all its offices of JWT come together and discuss the previous month's work. An internal website through which employees can view the works of their colleagues across all regions is in the offing. A program called the *Lunacy* showcases the best work of every office, which in turn is ranked by the worldwide creative council. The intention is to boost the good work and encourage them to create better ads.[6]

---

5 Purvita Chatterjee, "People, Fun and Lowe", www.blonnet.com

6 Ajita Shashidhar, "People Don't Have Time to Watch Bad Advertising", www.thehindubusinessline.com

To Instill Discipline at Work

The canteen hasn't been restocked today. Because the guy who was supposed to do it came late and hasn't found the time to do it yet. He's promised to come on time henceforth. We hope you will too. Please follow office hours.

The commode hasn't been cleaned today. Because the guy who was supposed to do it came late and hasn't found the time to do it yet. He's promised to come on time henceforth. We hope you will too. Please follow office hours.

This here is yesterday's milk. Because the guy who was supposed to replace it with today's, came late and hasn't found the time to do it yet. He's promised to come on time henceforth. We hope you will too. Please follow office hours.

These urinals haven't been cleaned today. Because the guy who was supposed to do it came late and hasn't found the time to do it yet. He's promised to come on time henceforth. We hope you will too. Please follow office hours.

These are a series of posters put up at the Lowe office in Mumbai to make employees reach the office sharp at 9.30 a.m. More than a disciplinary move, the initiative is part of a bigger HR plan, breaking away from the tried and tested methods of making employees come on time.

Addressing 'creative' employees in an agency is different from dealing with a typical employee in any other industry. After all, creative employees have to be driven by emotion and drama to drive home a message. What could have been driven home through a memo had to be done through this in-house poster campaign.

Sujaya Banerjee, vice-president, Corporate—HRD & Personnel at Lowe, states that "We had to tactfully make it clear that we didn't want to take away their freedom but initiate discipline at work. What took away the edge from the pain was explaining to them that coming early to work only meant that they had more time for their social life outside work."

She adds, "The profile of people is different in advertising. They are educated and talented mavericks who are non-compliant by nature—brilliant in a different way." Implementing HR policies for the 750 employees across the Lowe group is thus a challenge.

Source: "People, Fun and Lowe", Purvita Chatterjee (www.blonnet.com).

To keep the atmosphere charged, Lowe has initiatives that infuse fun in workplace. Lowe has regular beer 'n biriyani evenings, Independence Day celebrations, or talent contests where employees compete against each other for prizes. Employees celebrate festivals (*Ce`Lowe'Brations*) in a novel way and as a part of employee welfare activities it has formed clubs for games like cricket, soccer, go-karting, trekking and bowling. Other initiatives include, *Lintas Box office*, where employees are offered tickets to watch movies with their family and friends, *Lingainz*—where the agency pampers them with gift vouchers and discounts companies like SOTC, ICICI, etc., on purchase of products and services. A podium where senior managers and renowned personalities exchange and share ideas, insights over lunch, forms one of Lowe's HR initiatives. To give its employees a secure feeling about their career, Lowe has a three-tier hierarchical system where the employees are categorized based on the roles they are expected to play in future. The brand services manager that evolves into the brand services director who then graduates to become a vice president within the agency, thus chalking out clear career progress plans for its talented staff.[7]

Ogilvy & Mather as a part of its Knowledge Management initiative, started *Ogyani,* a platform to share its enormous knowledge pool and expertise, which it feared would sink into oblivion considering that the acquired knowledge being lost every time an employee left the organization. *Ogyani* invited its staff to post and find documents, presentations and creative work, and also interact with people who have expertise ('gyanis') in particular consumer segments or product categories. Incentives were offered and contributors rewarded for their efforts to encourage participation and usage.[8]

This kind of knowledge sharing within ad agencies will encourage professionals to come up with new and better ideas. The thought of their innovative efforts being discussed and looked up at, will motivate and also give immense satisfaction to the people. Also, the competitive spirit arising out of this will benefit agencies in attracting the big accounts and increasing their pie.

Conclusion

Indian advertising is making its presence in the international awards functions like the Cannes, with ads not only being nominated, but also winning some awards. Our creative talent is being recognized globally and the international fraternity is opening its doors for Indian ads. The picture seems impressive with the ad men getting opportunities to work on foreign assignments. As the job demands greater levels of creativity and innovativeness, the ad personnel expect to be compensated well. Also the HR personnel need to realize that if they wish to attract or retain good talent within the organization, they will have to opt for

---

7 Purvita Chatterjee, "People, Fun and Lowe", *www.blonnet.com.*

8 Kunal Sinha, "Knowledge, Entertainment, Networking", *Journal of Knowledge Management Practice,* May 2004.

people-centric policies. They need to frame policies that are in line with practices that are followed by service industries like software or financial services to fight poaching and job-hopping, else as Biju Joseph Dominic says, the ad agencies will have to put up notices outside their offices saying 'Trespassers will be hired'.[9]

(Shalini Govindan is a Research Associate in Icfai Books, a division of the Icfai University Press. She can be reached at shalinikeerthi@yahoo.com)

References

1. *The Hindu Business Line*
2. *ET Strategic Marketing*
3. *Agencyfaqs.com*
4. *Business World*
5. *Economic Times*
6. *www.indiainfoline.com*
7. *www.exchange4media.com*
8. *www.domain-b.com*
9. *www.indiatelevision.com*

[9] Biju Joseph Dominic, "Face It: No One's Willing to Work for Ad Agencies Anymore", www.etstrategicmarketing.com

12

Employment Scenario and Human Resource Strategies in Tourism Industry

H Rajashekar and Suresh Poojary

Travel and Tourism is the world's largest industry and thus the largest generator of jobs. Undoubtedly, tourism is a growing international industry that makes a significant contribution to employment. There is no widely accepted categorization of tourism employment. It creates mostly unskilled and semi-skilled jobs; employs young people with females dominating the workforce. Untrained, unmotivated, underpaid and unorganized labor force bears high labor turnover in the industry. Standard practice of Human Resource Management and Development is found lacking here.

Tourism[1] or hospitality business, a tertiary sector activity, has been given the status of the industry even prior to the liberalization of the economy in the 1990s. Tourism is an industry concerned with wooing people to a destination,

1 Tourism comprises the activities of persons traveling to and staying in places outside their usual environment for not more than one consecutive year for leisure, business and other purposes not related to the exercise of an activity remunerated from within the place visited. United Nations and World Tourism Organization: Recommendations on tourism statistics. United Nations Services M, No. 83, New York 1994, pp. 9, 20 quoted in WTO: Tourism Satellite Account (TSA): The conceptual framework, part of the World Conference report on the measurement of the Economic Impact of Tourism (Nice, France, June 15-18, 1999).

transporting, accommodating, and entertaining them upon arrival and sending them back with memories of lingering experience (Manjula Chaudhary and DS Bhardwaj: 1997). It is a mega industry, which is instrumental in blending the socio-cultural relations, a tool for economic development, a vital force for national integration and international peace and harmony, eradicator of poverty and social evils and a facilitator for human resource development. It is considered to be one of the easiest and most viable development options available to the developing countries. Tourism today is globally recognized as a major economic contributor and employment generator and it is regarded as a multi-faceted economic asset (Selvam: 1989; KC Sharma: 1996).

Current Picture of Employment in Tourism

The most significant feature of the tourism industry is its capacity to generate large scale employment. Its ability to employ a large number of women and young members of the workforce is of social benefit.

Tourism generates:

1. Direct employment resulting from visitor expenditure in the tourist services.
2. Indirect employment in the tourist sector, not resulting directly from visitor expenditure.
3. Induced employment resulting from the effects of the tourism multiplier (Mathieson and Wall: 1982).

The employment impact of capital investment in tourism is so strong that no developing country can afford to ignore the tourism industry. Tourism has a very positive capital-labor ratio. An investment of 1 mn rupees (at 1985-86 prices) would create 89 jobs in the hotel and restaurant industry, compared to 44.7 jobs in agriculture and 12.6 jobs in manufacturing industries. The average for the whole tourism industry is 47.5 jobs for an investment of 1 mn rupees (Khanna: 1999). This indicates the labor intensive nature of jobs created by tourism industry and related industries.

It has been estimated that one man-year of employment is created for about every three foreign tourist arrivals. Similarly, one man-year of employment is

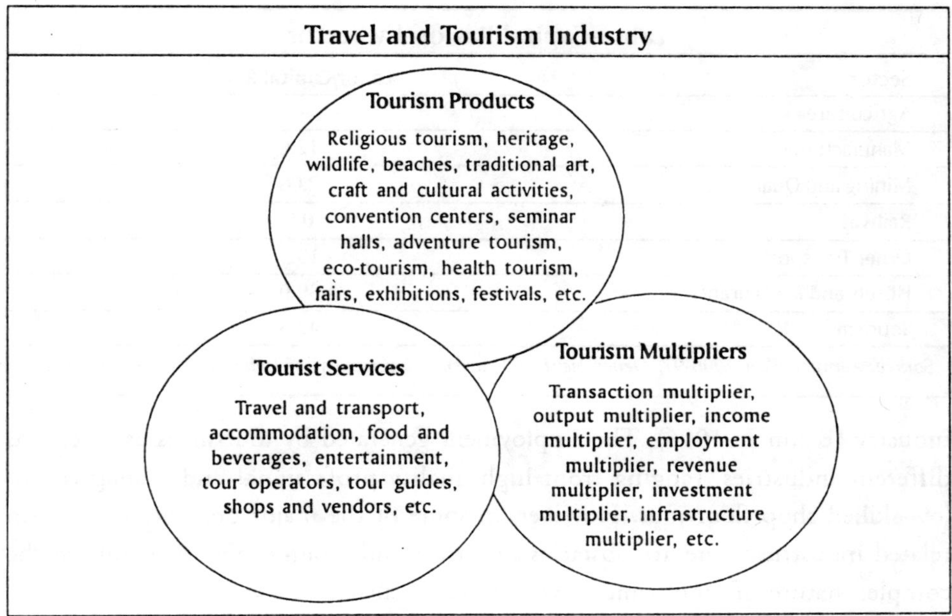

created for about every 38 domestic tourist arrivals.[2] The employment multiplier for the leisure industry is 2.36 i.e., a direct employment of one person in tourism creates jobs for 1.36 persons in other sectors of economy (Department of tourism, Government of Karnataka: 2005). According to WTO and World Tourism and Travel Council (WTTC), tourism generates almost 212 million jobs (direct and indirect) accounting for 10.7% of global workforce (GOI, Department of Tourism: 2004). As per the estimates of the Department of Tourism, Government of India, the tourism sector currently employs 4.1 crore persons, 2.4 crore directly and 1.7 crore indirectly. It contributes about 5.6% to the Indian economy. According to WTTC, tourism supports 9.3 million direct jobs in India, and by 2010 this is expected to rise to 12.9 million jobs. The tourism economy also supports 17.4 million indirect jobs in India, which is 5.8% of total employment. By 2010, this is expected to rise to 25 million jobs or 6.8% of total employment.[3]

Complex Nature of Tourism Employment

Industry structuring and human resource provision as they exist in the tourism industry have given rise to general personnel and specific skill shortages in the

---

[2] "Human Resource Development Requirements of the Tourism Sector in India", at www.unescap.org

[3] Assocham, "Second Annual Travel and Tourism Summit," November 3-4, 2000, New Delhi, Back ground Paper, p. 7.

Labor-Capital Ratios by Sector	
Sector	**Labor/Capital Ratio**
Agriculture	44.7
Manufacturing	12.6
Mining and Quarrying	2.06
Railways	0.9
Other Transport	13.8
Hotels and Restaurants	89.0
Tourism	47.5
Source: Annual Plan 1996-97, Department of Tourism, Government of India at www.unescap.org	

industry (Baum T: 1996). The employment generated by tourism is as diverse as different industries, ranging from high-quality professional and managerial to low-skilled shop floor jobs. However, in some of the major branches of tourism related industries there are obstacles to attract and retain the workers due to the complex nature of employment, which are discussed below:

- Heterogeneous or wide range of employing organizations involved in the tourism sector covers both public and private sectors.
- The bulk of employment and the scale of operation of tourism sector are in the hands of relatively small employers engaged mostly in micro family owned businesses.
- Much of the employment is mostly seasonal; many tourist attractions are closed during winter or rainy season.
- The sector generates semi-skilled and unskilled jobs employing young people, particularly students, as potential workforce. Part-time employment is common. Female workforce dominates in many areas of tourism.
- Employment security and opportunity for progression is limited.
- Specialist qualifications are not required in order to operate. As a consequence, the standards of managerial expertise and competencies are variable and low. Only a few organizations would be said to operate with good people management policies and practices.

- The sector offers the employees reward packages that are lower than those found elsewhere in other service industry.
- Working conditions are very weak. This is the sector where quality service is expected from employees, but employees are receiving the poorest remuneration and working in the least attractive working conditions.
- Most of the employees are appointed on adhoc and temporary basis.
- There is no trade union presence in the sector, which results in least bargaining power with the employees.
- As the tourism workforce is highly untrained and unmotivated, the sector suffers from high level of labor turnover.
- The sector has a reputation for not having good training practice and employing unqualified/less qualified and under-trained workforce.
- A variety of forms of restructuring has started, which affects the tourism sector, including greater outsourcing and franchising. Some sections of the workforce is being de-skilled.

Suggested Strategies

Human Resource Development is of vital importance in the tourism industry. People engaged in tourism deal with the people and cater to their needs. They are the ones who create experience—good or bad and therefore, determine the quality of the products offered to the tourists. The tourism sector requires not just a human touch, but a service with a smile as a good value. The study by Baum Tom, Amoah Vanessa, and Spivack Sheryl (1997) developed an argument that human resource management is more than a strategic and operational concern for companies competing within the hospitality market place. It considers human resource management as a strategic dimension within the wider enhancement of quality and market positioning of tourism at the level of organizations, specific destinations, and regions within countries or whole nations. Thus, there is a wide scope in the sphere of vocational education and professional training in the constituent industries of transportation, accommodation, tour operation and related activities. Some of the strategies for attracting and retaining talented and qualified employees in the tourism industries are discussed below.

Recruitment of New Employees

Systematic manpower planning must be designed on all levels of the organization. Recruitment and selection of employees must be done on a scientific basis. Standard training and development programs must be evolved to make the employees multi-skilled so as to meet the requirements of the industry.

Skill Requirements Concerning the Employees

Tourism employees must posses multiple skills to perform multiple jobs. The industry must recruit its employees with International Air Transport Association (IATA) qualification. Guide training and time to time refresher courses to the existing guides must be conducted by the tourism industry. It is also suggested to impart training in job specified skills, communication skills in Indian and foreign languages and foreign exchange knowledge, training on background study of tourism products, and customer care skills to the employees. It is also expected to professionalize the industry by providing more opportunities for training and development of its employees.

Industry–Institution Linkage

The tourism courses offered by the Universities/Colleges and training institutions are more of theoretical emphasis than practical. The tourism curriculum is inadequate to meet the challenges of the industry. Therefore, more practical oriented curriculum must be designed along with the theory updates to make qualitative improvement in tourism education. Industry-academia interaction is suggested to reduce the skill gap between the required and available human resources. Thus, tourism education must match the industry requirements. Therefore, industry-institutional linkage is very necessary for the success of any tourism course. The industry-academia interaction and consultation should start right from the stage of course curriculum formulation.

Private Sector Participation

The private sector should also be involved to play an active role in ensuring the maintenance of the highest international standards of management and services, both through access to international skills and experience, to ensure competitiveness and the implementation of training and career structures capable of supporting the development of skills.

Attraction and Retention of Qualified Employees

Employees of the tourism industry are highly de-motivated and dissatisfied because of poor pay, insecurity and uncertainty of job, unsocial working hours and lack of career structures. Attractive remuneration package must be devised, which must be competitive enough to attract the qualified people to the industry. Along with attractive remuneration package, employees must be provided with career development opportunities. An effective grievance procedure is also suggested in the industry.

Conclusion

Travel and tourism is the largest employer in the world. Tourism is considered as one of the popular development alternatives available to a number of poorer communities and has been suggested as a potential source of sustainable development. It is argued that there is a direct link between tourism, sustainable development, and world peace. However, human resource has an important role to play in developing and managing tourism in a sustainable manner. The development aspect needs to be given more importance as a strategy for sustainability in tourism. But it was observed that tourism workforce is highly unskilled, untrained and unmotivated; the sector suffers from a high rate of labor turnover. The research findings indicate under-investment in training and development with approximately half of the employers not having either a training policy or a policy on continuing professional development. Poor pay, unsocial working hours and lack of career structure were the primary reasons cited for leaving the industry. Tourism workforce must be brought to the mainstream of service occupations and educated to organize themselves for better bargaining power. Career advancement and career planning mechanism with a good practice of human resource management and development must be designed to make the employees aware of the need for their development.

(H Rajashekar, Reader, Department of Commerce, University of Mysore, Manasagangotri, Mysore-6. The author can be reached at rajashekarh1@yahoo.co.in

Suresh Poojary, Lecturer, Department of Commerce, St. Aloysius College, Mangalore. The author can be reached at sureshsucha@sify.com)

Tourism Industry – HR Challenges

Travel and tourism has emerged as substantial economic and social activities in the modern world with tremendous impact on the economy. They are seen as a valuable means for economic development and employment creation, especially in regions that are rural or less developed. Tourism has also become an instrument for sustainable human development with the aim to assuage poverty, regenerate the environment, create jobs in remote areas and help in the advancement of women and other disadvantaged groups.

In India, Human Resource Development in the tourism sector will face certain challenges as international tourists expect international standards of service and domestic travelers demand better quality services. Quality of services and improved infrastructure will be the key to the future success of tourism in India. The challenge is extraordinary, since India has to deal with many other issues in efforts for the betterment of the quality of life for its citizens.

Source: www.unescap.org

Section IV

Global Perspective

13

Talent Deficiency Syndrome®: Who Moved My Talent?

Vineet Tandon

Despite having a population of a billion plus, the shortage of skilled talent is becoming a major problem in India. The talent deficiency scenario in India can be used to India's advantage only if adequate policy-level support and industry participation is there. A forward-looking initiative towards creating a knowledge ecosystem shall help the Indian cause in the long run. This article addresses the issue of shortage of skilled talent that is becoming a major problem in India. The article also discusses the reasons for the sudden shortage and challenges[1] to overcome talent deficiency.

While the impact of avian influenza on the poultry industry has been huge, there is another bug that has hit the corporate headquarters of many companies. And the bug is TDS. No, it's not Tax Deduction at Source that I am referring to. I am referring to Talent Deficiency Syndrome® (TDS), which is fast spreading; and the effect it can have on the overall industry will be many times

1 Turning the Skewed Labor Model, Re-engineering the Educational infrastructure, Revisit Existing Educational Models, Knowledge Creation, Development of Knowledge Cities and More Government Participation.

Source: Effective Executive, May 2006. © Vineet Tandon. Reprinted with permission.

more than we can even comprehend. The cell phones of HR managers are no longer ringing nor are their inboxes filled with resumes of job aspirants. Rather, the trend has reversed where the HR managers go out calling the aspirants and sending e-mails to the potential candidates. And while "the customer is king" stood true at least for marketers, the job aspirant has become the king for HR managers. HR managers and headhunters are scouting for talent like crazy, and doing almost anything and everything to overcome the Talent Deficiency Syndrome®.

Jump in salaries, preferred location, perks and incentives all are assured. If the aspirant fits the bill of the job in demand, there is no stopping in terms of what can be offered.

Imagine a situation where you got up on a fine Monday morning and as you were going through the pages of your newspaper you found to your surprise an ad-insert, which was your offer letter for your dream job. Can't believe it! Added to your surprise you also receive a telephone call from the same company, asking whether you are interested to join and before you could respond, your doorbell rings—the pick-up car is there to take you for your first day at the office. Well, things couldn't get any better than this. You might be shocked at what I am asking you to imagine, but with the hunt for talent intensifying, the newer methods of job offers and recruitment might just be around the corner.

So what exactly is TDS? Talent Deficiency Syndrome® can be defined as a phenomenon where companies have more requirement for talent than what can be sourced from their immediate environment. The results are often explicit in the form of higher salaries, poaching, high attrition, empty corridors, ongoing induction and training, higher recruitment costs, inability to complete contracts, etc., all of which can directly affect a company's bottom line.

A Paradox

The article, "India: Desperately Seeking Talent", was published in *BusinessWeek*, November 7, 2005, which addressed the issue of how the fuelling growth has led to companies scrambling for talent. Very surprisingly, almost a year ago an article was published in May 2004 on *Rediff.com*, "Where have all the Jobs gone?",

Box I: Talent Quest

Talent Becomes a Luxury

Employers are having difficulty finding the right people to fill jobs despite high unemployment in Europe and the US, a survey by US-based staffing firm "Manpower" showed on Tuesday.

The survey conducted late in January showed that 40% of nearly 33,000 employers in 23 countries across the world were struggling to find qualified job candidates.

"The talent shortage is becoming a reality for a larger number of employers around the world," Manpower's CEO and Chairman Jeffrey Joerres said in a statement.

Source: Financial Express, February 21, 2006.

A Flood of Job Offers

The Managing Director of The Headhunters India, Kris Lakshmikanth, said, "There was one candidate who came to the negotiating table with seven offer letters and was attending her eighth interview that day." "After the offer letters are accepted, we can be sure that only 30% actually join the company," according to Arjun Dev, General Manager, The Headhunters.

Source: The Hindu Business Line, February 12 , 2006.

Now Campus Hiring Starts a Year Ahead

Out of 3,65,000 engineers who graduate every year, hardly 20% are suited to industry needs. They come calling earlier and earlier. IT companies, whose mainstay talent comes from campus recruits (almost 50-60% in biggies such as Infosys, Wipro and TCS), are landing in colleges in March-April this year to recruit students from the graduating batch of 2007.

Source: The Hindu Business Line, February 19, 2006.

which reflected on the findings of National Sample Survey that unemployment in India has increased over the years.

Just in one year's time frame, discussions in newspapers and magazines have changed from unemployment statistics to shortage of skilled talent; and TDS is the latest virus affecting the very survival of companies in the knowledge economy. It's not only in India that the talks are about talent shortage: Today, global media is talking about talent shortage, and unless something is done to correct it, not much help will actually be available for this syndrome.

This is very surprising and unfortunate that despite having a population of a billion plus, we are feeling scared by the sheer numbers various statistics are projecting in terms of demand for skilled talent.

Exhibit I: The Present Scenario of Education and Training in India

Sector-wise Requirement of Talent			Figures of Annual Intake of Various Approved Colleges by AICTE		
S.No.	Sector	Projected Demand	S.No.	Category	Annual Intake
1	Aviation	10,000 pilots by 2010	1	Engineering Graduates	439,689
2	Engineering	73 million by 2015	2	Diploma Engineers	265,416
3	Animation	100,000 by 2008	3	MCA	54,167
4	IT & ITES	1,000,000 by 2010	4	Pharmacy	24,672
5	Retail	2.5 million by 2010	5	Hotel Management	3,685
				Total	787,629
Compiled from various sources.			*Source: AICTE website list of approved institutions and their intake.*		

While the West does not have enough population to meet the demands of the industry, we have the population, and also the required number of skilled workers to fill this gap. While the West is ageing, India is getting younger. So why can't we create a pool of talented workforce that will meet the demands of the industry? Why do we have a situation where some people are desperately seeking jobs, while there are others (very few in numbers) who have more jobs than they can possibly do? Who is to be held responsible for this scenario and what is the way out?

Exhibit I represents a work pool of almost 8 lakh skilled workers. Besides this, there are MBAs who alone would be around one lakh in number (if we take the calculation as 1000 management colleges with 100 intake for each) and simple graduates passing out from colleges like plain BA and B.Com graduates who would be the highest in numbers, taking the figure to around 15-20 lakh graduates.

Now IT and ITES alone would require 10 lakh skilled people in a very short time. So, we can clearly see that we need more skilled talent than we can possibly supply and, therefore, this TDS.

Why the Sudden Shortage?

The shortage looks sudden; but it is not so. With the economy doing well and the different sectors moving on the path of making it big the hunt for talent was expected to happen. And there are no shortcuts either. One can only address it over a period of time.

Let's look at some of the findings of the 60th round of National Sample Survey Organisation(NSSO) survey on employment and unemployment.[2]

- About 72% of the households belonged to rural India and accounted for nearly 75% of the total population.
- The unemployment rate went up between 1993-94 and 2004. On the basis of current daily status (unemployed on an average in the reference week) during the reference period, unemployment rate for males increased from 5.6% to 9.0% in rural areas, and from 6.7% to 8.1% in urban areas.

Seventy-five percent of the total population still resides in rural India, which in effect means that only a quarter of the Indian population lives in urban India. This, in effect, also means that while the services sector contributes 52% towards the nation's GDP, less than 25% of the population contributes towards that, and the rest are only left behind. The survey points out the pathetic situation of unemployment in the country, highlighting the fact that while on the one hand we have talent deficiency, on the other hand, there is increasing unemployment in the country, which is really unfortunate.

What are the Challenges to Overcome Talent Deficiency?

The talent deficiency scenario in India is like the disease in pathogenesis stage where the causative agents have already affected the host. However, the solution to it does not lie in offering a prescriptive solution. The solution to TDS will lie in creating a proactive approach to overcome it rather than having a reactive solution.

Some of the challenges to overcome talent deficiency are:

Turning the Skewed Labor Model

One of the biggest challenges facing the talent scenario in India is the skewed distribution of population. While urban India needs far more talent to meet the

[2] Source: National Economic Survey 2005-06.

demands of the services sector, the supply of labor is higher in rural India. So there needs to be a radical shift in the supply of labor from rural India to the services sector. While the labor force from rural India cannot be immediately employed to meet the demands of the services sector, we definitely need to initiate a trend where and when this shift can be brought about. The idea is not to dump rural India onto the services sector, but to tap their unemployed youth to meet the demands of the services sectors in urban India. While this will not happen for a year or so, creating an environment that will mark the shift of labor from rural to urban areas will certainly help in meeting the demands of the services sector, and will also help in decreasing unemployment in rural India.

The data above is a clear indicator of the skewed talent scenario in India. While rural India's contribution to GDP has declined, the unemployment in rural India has increased. On the other hand, though the services sector's contribution to GDP has increased, there is still shortage of skilled talent in the country. Therefore, the need of the hour is to create a scenario where excess human resource can be tapped and the requirements of the knowledge economy can be met.

How can the model be worked? This will require long-term policy implementation, creating academic industry partnerships and constant focus to bring the shift. There has been a boom of academic institutions across the country, especially in metros and Tier-II cities. But, rural India is yet to experience the boom. The government should encourage development of academic programs in

Box II: IT Talent Needed

- India's contribution to the global talent pool of knowledge workers – 28%.
- India will face a shortage of 5,00,000 knowledge workers by 2010.
- India requires 10-12 integrated knowledge centers by 2010.
- IT/BPO sector to create 1.6 million jobs by 2010.
- IT/BPO sector to provide indirect employment to 6.5 million people by 2010.
- IT Services sector will require 1,50,000 employees by 2010.
- BPO Services sector will require 3,50,000 employees by 2010.
- Majority of 2,50,000 engineering degree/diploma holders enter IT sector.
- Total demand for IT professionals, (more than 1.1 million) will exceed supply in 2007-08.

Compiled from various sources.

rural areas. While *Sarva Shiksha Abhiyaan* and other schemes are welcomed, the government needs to think of a fresh paradigm altogether for developing a modern and vibrant India. The government should promote incentives for the establishment of educational facilities in rural areas. The emergence of educational opportunities and creation of a knowledge environment will mark the beginning of the creation of an actual knowledge economy in India.

Re-engineering the Educational Infrastructure

There has been an impressive growth in the area of higher education with an increase in annual student enrolment from 7.26 million in 1997-98 to 9.95 million in 2003-04. Enrolment of women students rose from 2.45 million in 1997-98 to 4.03 million in 2004-05, constituting 40.22% of the total enrolment.[3]

However, the present educational infrastructure in India can hardly meet the demands of the industry. We are able to produce around 15-20 lakh graduates out of a population of one billion plus. This needs to change. The government needs to think beyond just achieving the literacy rates. There is a need to create more colleges and polytechnics in the country than what we currently have. Besides, we also need to have an independent agency that gives rating to various educational colleges in the country. These ratings should be based on factors like the level of intellectual capital, R&D facilities, academic infrastructure, faculty-student ratio, academic industry interface and the like. We need to introduce more and more vocational courses, which can offer direct employment opportunities. Thus, there is a need to re-engineer the complete educational infrastructure. While policy initiatives like increasing budgetary allocations for education and employment are the need of the day, there is also an explicit desire to look forward to India's progress in terms of globalization and economic progress.

Revisit Existing Educational Models

There is also a need to revive the existing education models. It has been a common observation in the industry and across the sectors that not all the college graduates are employable. They are taught from outdated curriculum and do not have the necessary skills that will increase their employability. In most of the cases the learning models used are based on what have continued in the past. In today's

[3] Source: Economic Survey, 2005-06.

dynamic environment the need is to create a dynamic curriculum, which makes sure that the skills needed by the industry are nurtured. It's no point for anyone doing a four year BTech program only to realize later that whatever was taught, hardly added any value. Towards this objective there is a clear requirement of effective academic industry participation. The industry needs to partner with academic institutes to develop curriculum that will serve the demands of the jobs created in future. The idea is to create a learning environment, which will help in developing skill sets for future requirements, and not just address the needs of the present.

Knowledge Creation

Another way to address TDS is by building a pool of knowledge creators. Knowledge creators are people who are specialists in their respective domains. However, creating a pool of knowledge creators is itself a huge challenge. The research and development scenario is not very attractive in India. Not many academic institutions are involved in R&D activities, and not much emphasis is being paid on developing the research base in the country. We need to understand that knowledge economy will require knowledge creators and that alone will provide India the cutting edge in the coming years.

Development of Knowledge Cities

There is indeed a requirement to develop and build knowledge cities. These cities should serve as centers of excellence, and will be the focal point to initiate all activities related to development of knowledge pool. They will develop local talent by providing knowledge related services to the talent pool available there. There should ideally be one knowledge city in every state capital. Each state should then work out its own knowledge strategy for deploying the resources both economic and human to the best of its potential. This will, in turn, create various centers of excellence across the country and, thus, will help in uniform development of the knowledge pool. For instance, each state can use its own natural resources to create a learning environment that will serve the twin purposes of knowledge development and deployment of natural resources. For instance, Chhattisgarh state, which is rich in a variety of herbal medicines, can create a knowledge strategy whereby they can bank upon their vast natural resources for herbs and at the same time start developing centers of excellence in herbal R&D.

This will make sure that the entire value chain of creating herbal products right from production to marketing and distribution is addressed and the benefits are distributed across the talent pool at all levels.

More Government Participation

The government should take advantage of and utilize the country's human resources rather than write it off as a liability. To reverse the trend from rural unemployment to employment, the government needs to come up with policies that will promote the creation of a talent pool in the country. Some of the measures that the government should take up to address TDS are:

1. Have a new paradigm for knowledge creation. Entire new approach, which will shift the focus from achieving mere literacy to gaining a society full of knowledge workers. This will bring about the transition needed to reduce rural unemployment.
2. Promote incentives for the creation of educational infrastructure in rural areas.
3. Create a knowledge ministry headed by a knowledge minister, who will spearhead the creation of knowledge-building initiatives in the country.
4. The Government of India, should have a knowledge vision statement, which will clearly spell out Indian leadership in the knowledge economy.
5. Create an independent rating agency for colleges, which will help in creating standards of educational excellence in the country.
6. Create an environment that will promote research and development in the country.

Conclusion

The talent deficiency scenario in India can be used to India's advantage only if adequate policy-level support and industry participation are there. While the solution to talent deficiency cannot be immediately addressed, a proactive approach and forward-looking initiative towards creating a knowledge ecosystem shall help the Indian cause in the long run.

(Vineet Tandon, is working as Senior Communication Analyst at Oracle Corporation. He can be reached at vineet.tandon@gmail.com).

Talent Crunch: Posing a Challenge

– D Satish and Surendar Vaddepalli

An increasing number of companies are relocating/establishing their manufacturing base or their back-office hub in India. Some of them are also setting up their R&D centers in India to leverage on the latter's low-cost skilled workers. Many companies are realizing the benefits of setting up offices here. But, of late, the pace of the number of companies coming to India has increased, and the companies already existing in India are expanding their operations, adding to their headcount. The demand for qualified labor at all levels is increasing at a faster rate when compared to the supply, with impressive growth being witnessed in both manufacturing and service sectors. As per the industry estimates, nearly 500 CEOs and 5,000 VPs will be required in the next 18 to 24 months. The number of employees needed in the lower ranks will also be more.

As increasing number of contracts poured into India, shortage of talent was first felt in the Information Technology (IT) and Business Process Outsourcing (BPO) industries. Some of the other sectors, which are having a serious talent crunch presently include airlines, telecom, biotechnology, healthcare and hospitality sectors.

Causes for Concern

Though India has an abundant supply of manpower, there is a severe shortage of skilled and talented workforce. Most of the students coming out of colleges every year are not employable because of their inability to fulfill the stipulated standards required by the organizations. Except some good institutes, lack of adequate infrastructure in universities and educational institutions and non-availability of expert faculties are some of the factors responsible for students' inefficiency to fit into the jobs available.

Despite many schools and institutions using English as the medium of education, people with acceptable levels of spoken English have also become scarce. Spoken English is a key factor in the outsourcing industry, which is expected to face a shortage of English-speaking professionals, with a large number of outsourcing contracts coming to India. Nasscom foresees a shortfall of skilled workers for the IT and BPO industries in the next five years. While these sectors together employ seven million people at present, the shortage is expected to be nearly 2,06,000 skilled workers by the year 2009.

The aviation sector is also witnessing a lot of activity with around 450-500 new aircraft likely to join the sector in the next five years. The industry is already facing a shortage of pilots, and an additional 2,000 pilots, 10,000 engineers and logistics staff will be required to fill up the positions generated by the proposed fleet induction. Also, there is a scarcity of aviation training institutions and facilities. Moreover, the new airline operators do not have training institutes of their own. The high expenditure involved and the minimum time available to become a pilot are also aggravating the problem.

Another industry which will face the brunt of skilled manpower shortage is the retailing industry. With the entry of foreign retailers into the Indian retailing industry, the latter is more organized now, with numerous malls mushrooming all over. This is sure to generate a big demand for skilled manpower. As there is a scarcity of skilled manpower, new players entering into the industry are offering good pay packets to attract talented workforce from the existing companies. Companies are also looking for Indian expatriates to fill up the senior positions. Recently, Reliance Industries mandated a global sourcing firm to hire Indian expatriates for senior positions in its retail foray.

Contd...

Contd...

The healthcare sector is growing at a very fast rate with the number of patients coming from abroad for medical treatment constantly increasing. However, the growth of super-specialty hospitals and an increasing demand for healthcare have led to a dearth of top-quality surgeons, trained nurses and technicians. The available number of seats in medical colleges in proportion with the growing population is dismal.

After software, biotechnology is expected to be the next big hit of the Indian industry. It is knowledge-intensive and India has a great opportunity, with investments flowing in to encourage research in this field. Here too, scarcity of research scholars in the relevant field is feared to hinder growth. In the manufacturing sector also, a workforce of 73 million will be required by 2015, due to the growth in steel, infrastructure, and oil and gas industries. The gap between demand and supply of workforce is getting wider and the numbers required for filling in the vacancies is only increasing.

Measures to Overcome the Crunch

In this changing environment where there is a shortage of skilled labor, retaining the existing employees becomes all the more important.

The workforce can be retained by providing a congenial work environment and by offering incentives. Employers can set up work-based training programs and thus create qualified talent to suit their requirements. By reskilling and upskilling the individuals, and by redesigning the jobs, employers can create the required talent to fill up the emerging positions. In this way, the companies can contain tacit knowledge within the organization itself. P V Kannan, CEO of 24/7 Customer, says, "The industry takes young, raw talent and in a span of five to six years creates business leaders out of the young individuals."

The employers and governments are taking necessary steps to overcome the estimated shortage of manpower by improving educational and training facilities. Supplemental training system is being adopted in collaboration with specific institutions: Employees gain exposure and training in the areas relevant to the job requirement.

Business houses too are taking more initiative in training freshers and those who lack the required skills. A few of these business houses are even setting up institutions on their own to fill the gap of talent shortage. Recruiters have started conducting certain training courses for their customers when their potential recruits fall short of certain required skills. Ajai Bhatnagar, Principal Consultant, BPO Consultant India, says, "There are no quick solutions to human resource constraints, else China would have beaten us hands down in the game of global service outsourcing nation."

By tapping the previously untapped areas, the total talent pool can be exploited. Many of the businesses are adopting different methods such as part-time work and flexible job schedules for the older and senior employees.

Role of the Academia

The education system has a greater role to play in fulfilling the expectations of India's prospects. Unless some changes are brought into the education system, the current boom in job market cannot be sustained. There are nearly 330 universities and 17,000 colleges in India that are funded by the government. Most of the funds are being used to subsidize student fees rather than being spent on improving the infrastructure.

Sufficient budget allocations for education, training and R&D will facilitate in reducing the intensity of the problem. To create a better-qualified talent pool, certain policy decisions, such as

Contd...

Contd...

greater investment in education and training are crucial for the country's economic progress. Also, paying the right salaries at the right time to the faculties and retaining those who are skilled is equally important.

A public-private partnership model among higher educational institutes can lead to greater differentiation, which leads to the production of top-quality graduates. While HP has an alliance with Jadavpur University, Kolkata, Genpact has an alliance with Osmania University, Hyderabad, to facilitate exchange of knowledge with each other. Cisco has established over 130 networking academies in 20 states, benefitting more than 6,000 students. TIBÇO and IIIT (Pune) have announced an academic partnership, where the former would provide business integration software free of cost to hone the required skills in the students. Accenture and XLRI have set up the Accenture and XLRI-HR Academy, especially to provide training to the IT/ITES industry.

By following an international curriculum and utilizing the services of experts as faculty, the quality of education can be enhanced, which will lead to improving the skills of the students. To ensure a steady supply of skilled professionals, Nasscom has started an "IT Workforce Development Initiative", which attempts to bring changes in the interface between academia and industry. It has suggested deregulating higher education, setting up of higher education zones and funding them, based on the demand for the colleges and universities. The time has come to bring about changes in our education system if we have to capitalize on the opportunities. A greater responsibility rests on the shoulders of industry experts, academicians, administrators and policy makers. As Shikha Suman, CEO, Suvi Inc., Research and Management Consultants, said, "Young should put their efforts in areas, which will enhance their employability."

Source: Chartered Financial Analyst, July 2006.

14

China's Rising Cost of Business: The Human Resources Factor

Souvik Dhar

China's enormous pool of low cost manpower had enabled it to develop as a manufacturing base for companies across the globe. However, since 1998, the situation seemed to be fast changing with China facing a shortage in the availability of skilled manpower. Experts predicted that this would lead to an increase in the cost of available manpower and therefore increased costs for businesses. They feared that this would result in China losing its competitive advantage as a low cost manufacturing base. However, some experts were of the opinion that the shortage of manpower was merely a temporary phenomenon and China would continue to be a low cost manufacturing base. The case helps in understanding China's competitive advantage as a low cost manufacturing base because of the availability of low cost manpower and the reasons for increase in manpower cost since 1998. The case provides scope to discuss whether China would lose its competitive advantage as a low cost manufacturing base for global companies.

"China's population is so vast that it can stay smart and cheap—a formula that's making it a new superpower in high-tech manufacturing... There's enough talent in the poor interior that prices will stay relatively low... It begins with the millions who abandon farming or menial jobs in small towns and provide a constant stream of cheap factory labour."[1]

– An article in *The Wall Street Journal*, March 14th 2002.

"It's not the end of the great China manufacturing story. But you're no longer going to be talking about China having labour so radically cheap that it will capture all the investment flows. This is an opening for Vietnam, it's an opening for India and Cambodia."

– Jonathan Anderson, the Chief Asia-Pacific Economist for UBS.

China's vast pool of low-cost manpower enabled it to be established as a manufacturing base for companies from across the world. Because of their low manpower costs, Chinese businesses were able to flood the global market with low-priced products.

However, the situation was changing as the Chinese businesses were increasingly facing shortage of manpower. Experts were predicting that shortage of manpower, witnessed since 1998, would lead to increased costs for the businesses and this would lead to China losing its comparative advantage as a low-cost manufacturing base for the global companies.

However, some experts were of the opinion that shortage of manpower was merely a temporary phenomenon and China would continue to hold its advantage as a low-cost manufacturing base for businesses.

China's Manpower Cost Advantage

Since 1978, when China began to liberalise its economy, its GDP grew from Rmb 362.4 billion to Rmb 13.7 trillion in 2004 (Exhibit 1).[2] Such a high growth in GDP was made possible due to huge Foreign Direct Investments (FDI) into the Chinese economy. Two factors were responsible for the Chinese economy attracting heavy flow of FDI. The first was China's enormous potential as a consumer market with its huge population. The second was an unlimited supply of labour and the resultant low costs. According to a survey by US Bureau of Labor Statistics, average hourly compensation for factory workers in China in 2002 was $0.64, as compared to $21.33 in US and $17.47 in UK (Exhibit 2).[3] The survey also concluded that in 2002 China had 38 million city manufacturing workers and 71 million suburban and rural manufacturing workers.[4] An article in *Financial Times* noted, "In Singapore, Malaysia and other South East Asian countries, wage inflation followed as labour resources were stretched. In China, the supply of labour seems almost inexhaustible."[5]

Abundant availability of low-cost labour resulted in many foreign companies setting up their manufacturing bases in China. Initially foreign companies used China as a source for simple, labour-intensive products. Eventually they began using China as a production base for high technology products. Jim Hemerling, a Senior Vice President in The Boston Consulting Group's (BCG) Shanghai office, observed, "Sourcing in China started with low-tech products but it has evolved beyond that. Now, in addition to traditional products, another huge area is consumer electronics. I believe the next big wave will be industrial goods, with companies like ITT, Siemens, Honeywell and ABB leading the way."[6]

In 2004, technology exports accounted for 27% of total exports of China, up from 23% in 2003. According to a Bloomberg report, China's export of technological products in 2004 increased by 72% to $45.4 billion in comparison to 2003.[7] Till December 2004, China's foreign trade increased by 21% to $620 billion, as compared to 2001 making it the world's fifth largest trading nation.[8] Jack Perkowski, CEO of ASIMCO Inc., a component maker operating in China, remarked, "If you want to be making engineer products, which auto components are, there is no better place to be doing it than China. You not only have a vast labor supply, but you also have a growing pool of high quality engineers."[9] According to *The Wall Street Journal*, 50% of cameras, 30% of air conditioners and TVs, 25% of washing machines and 20% of refigerators of the world were produced in China in 2004.[10] China also continued its dominance in exports of labour-intensive products and accounted for 95% of toys and 85% of shoes sold in the US in 2004.[11]

However, the situation was changing and companies in China were finding it difficult to recruit low-cost manpower as Vincent Gauthier of Hewitt Associates, a human-resources consultancy, remarked, "If you think that China is a cheap place for labour, think again."[12]

Increase in Manpower Cost

Since 1998 Chinese businesses were finding it increasingly difficult to recruit low-cost factory and manual workers. The shortage was attributed to decrease in migration of manpower from the country's rural region, a major supplier of cheap manpower in the past (Exhibit 3). Roy Chung, Managing Director of Hong Kong-based Techtronic, a power-tool maker who supplies to Sears Roebuck & Co., and Home Depot Inc., and employs about 12,000 people in Guangdong, said, "Fewer workers are coming down from rural areas than in the old days."[13]

This was because the Chinese farmers were considering their earnings from agriculture to be higher than those provided by factory jobs in urban areas. The Chinese farmers' increasing financial prosperity from agriculture was due to the increase in agricultural subsidies and grain prices. As a result, income growth in rural areas was found to outstrip income growth in urban areas. A 27-year-old native of Chengnan in Northern Guangdong, remarked, "Most young people in my village don't want to leave because they can make money from the land."[14] China's one-child policy was also considered to be responsible for this change, as the Chinese farmers wanted their only child to remain with them and help them in their family occupation rather than migrate.

The businesses were also facing a poor supply of skilled manpower, needed for shoes and leather, garment, toys, furniture and electro technical factories in the Yangzhe River delta, the Pearl River delta and Fujian. From the second quarter of 2003, supply of skilled technical workers started falling short of market demand. In November 2003, Shanghai Municipal Economic Commission estimated that the city would be facing a shortage of 8,000 technicians in the next three years in the fields of craft designing, machine tool operation, electric equipment and optimisation of optical, mechanical and electronic synthesis. Zheizang province was also expected to face a shortage of 300,000 logistics workers in transportation and warehousing by 2006.

The businesses were also facing shortage of employees suitable for managerial positions. Jeff Barnes, Chief Learning Officer at General Electric in China, said,

"Issue we have is finding mid-level and top-level leadership."[15] Lack of quality education for the generation growing up during the Cultural Revolution of 1966-76 and the shortage of business schools in the country were cited as the reasons for this. The shortage of manpower—unskilled, skilled and managerial level—had led to increased salaries and wages, resulting in increased costs for businesses. Jonathan Anderson (Anderson), the Chief Asia-Pacific Economist for UBS, remarked, "It's a serious situation if you're a manufacturer, because now you have got to compete on wages. You can't just put up a sign and expect workers to come knocking. That game is over."[16] Since 1998, salaries were rising at an average annual rate of 7%.[17] Statistics revealed that salaries for middle and high-ranking staff at foreign companies were rising more rapidly than the Consumer Price Index. The average salary increase on an annual basis was 6%-10% in 2004, compared to increase in inflation rate of around 2%.[18] Top-level salaries reached global levels and salaries paid to senior managers in the Mainland in 2004 were comparable to the salaries paid to their counterparts in Hong Kong. Wages for factory workers also showed significant rise. In China's Pearl river delta industrial region, wages increased by about 50% in 2004, when compared to the figures a couple of years earlier.

In addition to increased salaries and wages, companies' expenses for providing various benefits to their manpower also increased. In its efforts to establish a nation-wide social welfare system, the Chinese government passed legislations requiring the business enterprises to increase their contributions to employees' and citizens' social welfare fund. The domestic housing commission also enforced businesses to contribute towards housing funds for employees. The increased contributions made by businesses towards statutory benefits of their manpower constituted 40% of payroll for low-level and middle-level jobs. Shortage of manpower also resulted in high turnover rate. According to a research carried out by Hewitt Associates, employee turnover rate in China increased to 11.3% in 2004, compared to 8.3% in 2001.[19] Anthony Wu, head of accounting firm Ernst & Young in Hong Kong and China, remarked, "The biggest issue is retention of people. Retention is much cheaper than recruitment."[20] This had further increased manpower costs of businesses in China.

Due to the increased costs, it was feared that Chinese businesses could lose their low-cost advantage in future creating serious repercussions for Chinese economy. Gus Kang, Human Resources Consulting Director for PricewaterhouseCoopers China, said, "Investors should take the high cost of local labour into serious consideration."[21]

Future Repercussions

Investors were worried that increase in manpower costs would certainly lead to increase in prices of China's exports. Anderson of UBS observed, "Very gradually manufacturing prices of goods from China will go up. They have been falling the last five or six years (from 1998 to 2004). That won't happen anymore."[22] The first casualty of rising costs was expected to be the low-margin manufacturers of toys and clothing. In 2004, several toy manufacturers in the Dongguan manufacturing hub closed down their operations and some shifted their operations to Vietnam. Loh Sai Kit, Director of Yiu Fai Toys Factory in Dongguan, remarked, "It just didn't make financial sense for them to go on and try to honour their agreements."[23] Increase in costs was also expected to force the Chinese businesses to pass on their additional costs to their customers, as most of them operated with wafer-thin margins. Factories in Guangdong and other east coast provinces were contemplating to pass along a part of their increased costs to their foreign buyers, accustomed to rock-bottom prices. Andrew Tsuei, Wal-Mart's Vice President for global procurement, remarked, "(Wal-Mart has managed to keep) cost increases to a minimum through negotiation and leveraging our volume. However, we're seeing signs of more increases around the corner."[24] As foreign customers would be required to pay more for their purchases from the Chinese businesses in the future, they could shift their manufacturing bases to other cheaper destinations.

Experts predicted that China could lose its labour cost advantage by 2014 to other low-cost countries like India, Bangladesh and Eastern European countries, which could emerge as less expensive manufacturing bases. As factory costs could be written-off usually after a period of three to five years after being set-up, companies could close down their manufacturing facilities in China and re-establish them in other low-cost countries. Experts fear that the trend, which started with manufacturing bases being shifted from Japan to Korea to China, could again be repeated with China as the loser.[25]

The continued increase in manpower costs could also give rise to social problems. Increase in wages and salaries would result in political instability as the gulf between the rich and poor would continue to grow at an alarming pace.

Besides, according to Goldman Sachs' Chief China Economist, Hong Liang, increase in prices of products manufactured in China would also have global implications. Being the low-price trendsetter for plenty of goods globally, China's costlier exports would lead to potential increase in prices of everything from consumer products to mortgages for customers across Europe and US and therefore would result in inflation on a global basis.[26] However, not all experts believed that shortage of labour and the resultant increased manpower cost would be detrimental to the future growth prospects of China.

Some experts were of the opinion that shortage in supply of manpower, especially unskilled manpower, was merely a temporary phenomenon. According to them, there were plenty of workers available in Chinese hinterland, surplus rural labour was estimated to be 150 million in 2004, and once these potential workers know about the increased demand from the country's industry, migration to urban areas would again start. This would solve the short-term problem of shortage of manpower being faced by Chinese businesses.[27]

The problem of shortage of skilled manpower was also expected to be solved in the near future. A senior Chinese researcher, Lu Zheng, Director of the Institute of Industrial Economics under the Chinese Academy of Social Sciences, opined that in China there were 2.5 million college students waiting to enter the job market in the near future. Also, 60% of these students were undergoing training in science and technology and once qualified they would solve the problem of China's demand for technically qualified manpower.[28]

A BCG report, titled "*Capturing Global Advantage — How Leading Industrial Companies are Transforming their Industries by Sourcing and Selling in China, India and Other Low-Cost Countries*" published in 2004, suggested that in spite of increase in manpower costs, China would continue to hold its advantage as a low-cost base for manufacturers. The per-hour cost for a Chinese worker in 2004 was below $1, as compared to $15 to $30 for American and European plants.[29] This cost was also two to eight times cheaper than wages prevailing in other countries like Mexico and those in Eastern Europe.[30] The BCG report even predicted that by 2014, the gap in manpower costs between China and the developed countries, which had resulted in companies from developed countries to shift their manufacturing bases to China, would rather expand. Three reasons were cited for such a scenario to take place.

First was that companies operating from low-cost countries like China were able to lower their purchasing costs and would continue to do so in the future. So, even if cost of manpower in China increases substantially in the future they would be able to absorb such increases without passing the increased cost to their customers. Second reason was that China still had a huge number of unemployed people, who would provide an endless supply of cheap manpower for a long time in the future. The third reason was that the wage-gap between the developed countries and China, perceived to be as high as 20:1, would hardly disappear even if wage levels increase by double digits percentage in China. Further, they believe that China's cost advantage in comparison to Mexico and Eastern European countries would remain, as these countries were also expected to experience increase in manpower costs. In addition, as their base costs were much higher than that of China, so absolute manpower costs in China would continue to be lower.[31]

Experts were also of the opinion that China's manpower cost level was still below many other countries and increases in wage levels were usually being witnessed by small Taiwanese and Hong Kong-based exporters with their manufacturing facilities in China. For other companies, like the American ones, which were already paying wages to their manpower higher than the average, were not finding any difficulty in attracting or retaining the required manpower. Patrick J Powers, Director of China operations at the US-China Business Council in Beijing, said, "American companies are widely considered to be highly attractive employers."[32] So, analysts were confident that the fear of China losing its status as the world's workshop to other low-cost countries is far from reality.

(Souvik Dhar is a Team Leader at Icfai Business School Case Development Centre.)

Endnotes

1 "China is the Unqualified Cost and Quality Leader for Offshore Manufacturing", *www.chinafacturing.com*

2 "GDP Growth 1952-2004", *www.chinability.com,* April 6th 2005.

3 "Hourly Compensation Costs for Production Workers in Manufacturing, 30 Countries or Areas, 40 Manufacturing Industries, Selected Years, 1975-2002", *www.bls.gov,* May 18th 2004.

4 Coy, Peter "Just How Cheap is Chinese Labor?", *www.businessweek.com,* December 13th 2004.

5 Chan, John "Chinese Capitalism: Industrial Powerhouse or Sweatshop of the World", *www.freeindiamedia.com,* May 10th 2004.

6 "Sourcing From China: No Longer Just for Shoes, Toys and Clothes", ***http://*** *knowledge.wharton.upenn.edu,* April 20th – May 3rd 2005.

7 Ibid.

8 "Chinese Capitalism: Industrial Powerhouse or Sweatshop of The World", op.cit.

9 "China's Low-Cost Labor May Keep Pricing Pressure on Global Suppliers", *Autoparts Report, www.findarticles.com,* December 4th 2002.

10 "Chinese Capitalism: Industrial Powerhouse or Sweatshop of The World", op.cit.

11 "Sourcing From China: No Longer Just for Shoes, Toys and Clothes", op.cit.

12 "China's people problem", *www.economist.com,* April 14th 2005.

13 "China's Rising Rural Incomes Create Labour Shortage", *http://chinese-school.netfirms.com,* August 19th 2004.

14 Roberts, Dexter and Balfour, Frederik "Is China Running Out of Workers?", *www.businessweek.com,* October 25th 2004.

15 "China's people problem", op.cit.

16 "Labour Shortage Continues to Challenge Factories", *www.cbiz.cn,* November 11th 2004.

17 Zhu, Ruby "Is China Losing Its Cheap Labour Advantage", *www.tradelink-ebiz.com,* November 2003.

18 "China's People Problem", op.cit.

19 Ibid.

20 Ibid.

21 Liang, Xiao "Cost of Skilled Labour on the Rise", *http://app1.chinadaily.com.cn*, December 20th 2001.

22 "Is China Running Out of Workers?", op.cit.

23 Fong, Mei "A Chinese Puzzle Surprising Shortage of Workers", *www.chinalaborwatch.org*, August 16th 2004.

24 Wiseman, Paul "Chinese Factories Struggle to Hire", *www.usatoday.com*, April 11th 2005.

25 "China's Rising Cost of Labour", *www.electronicsweekly.com*, January 13th 2005.

26 "A Chinese Puzzle Surprising Shortage of Workers", op.cit.

27 Ibid.

28 "Researcher: China Enjoys Comparative Advantage in Labour Cost", *http://english.people.com.cn*, November 7th 2002

29 "China's Advantage in Low Labor Cost Will Remain in Coming Decade, Report", *http://englisg.people.com.cn*, September 7th 2004

30 Ibid.

31 Ibid.

32 "Is China Running Out of Workers?", op.cit.

Exhibit 1: China's Gross Domestic Product from 1978 to 2004 (in Rmb Billion)

Source: "GDP growth 1952-2004", www.chinability.com, April 6th 2005.

Exhibit 2: Average Hourly Compensation for Factory Workers Across Countries for the Year 2002 (in US Dollars)

Country or Area	Year 2002
United States	21.33
Brazil	2.57
Canada	16.02
Mexico	2.38
Australia	15.55
Hong Kong Sar (1,2)	5.83
Israel	12.14
Japan	18.83
Korea	9.16
New Zealand	8.89
Singapore	7.27
Taiwan	5.41
Austria (3)	21.08
Belgium	22.79
Denmark	24.23
Finland (4)	21.56
France	17.42
Germany, Former West	26.19
Germany, Unified	25.08
Ireland	15.08
Italy	14.93
Luxembourg	18.91
Netherlands	21.74
Norway	27.40
Spain	12.04
Sweden	20.18
Switzerland	24.11
United Kingdom	17.47

(1) Hong Kong special administrative region of China.

(2) Average of selected manufacturing industries.

(3) Excluding handicraft manufacturers. Excluding all printing & publishing and miscellaneous manufacturing.

(4) Including mining & electrical power plants.

Source: "Hourly Compensation Costs for Production Workers in Manufacturing, 30 Countries or Areas, 40 Manufacturing Industries, Selected Years, 1975-2002", www.bls.gov, May 18th 2004.

Exhibit 3: Share of Rural and Urban Labour in Selected Chinese Industries from 1990 to 2001 (in millions)

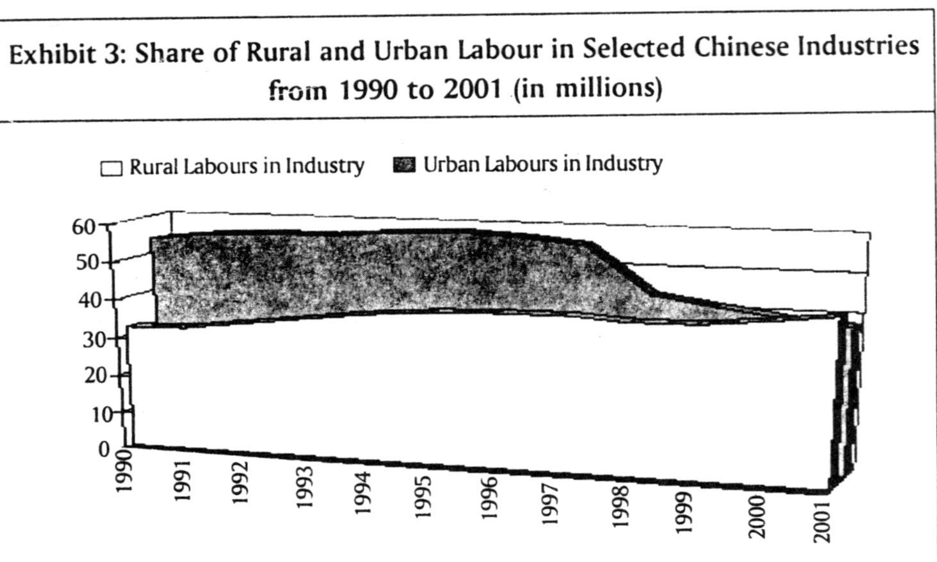

Source: Li, Sheng "Low Wage and Low Labour Standard in China: Substitute Explanation of Race-to-the-bottom", www.econ.utah.edu

15

ARTICLE SUMMARY

Forecasting Labor and Skills Shortages: How can Projections better Inform Labor Migration Policies?

Rajarshi Ghosh

Various vital sectors of the European Union states are in acute crunch of labour, especially skilled ones. To compensate the shortfall, migration of labour from transition economies is employed. However, such a stance is met with resistance from local residents. In this backdrop, the present paper tries to estimate the demand for labor in the aforementioned countries that could be met through migration along with appropriate policies to control it within permissible limit.

Introduction

Majority of the European Union (EU) states are facing labor and skill shortages in various sectors, along with high rates of unemployment. The sectors are IT,

This is the summary of the research paper. "Forecasting Labor and Skills Shortages: How can Projections betterInform Labor Migration Policies?" The research paper is written by Christina Boswell, Silvia Stiller and Thomas Straubhaar and published by Hamburg Institute of International Economics (HWWA).

health, consumer and commercial services, education, construction, and engineering to name a few. The root cause is the mismatch between available and demanded skills and or insufficient mobility of the EU residents, for which reasons could be many. Labor migration is a common tool employed by EU to address such skill and labor shortages.

However, labor migration policies usually face objections from the residents and may be politically uncomfortable. Therefore, it would be very useful if the gaps in the labor market are correctly estimated and migration is encouraged to that extent. The purpose of this paper is to analyze whether shortage projections can help formulate appropriate migration policies.

Labor and Skills Shortages: What are They and Why do They Occur?

The reasons behind labor and skill shortages could be various:

1. Consistent increase in labor demand outpacing supply levels.
2. Fall in labor supply greater than the fall in labor demand.

Now, what causes excess demand in the labor market?

There are two reasons:

A. **Industrial Effect**

   a) Overall growth in the economy increases the demand for labor.

   b) Growth in specific sectors of the economy raises the demand for labor of that sector with specific skill sets.

B. **Employment Effect**

   a) Once production decision is made in a particular area, the labor market in that area witnesses corresponding demand for skills and education.

   b) Technical change and innovation also affects demand for particular skills and occupations.

c) Change in regulations e.g., environmentalists are more in demand nowadays.

d) Degree of competition in the particular sector influences labor demand as competition demands high degree of innovation on the part of the firms.

The following factors influence labor supply:

a) Demographic trends—size, age and gender ratio of the labor force.

b) Expected labor force participation rates.

c) Net immigration.

d) Individual education and training decisions.

e) Job preferences of residents.

f) Intra and Inter regional mobility.

However, one should always remember that labor supply and demand are inter-linked e.g., labor demand influences work and education decisions and shortages influence manpower rationalization.

Current Trends Influencing Shortages in EU Labor Markets

Labor Demand

There are four Influencing Factors:

a) **Economic Growth** – Effect of economic growth on labor demand depends on labor intensity of the growth sectors, technical progress and unexploited production potential; and whether the growth is temporary or permanent.

b) **Structural Change** – As an economy advances, the service sector begins to play a prominent role over industry and agriculture. The sectoral changes can be due to various factors including demographic change, change in consumer tastes and the international division of labor. This influences labor demand accordingly. It is likely that the transition of the EU economy will create mismatches in the labor market.

c) **Location of Production/Services** – Labor-intensive production is likely to shift out of EU (labor scarce) to countries with cheaper labor. But this may intensify skilled labor production in EU and increase the demand for such labor.

d) **Technological Development and Innovation** – Development of Information and Communication Technology (ICT) creates demand for niche labor and can create skill shortages. But this can be useful also in the sense that regional imbalances can be taken care of without migration (people can work via ICT). Innovation affects labor demand by making the production process lesser or more labor intensive.

Labor Supply

There are four Influencing Factors:

a) **Population Trends** – There is a rise in the average age of the population and decline in the proportion of the population in employment—the population in EU is ageing and dependency burdens are also increasing. Studies argue that this will reduce labor supply.

b) **Participation Rates in Workforce** – The trend is higher schooling and tertiary education—this has increased the entry age and there is also a tendency to retire early. Though this is likely to cause labor shortages there has been an offsetting trend by way of increased female participation in work.

c) **Immigration** – There is a distinct demand for low skilled immigrant labor in EU to perform chores which resident workers are unwilling to.

d) **Education and Qualification** – More qualified people seek higher-level work and that is more financially rewarding. Accordingly labor shortages are occurring in lower level work. Shortages could also be due to reluctance on part of labor to move within the EU, but this is doubtful because all EU states are facing similar problem of ageing society.

Methods for Estimating and Projecting Shortages

The popular method for estimating labor and skills shortages is surveys—employer or employee surveys. Four different types of surveys are described:

A. European Union

In 1999 the Directorate General for Economic & Financial Affairs carried out a survey on employers and employees to assess their views of the evolving labor market. This type of survey reveals the skills that are in demand and influence of technology on labor skills.

B. Germany

In 2001, The Institute for the Study of Labor conducted an International Employer Survey to understand why foreign labor was recruited to fill the skill gaps. This type of survey throws light on the supply side measures needed to combat skill shortages including reforms of the education system.

C. UK

Employers Skills Survey was carried out in 2002 to find the difficulties faced by employers in filling the skill gaps and could give an idea as to what sort of short-term policy measures could help, including migration.

D. USA

US Bureau of Labor Statistics carries out a Job Openings and Labor Turnover Survey, which measures labor market tightness and efficiency.

Projecting Future Shortages

There are theoretical, methodological and data problems in forecasting shortages yet projections are attempted in a bid to get as close to reality as possible and minimize mismatches in the labor market.

While studying different projections one has to keep three factors in mind:

a) whether the time frame of the projections allow adequate time for policy action.

b) whether the disaggregation of shortages by sector, occupation or skills is sufficiently detailed.

c) whether the projections incorporate reactions to policy action on labor shortages.

Best Practices in Projecting Shortages

Australia

The method proceeds in five stages:

1) A macro scenario is considered including GDP forecasts derived from a five year Business Outlook.
2) GDP and its components are transformed into output and employment by industries.
3) National projections for output and employment are split up into regional forecasts.
4) Employment projections on industry basis are converted to occupational forecasts.
5) From stage 4 employment forecasts by age, sex, qualifications are derived.

Canada

The Human Resources Development Canada (HRDC) produces the Canadian Occupational Projection System (COPS). The COPS model integrates demand and supply sides of the economy to project requirements for 139 occupations and five broad skill categories. The five components of COPS are:

1) Demand: New Openings = Expansion + Replacement.
2) Supply = School Leavers + Immigrants + Re-Entrants.
3) Equilibrium: Demand = Supply.
4) Excess Supply = (Supply + Unemployed) – New Openings: Surplus if > 0, Shortage if < 0.
5) Outlook: Change in Excess Supply.

Germany

Institute for Employment Research generates employment projections. They use a complex econometric model where 59 different sectors are analyzed in detail with around 600 sector specific variables as well as common economy specific variables, to generate employment forecasts. Individual sector forecasts can be aggregated to get the economy forecast. However it is difficult to derive skill gaps from this model as labor occupations or qualifications are not considered here, these estimates are made separately through 'trend extrapolations'. To project labor supply, long-term population trends and estimated participation rates were used. The method of projection by Institute for Economic Research, Munich is also mentioned in the paper.

Netherlands

The Research Centre for Education and the Labor Market (ROA) usually makes the employment projections. Projected job openings reflect expansion of demand as well as replacement demand. The school leavers and the unemployed, seeking a job provide the supply of labor. By corresponding labor demand with supply, ROA can then create an indicator for the future labor market for each occupation/qualification set.

United Kingdom

The Warwick Institute for Employment Research has made employment projections in collaboration with Cambridge Econometrics. The three steps followed are: 1) estimating employment changes in the economy 2) estimating changes in the relative share of different industries and then 3) estimating changes in the relative shares of various occupations within each industry. An econometric model incorporating over a thousand technical and behavioral factors is used to arrive at the above results. The Institute has also estimated labor supply of the highly skilled.

USA

The US Bureau of Labor Statistics makes projections of employment and labor force. The estimates of Labor Demand are based on: 1) aggregate macroeconomic growth 2) GDP disaggregated by consuming sector and product 3) Inter-industry relationships 4) Industry output and employment and 5) occupational employment. Labor Supply is estimated from the size, demographic composition of the labor force and participation rates.

Evaluating the Methods

The following issues evolved from the study of the methods:

1) **Level of Disaggregation** – Labor market forecasts, skill set wise, need very high degree of differentiation than used by the forecast methods. However, there are continuous improvement efforts to achieve the same. A bottom up approach may be more useful than a top down approach and one of the methods used the same.

2) **Integration of Demand and Supply Models** – Most of the studies had separate estimates for labor demand and labor supply. The best is to derive them from one model because of the interdependency between them.

3) **Integration of Factors Determining Participation Rates** – Economic development, demographic trends and participation rates are usually interlinked, but the practice is to project participation rates separately.

4) **Extrapolation from Past Trends** – Usually, the models project the future labor market on the basis of the past developments. Projections need to be supplemented by a survey of the labor market and an analysis of the factors influencing labor demand and supply.

5) **Data** – The more the disaggregated forecast, the more is the data needed and extensive surveys would help here.

6) **Scenario-Mapping** – Predicting probable scenarios of the future labor market may be helpful in policy making.

7) **Time Frame** – Estimates should be short- medium- as well as long-term. A study of all these can help in matching policy formulation.

In spite of any shortcoming, projections are invaluable in formulating a migration policy.

Implications for Policy and Research

The utility of the methods outlined above depends upon the shortages referred to: aggregate shortages and skills shortages.

Aggregate Shortages

Overall economic growth and/or demographic changes cause labor shortages and are relatively easier to estimate. Whether migration can attend to the problem of declining and ageing populations is much debated and EU states usually like to increase resident work life, increase resident participation in work and encourage higher births in the EU. Though migration is not high priority for them they may have to fall back on selective migration in specific sectors (e.g., health) to fill the gaps. However, they have to be cautious that advent of low skilled foreign labor does not delay adoption of more capital-intensive technology.

Skills Shortages

As observed, these are not very easy to predict as skill and occupational requirements vary over time and are influenced by technological changes. But, the broad trends in occupation and skills demanded could be predicted on the basis of industry, ICT and consumer preference trends. It is observed that the essential skills needed are a general capacity for flexibility and lifelong learning and EU states have accordingly focused on building a strong foundation in primary and secondary education, which can enable one to continue lifelong learning. However, flexibility is needed on part of workers as well as the education system and this warrants timely and accurate information.

Even if skill shortages are accurately predicted they can induce changes in human behavior and cannot guarantee supply of requisite labor. This makes selective migration helpful to the EU. Notwithstanding the advantages, political sensitivity of migration tends to affect policy formulation.

(Christina Boswell, Silvia Stiller and Thomas Straubhaar, Hamburg Institute of International Economics (HWWA).)

(Rajarshi Ghosh worked as a Consulting Editor at Icfai Business School Research Centre, Kolkata.)

16

Addressing the Challenges of an Aging Workforce: A Human Capital Perspective for Companies Operating in Europe

Eric Lesser, Carsten Hausmann and Steffen Feuerpeil

European governments and organizations that operate in European countries are now faced with addressing the challenges of an aging workforce, as they built their economies using a labor force fueled by one of the largest demographic booms in history. While many countries around the world are addressing the challenges of an aging workforce, generous state pensions and declining birthrates over the years have further exacerbated this issue in many European nations. The aging of the existing workforce, combined with shrinking pools of new employees, poses a number of problems for a range of organizations, particularly those in the public sector and in mature industries such as petroleum and chemicals, mining, and aerospace and defense. First, many companies are finding it increasingly difficult to hire new employees within certain disciplines. Then, even if they can find qualified candidates, the firms must still invest in training to further increase their

Source: http://www.935.ibm.com/services/us/.

productivity. This article focuses on the impact of changing demographics from the European perspective and how companies across Europe and worldwide are developing innovative solutions to address this issue.

Introduction

Many European countries are wrestling with a common challenge: the graying of their populations. Because they built their economies using a labor force fueled by one of the largest demographic booms in history, both European governments and organizations that operate in European countries are now faced with addressing the challenges of an aging workforce. While many countries around the world are facing this situation, generous state pensions and declining birthrates over the years have further exacerbated this issue in many European nations.

"It is not an overstatement to say that the demographic situation regarding the ageing workforce is one of the most pressing issues confronting Europe today."[1]

– Anders L Johansson, National Institute for Working Life, Sweden.

The aging of the existing workforce, combined with shrinking pools of new employees, poses a number of problems for a range of organizations, particularly those in the public sector and in mature industries such as petroleum and chemicals, mining, and aerospace and defense. First, many companies are finding it increasingly difficult to hire new employees within certain disciplines. Then, even if they can find qualified candidates, the firms must still invest in training to further increase their productivity. For example, in a 2002 study of over 500 German companies, 23 percent stated that the aging of their workforces represented a problem for their organizations.[2] In addition, 39 percent indicated, that they were facing challenges associated with shortages of qualified labor, and 27 percent stated they needed to focus on additional training.[3] These shortages can place key capabilities at risk, as indicated by an HR executive of a major chemicals firm:

Last year we needed twenty-five chemical engineers in one country. But of the total pool of graduates, those who had the capabilities to work in a global operation, there were maybe eighty, and we got only three.[4]

A less visible, but no less dangerous problem, is the loss of expertise resulting from mature workers leaving the organization without passing on their knowledge to others. As greater numbers of "knowledge workers" retire, they take with them insights about managing key customer relationships, handling exceptions to critical processes and a host of other experiences that can cost organizations significant amounts of time, energy and resources to recreate or replace. More often than not, the transfer of this knowledge is ignored, placing the organization in a position to repeat prior mistakes and expose itself to additional financial and operational risk.

This report examines the impact of changing demographics from the European perspective and how companies across Europe and worldwide are developing innovative solutions to address this issue. In addition, key questions are presented that executives should be answering to make sure that their organizations are prepared to address these new demographic issues.

The Aging Workforce: A European Perspective

The topic of mature workers continues to gain importance and urgency in European Union (EU) member countries. Over the next two decades, the number of people in the 50-64 age group will increase by 25 percent, while those in the 20-29 year age group will decrease by 20 percent.[5] Over the last several years, the focus of the EU has changed from preventing age discrimination to mobilizing the aging workforce. In recent summits, EU leaders have set two goals to encourage member countries to focus on this aging workforce problem. At the 2001 European Council, EU members agreed on a goal of achieving a 50 percent employment rate for older workers (55-64 years).[6] In 2002, the Barcelona European Council identified the retirement age of older workers as a common European problem and concluded that the exit ages of older workers for each country in the EU should be raised by five years by 2010.[7] A recent report by the Commission of the European Communities indicated that while some advances have been made in reaching these targets, overall, the EU is "still far short of both targets, and much stronger efforts are needed to make the necessary progress towards both targets."[8]

Figure 1 summarizes the current status of the 25 European Union countries with respect to their progress toward the Stockholm and Barcelona targets as of 2002.

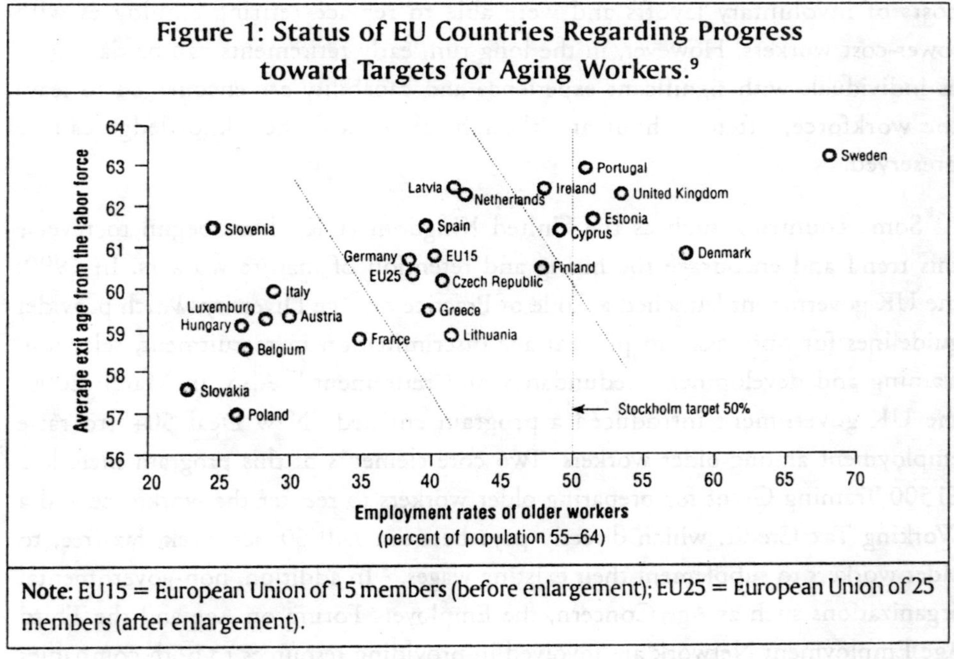

Figure 1: Status of EU Countries Regarding Progress toward Targets for Aging Workers.[9]

Note: EU15 = European Union of 15 members (before enlargement); EU25 = European Union of 25 members (after enlargement).

Two important factors have promoted the trend toward early retirement in European countries. First, the combination of state pension plans, coupled with early retirement and other social programs made it relatively attractive for individuals to retire early. In addition, companies looking to reduce headcount in European countries have traditionally offered early retirement packages as a way of avoiding layoffs. In many ways, early retirement was seen by governments and companies as a way of mitigating the impact of high unemployment, as less expensive younger workers were able to move into jobs vacated by older employees.[10]

In fact, a recent EU study showed that while approximately 33 percent of all retired individuals between the ages of 55-64 indicated they left their last jobs or business as part of normal retirement, almost 20 percent (or three million people per year) cited early retirement as the main reason.[11] From a short-term perspective, both employers and employees appeared to have benefited from this arrangement, as retiring employees received benefits while employers avoided the expensive costs of involuntary layoffs and were able to replace retiring employees with lower-cost workers. However, in the long run, early retirements can be damaging as individuals with significant experience and capability are encouraged to leave the workforce, often without any thought as to how their knowledge can be preserved.

Some countries, such as the United Kingdom (UK), have begun to reverse this trend and encourage the hiring and retention of mature workers. In 1999, the UK government launched a Code of Practice on Age Diversity, which provides guidelines for businesses to prevent age discrimination in recruitment, selection, training and development, redundancy and retirement.[12] Also, in March 2000, the UK government introduced a program entitled "New Deal 50+" to raise employment among older workers. Two core elements of this program include a £1500 Training Grant for preparing older workers to reenter the workforce and a Working Tax Credit, which directly pays between £40-60 per week, tax-free, to older workers to supplement their existing wages.[13] In addition, non-governmental organizations such as Age Concern, the Employers Forum on Age and the Third Age Employment Network are involved in providing resources to both companies and workers regarding the benefits of the aging workforce.

What should Companies do?

Based on our research and working with companies on their workforce strategies, we recommend that companies consider the following six strategies for addressing the challenges of an aging workforce:

- Redirect recruiting and sourcing efforts to include mature workers.
- Retain valued employees through developing alternative work arrangements.
- Preserve critical knowledge before it walks out the door.

- Provide opportunities for workers to continually update their skills.
- Facilitate the coexistence of multiple generations in the workforce.
- Help ensure that mature workers are able to use technology effectively in the workplace.

Redirect Recruiting and Sourcing Efforts to Include Mature Workers

Given the shift in workforce demographics, companies are quickly finding shortages of workers from labor pools where they normally would draw younger employees. ASDA, the UK's largest retailer, has recognized the value of attracting mature workers on a part-time basis.[14] The company has over 20,000 employees who are over 50 years old, representing 19 percent of its workforce. ASDA conducts over 50 workshops at local job recruitment centers in the UK for anyone interested in continuing to work, not just those interested in working for ASDA. They also provide a number of flexible benefits targeted toward mature workers such as "Benidorm leave" (three months unpaid leave between January and March) and "Grandparent leave" (a week unpaid leave after the birth of a grandchild). Recently, the company opened a store in the UK where 40 percent of the associates were over age 50. ASDA has found that this focus on aging workers provided a number of organizational benefits. For example, stores with a higher proportion of older workers have absenteeism rates less than a third of ASDA'S average rate.[15] Also, in March 2003, ASDA was selected as one of the Britain's top ten companies to work for, and the UK's best company for flexible working.[16]

Attracting mature workers does not have to be limited to entry-level positions. Westpac, a major financial services institution based in Australia, was looking to increase its presence in the financial advising market. To accomplish this, it trained approximately 900 recruits who were over 55 years of age and looking to establish a second career. Noel Purcell, Westpac's general manager of stakeholder communications, noted that these older workers became an important asset because they related well with older customers, who sometimes felt that younger staff were not experienced enough to address their financial concerns.[17]

Other examples of companies interested in sourcing older knowledge workers from outside their organizations are Procter & Gamble (P&G) and Eli Lilly.[18]

Together, they are the initial sponsors of *YourEncore.com*, a contracting agency focused on attracting retired research scientists, engineers and product developers who want to work on a project-by-project basis. Retirees are hired by *YourEncore.com* and are provided with marketing, accounting and administrative support. At the same time, *YourEncore.com* works closely with sponsoring companies to identify opportunities to use these resources on a part-time basis.[19] As sponsoring companies, P&G and Eli Lilly obtain access to a range of experienced personnel that they can tap into on an as-needed basis.

Retain Valued Employees through Developing Alternative Work Arrangements

While some companies are recruiting aging workers, other companies are developing alternative work arrangements to try to hold onto employees before they walk out the door. One organization that has made a commitment to retaining workers after they reach retirement age is the Aerospace Company, a US defense contractor. It developed a Retiree Casual program, where retirees can work on a project-consulting basis for up to 1000 hours per year and earn roughly the same base salary they earned prior to retirement, depending on roles and responsibilities. About 500 Retiree Casuals are eligible to work, while 200 are working at any given time. Most individuals in the program work two days per week, but some work full-time for six months straight. Most of the workers in this program are in their mid-sixties, but some continue into their eighties. The program has proven beneficial not only for the participants, but also for the company as a whole. As George Paulikas, a retired executive vice president and a program participant said, "The Retiree Casual program keeps expertise around and helps transfer it to others. People often remark that we don't have many consultants around here. Actually, we do, but they are called retirees, and they already know the business inside out."[20]

In addition to retaining workers using part-time work schedules, companies should also explore, when appropriate, the use of telecommuting as a way of encouraging mature workers to remain with the organization. Avoiding the time, costs and difficulties associated with commuting full-time can be a powerful incentive for individuals, particularly where traffic and weather conditions make regular travel inconvenient. While telecommuting can provide challenges in terms of social isolation and difficulty in coordinating remote activities, a regular schedule of office visits, coupled with appropriate training and support for remote workers, can help overcome these hurdles.

Preserve Critical Knowledge before it Walks Out the Door

When individuals leave an organization, the organization often loses a career's worth of experiential knowledge. This can range from e-mails, reports and documents that employees have accumulated, to tacit knowledge about how to do their jobs effectively. Too often, this knowledge leaves the organization without any attempt to identify, capture and share it with others. As a result, remaining employees often search futilely for answers to questions that have already been answered, recreate analyses that have been conducted many times over or simply fail to heed previously learned lessons that were never formally identified and captured.

A number of firms have focused on techniques to stem this hemorrhage of corporate insight.[21] One set of techniques focuses on eliciting the experiential, or tacit, knowledge of employees. Through detailed interviewing and/or documentation, companies are trying to capture these insights in an explicit form that can be stored for future use. Other companies have tried mentoring arrangements and fostering communities of practice to encourage mature workers to pass down the knowledge from their generation to the next. This type of knowledge exchange can be especially useful when the decision rules and experiences cannot be easily captured or written down without losing the essence of the knowledge.

Bosch, a German provider of automotive, industrial and consumer products, introduced an interesting method for retaining critical knowledge in the organization. Older workers who possess critical knowledge and are about to retire are asked to take part in a special program. Prior to retirement, these employees fill in a form about the knowledge they gained during their careers. This information is synthesized and captured in a database used by project managers around the world. If these project managers have a difficult project that requires specialist knowledge, they can search the database to determine if there are retired workers that fit their needs. These people are then asked to work for a short period of time during the project and support the team by bringing in knowledge gained during their previous tenure with the company.[22]

To retain valuable experiences, share lessons learned, expand the organization's knowledge base and improve operational and product quality, The World Bank captures videos and audiotapes of selected individuals and groups involved in challenging projects. Using storytelling techniques, the Bank seeks to uncover new knowledge from the practitioners in developing countries. Interviewees are encouraged to focus on telling stories, rather than providing general observations, so the material will be more interesting for the intended audiences. This knowledge retention initiative uses subject matter experts to conduct interviews, as well as to screen and edit the videos and audiotapes, pushing relevant insights and content to audiences through a variety of media.[23]

In concert with its well-conceived elicitation technique, The World Bank's knowledge dissemination process also contributes to its success. Both audio and videotaped interviews are posted to a website and burned onto CD-ROMs, with any documents referred to during the interview appearing as hot links in the final text. The World Bank also pushes these debriefings to a distribution list of targeted members, rather than simply passively posting them on the Internet. For reinforcement, they also make interviewees available for follow-up and mentoring.[24]

Provide Opportunities for Workers to Continually Update their Skills

Executives are recognizing the need to refresh the skills of those workers whose formal training may have ended years, if not decades, earlier. Lufthansa, the German airline, recognized that many of its older workers were not participating in learning activities. An annual evaluation of its training showed that the company had not offered systematic training opportunities for older workers for more than 10 years. To address the learning needs of managers older than 45, the company started an initiative called the "Added Experience Program."[25]

The objectives of this program are threefold: to transfer informal skills that have not been taught and that are necessary in the working environment; to create a dialogue among participants that facilitates the exchange of valuable experiences and enables managers to increase the size and scope of their personal networks; and to allow top management to learn about, and tap into, the know-how these experienced managers brought to the table. The program lasts for one year and consists of a number of one-week modules. The participants stay in the same cohort throughout the year to build a level of trust that is needed to share lessons learned and good practices.

Facilitate the Coexistence of Multiple Generations in the Workforce

Age is often overlooked when addressing the subject of employee diversity. Yet, the viewpoints and perceptions of different age groups can present significant barriers in a workforce where age differences can span 40 years or more. For example, preconceived biases about the willingness of older workers to learn and embrace new technologies can limit their opportunities, discouraging mature workers from refreshing their skills. At the same time, younger workers may be perceived as not willing to "pay their dues" before advancing in the company. This can dampen the enthusiasm of new employees and result in low morale and early attrition.

Her Majesty's Land Registry (HMLR) in the UK provides an example of an organization that recognized the importance of balancing the different needs, interests and work styles of different generations. An organization of about 10,000 employees responsible for managing the record keeping of real estate deeds in England and Wales, HMLR recognized that it needed to review and raise its staffing levels to meet increasing demand for services. An extensive demographic segmentation exercise across the whole organization confirmed a decline in recruitment of 16-24 year olds, as well as a difficulty in filling some vacancies. Further research showed that many managers held "stereotyped attitudes," and that the organization was focusing much of its recruitment resources solely on attracting younger workers.[26]

To address the issue, HMLR took a number of actions, including:[27]

- Monitoring age profiles by local office and grade level every six months.
- Monitoring recruitment and promotion decisions to prevent age discrimination.

- Incorporating age profiling results into the annual diversity report.
- Engaging key business unit managers in its age diversity challenges.
- Creating a mandatory diversity training program for managers (with scenarios and role-playing) designed to address age-related issues as well as other diversity challenges.

HMLR recently won an Age Positive award from the UK Department of Work and Pensions for its analytical approach to addressing the multi-generational workforce.[28]

Some companies have engineered ways to bring together older and younger workers to leverage their respective talents. For example, General Electric, at the dawn of the e-commerce era, matched 500 of its most senior managers with junior employees to learn about the potential for Internet technologies.The "junior" mentors and the "seniors" were paired based on knowledge and personality traits, and then spent two to four hours per week together, discussing the ins and outs of the World Wide Web. As a result of this process, the senior executives gained new insights that were critical to moving their businesses into the Internet age, while the junior employees were able to gain access to a network of executives that, under normal circumstances, would be difficult to obtain.[29]

Help Ensure that Mature Workers are Able to Effectively Use Technology in the Workplace

One of the primary misperceptions of many employers is that older workers have more difficulty learning and adopting new technologies. However, a number of research studies have demonstrated that age alone is not directly linked to the adoption of computer use in the work environment.[30] For example, a recent case study involving mature workers at the UK retailer Tesco found that, while not all older workers were initially comfortable using new technologies, many quickly adapted to it. Motivation was cited as one of the primary drivers for adopting new technologies. As one manager stated, the mature workers were the ones "studying the literature, making use of telephone help-lines and suffering the restless nights making sure they could do the job."[31]

However, organizations should be cognizant of two issues related to the use of technology by mature workers. First, organizations need to consider the accessibility requirements of older workers. As individuals age, it may become more difficult to decipher smaller typefaces on a screen, understand the audio portion of a streaming video, or control the hand motions necessary to use a computer mouse or similar devices requiring precise movements. When designing systems, companies need to address the needs of potential user groups and provide alternative mechanisms for accessing, displaying and manipulating web pages and other applications. Furthermore, organizations need to evaluate the strategies associated with rolling out and training older workers on new applications. Organizations should consider building a cadre of influenced leaders to demonstrate to older workers that they are capable of learning the new technologies, and build in ample practice opportunities to build comfort and confidence among individuals who have less experience in using the technology.[32]

Moving Forward

Given the changing composition of the workforce in the next 5 to 10 years, the following questions can help companies identify key HR requirements to avoid potential pitfalls and proactively address related issues:

- Does your company have a detailed understanding of its employee demographics, and of what key positions or job categories may be at risk in the near future?
- Has your company identified potential opportunities for attracting and retaining mature workers using part-time or alternative work arrangements?
- To what extent is retraining mature workers part of your company's overall learning and development strategy?
- Does your company have a strategy in place to preserve critical knowledge before it walks out the door?
- How effectively are age-related issues addressed within your company's overall diversity strategy?

- To what extent does your company address the accessibility needs of employees when designing or implementing new software?

Conclusion

The challenges associated with the maturing workforce often do not garner much executive attention. Like an individual suffering from hypertension, an organization with an aging workforce often feels no symptoms for many years. However, as the situation advances, companies will soon realize the pain associated with losing expertise, incurring higher recruiting and training costs, and managing intergenerational concerns. Firms need to take a proactive approach to address demographic changes, both within their organizations and across their labor markets, to avoid issues that could significantly hamper companies in the industrialized world.

(Eric Lesser is an Associate Partner with the IBM Institute for Business Value. He is responsible for conducting research and developing thought leadership on a variety of human capital management topics. Eric is based in Cambridge, MA and can be reached at elesser@us.ibm.com

Carsten Hausmann is a Partner with IBM's Business Consulting Services and heads up the Human Capital Management Practice in Central Region, EMEA. His team works with national and international clients on all aspects of HR from strategy, process and organization design and systems implementation to HR outsourcing. Carsten is based in Dusseldorf, Germany and can be reached at carsten.hausmann@de.ibm.com

Steffen Feuerpeil is a student of International Business Administration and Information Technology at the University of Cooperative Education, Mannheim. As a participant in IBM's University Education program, he has worked for IBM in several departments around the world. Steffen is based in Mannheim, Germany and can be reached at feuerpeil@de.ibm.com)

About IBM Business Consulting Services

With consultants and professional staff in more than 160 countries globally, IBM Business Consulting Services provides clients with business process and industry expertise, a deep understanding of technology solutions that address specific industry issues, and the ability to design, build and run those solutions in a way that delivers bottom-line business value.

References

1. Johansson, Anders L, "Work Organisation in an ageing Europe," European Agency for Safety and Health at Work, September 2004, *http://agency.osha.eu.int/publications/magazine/2/en/index_10.htm* (accessed November 29, 2004).
2. Buck, Harmut and Bernd Dworschak, "Ageing and Work in Germany—Challenges and Solutions," in Buck, Hartmut and Bernd Dworschak eds., *Ageing and Work in Europe.* Stuttgart: 2003, ISBN# 3-8167-6321-9. *http://www.management-issues.com/display_page.asp?section=blog&id=671, p. 27.* (accessed February 7, 2005).
3. Ibid.
4. De Long, David, "Lost Knowledge: Confronting the Threat of an Aging Workforce", Oxford University Press: New York, 2004, p. 35.
5. Von Nordheim, Frtiz, "ED Policies in Support of Member States Efforts to Retain, Reinforce and Re-integrate Older Workers in Employment," in Buck, Hartmut and Bernd Dworschak eds., *Ageing and Work in Europe,* p. 11.
6. Commission of the European Communities, "The Stockholm and Barcelona Targets: Increasing Employment of Older Workers and Delaying the Exit from the Labour Market," *Commission Staff Working Paper,* Brussels, April 2004, p. 2.
7. Ibid.
8. Commission of the European Communities, "Increasing Employment of Older Workers and Delaying the Exit from the Labour Market," *Communication from the Commission to the Council, the European Parliament, The European Economic and Social Committee and the Committee of the Regions,* March 3 2004, p. 3.
9. Ibid; p. 6.
10. Von Nordheim, Op. Cit., p. 10.
11. Commission of the European Communities, "Increasing Employment of Older Workers and Delaying the Exit from the Labour Market," p. 9
12. Age Positive—Facts and Figures, *www.agepositive.gov.uk/factfigures.cfm7sectionid =70* (accessed February 3, 2005).
13. Taylor, Phillip, "Policy Making Towards Older Workers in the United Kingdom," in Buck, Hartmut and Bernd Dworschak eds., *Ageing and Work in Europe.* Stuttgart: 2003, p. 71.

14. Case Study: ASDA Stores *http://www.agepositive.gov.uk* (accessed February 3, 2005).

15. "SAGA Predicts Thousands will Delay Retirement," Personnelzone Direct, October, 2003. *http://www.personnelzone.com* (accessed February 7, 2004).

16. Ibid.

17. Nixon, Sherrill. "Looming Labour Crisis Puts the Focus on Grey Force." *Sydney Morning Herald.* October 2, 2002.

18. "P&G, Eli Lilly to Use Expertise of Retirees," *Associated Press Newswire,* November 4, 2003.

19. *http://www.yourencore.com* (accessed February 10, 2005).

20. Dychtwald, Ken, Tamara Erickson and Bob Morison, "It's Time to Retire Retirement," *Harvard Business Review,* March, 2004.

21. For more information on techniques to preserve critical knowledge, see Casher, Amy and Eric Lesser "Grey Matter Matters: Preserving Critical Knowledge in the 21st Century," IBM Institute for Business Value Executive Brief, 2003.

22. Bosch Management Support, "Handfeste Unterstutzung statt allgemeiner Ratschlage-eine feste Verbindung auf Zeit," 2004, p. 2.

23. Retaining Valuable Knowledge: Proactive Strategies to Deal with a Shifting Workforce," *APQC Best Practice Report.* August 2002.

24. Ibid.

25. Euler, Petra, "Die "vergessenen Manager trainieren" in *Personalfuhrung* 1998, p. 1.

26. HM Land Registry - Engaging with Line Managers, *http://www.efa-agediversity.org.uk/case-studies/hmlr1.htm* (accessed February 7, 2005).

27. Personal Today Awards 2004, September 14, 2004. *http://www.personneltoday.co.uk/Articles/2004/09/14/25567/Personnel+Today+Awards+2004.htm* (accessed February 7, 2005).

28. Ibid.

29. GE Annual Report 1999; Schlender, B. *et al.* "The Odd Couple." *Business 2.0,* May 2000; Breen B, "Trickle-Up Leadership, " *Fast Company Magazine,* November 2001; Low L, "New Tricks for Old Dogs." *CIO Magazine.* October 15, 2000; Useem M, "Leading Up: How to Lead Your Boss So You Both Win," 2001, New York, New York: *Three Rivers Press,* p. 284.

30. Borghans, Lex and ter Weel, Bas, "Do Older Workers Have More Trouble Using a Computer Than Younger Workers?" Working Paper ROA-RM-2002/1E, Research Centre for Education and the Labor Market, University of Maastrich, February, 2002. *http://137.120.22.236/www-edocs/loader/file.asp?id=581* (accessed February 7, 2005).

31. Stoney Christopher and Mark Roberts, "The Case for Older Workers at Tesco: An Examination of Attitudes, Assumptions and Attributes," Carleton University School of Public Policy and Administration, Working Paper, No. 53, June, 2003. *http://www.carleton.ca/spa/Publication/WP%2053%20Stoney.pdf* (accessed February 7, 2005).

32. Morris, Michael and Viswanath Venkatesh, "Age Differences in Technology Adoption Decisions: Implications for a Changing Workforce," *Personnel Psychology*, Vol. 53, No. 2, July 2000, pp. 375-403.

17

The Aging of the US Workforce: Employer Challenges and Responses

Although corporate America foresees a significant workforce shortage as boomers retire, it is not dealing with the issue at present and may be underestimating the strategic challenges ahead. This article is a survey, that indicates that a little more than half of the respondents agreed that the aging workforce is an issue that must be addressed. While almost two-thirds said that retirements will lead to a "brain drain" in their organization, less than one-quarter said that it is an issue that is strategically very important. The main purpose of the survey is to understand how organizations are approaching the issue, whether organizations are identifying older workers that may be lost as they retire and how to determine the programs to retain employees so that their wisdom is transferred to the next generation.

Executive Summary

Corporate America clearly understands that it will face a workforce shortage as retirements increase and it is just beginning to understand the strategic challenges it will face as a result of those shortages. While more than half of the respondents

---

to the survey - entitled "The Aging of the US Workforce"—agreed that the aging workforce is an issue that must be dealt with because it will lead to a workforce shortage, and almost two-thirds said that retirements in their organization will lead to a "brain drain," less than one-quarter of those surveyed said that the aging of their workforce is an issue that is strategically very important to them. one-third of the respondents said that this issue is important to their organization's overall goals and strategy.

Strategically, corporate America is focusing resources on more immediate issues. Despite the low number of employers who think that the aging workforce is a very important issue today, an overwhelming 90 percent of them are committed to putting formal retention programs in place in the coming years to help address this issue as it becomes more prevalent.

However, in support of data from previous studies conducted by other organizations, our survey results do show that at least some employers are dealing with the issues raised by the aging of their workforce today. With an estimated 14.5 percent of respondents' workforces currently over age 55 and with just under 15 percent eligible to retire in the next five years, our respondents estimated that just over 10 percent of their current workers are likely to do so.

In the light of these looming retirements, just under 40 percent of respondents noted that their number one concern is the availability of talent over the next five years. Other highly ranked areas of concern included retention of key employees and talent management (i.e., ensuring that the right employees are in the right positions).

With these impending workforce shortages, the question becomes: Will corporate America move from productivity to "reductivity?" Letting the brain drain flow—i.e., not implementing retention plans or failing to consider how to leverage high-knowledge workers at retirement—can have a negative effect on overall productivity. We call this phenomenon reductivity—the systemic reduction in "business wisdom" that can extend learning curves, slow otherwise smooth processes, and cause duplication of efforts along the line of the "recreating the wheel" theory.

Based on the experience that Ernst & Young LLP has with many corporate clients, it is clear that governance and compliance issues—including the focus on Human Resource (HR) processes and systems in Sarbanes-Oxley Section 404 reviews—are of immediate concern to HR professionals. While many recognize that the aging workforce will be an issue in the coming years, today organizations are focusing their resources on dealing with these more pressing issues and will deal with the looming "wisdom withdrawal" when it becomes a more immediate concern.

For those who already have formal processes in place to transfer "business wisdom" from one generation to the next, succession planning, mentoring, and informal knowledge networks are the most common solutions, with mentoring showing the highest level of impact.

While a majority of our respondents (over 85 percent) had no formal programs in place to retain key employees, of those who did have programs, hiring retirees as consultants or contractors, retention bonuses, promoting a culture of generational diversity and pre-retirement planning programs proved to have the highest impact. With 90 percent of respondents stating that they intend to put some type of retention program in place, we can expect to see a number of the following formal programs grow in popularity over the coming years:

- Hiring retirees as consultants or contractors or creating an "on-call" pool of retirees.
- Creating flexible work schedules.
- Phased-in retirement.
- Creating flexible or special benefits.
- Mentoring.
- Continuous learning and training.
- Pre-retirement planning.
- Delayed retirement enhancements to pension plans.
- Workplace restructuring.
- Creating a culture that promotes generational diversity.

- Retention bonuses.
- Career counseling.
- Modifications to early retirement subsidies.

Survey Objectives

Few trends are as predictable and irreversible as the aging of the American population. What is much less certain, however, is the impact of this trend on the nation's workforce and on the human capital needs of US businesses and other organizations.

Ernst & Young LLP's Human Capital Practice, in conjunction with ExecuNet Inc., and the Human Capital Institute, conducted a survey of HR executives at organizations throughout the US.

The purpose of the survey was to determine how organizations are responding to the issues posed by aging workforces. The survey examines whether organizations are identifying older workers who possess "business wisdom" that may be lost as these workers retire, with a specific focus to determine whether organizations are developing programs to retain those employees so that their wisdom is transferred to the next generation.

The survey specifically explored:

- The extent to which employers are monitoring the age profile of their workforces, especially the distribution of older workers and their eligibility for, and likelihood of, retiring over the next five years.
- How each organization views its aging workforce and its importance to the organization's goals and strategies.
- Whether estimated retirements will cause a talent gap or "wisdom withdrawal" in specific organizational functions and levels.
- Whether organizations have formal processes in place to capture and transmit "business wisdom" and, if so, which ones are having a measurable impact.

- Whether organizations have measured the benefit costs associated with older workers delaying their retirement.
- Whether organizations have pre-retirement planning programs and, if so, what features these programs include.

Characteristics of Survey Respondents

Survey findings are based on responses from HR executives representing a cross section of some of the largest employers in the US in a variety of industry sectors. The survey was conducted electronically from November 11, 2005 to December 21, 2005.

Employer Size

Of those responding, 25.9 percent represented employers with 1,000-4,999 employees, 20 percent with 5,000-9,999 employees, and 12.9 percent with 10,000-24,999 employees. Employers with 25,000-99,999 employees comprised 9.4 percent of respondents and another 8.2 percent were employers with 100,000 or more employees. The remainder represented employers with fewer than 1,000 employees.

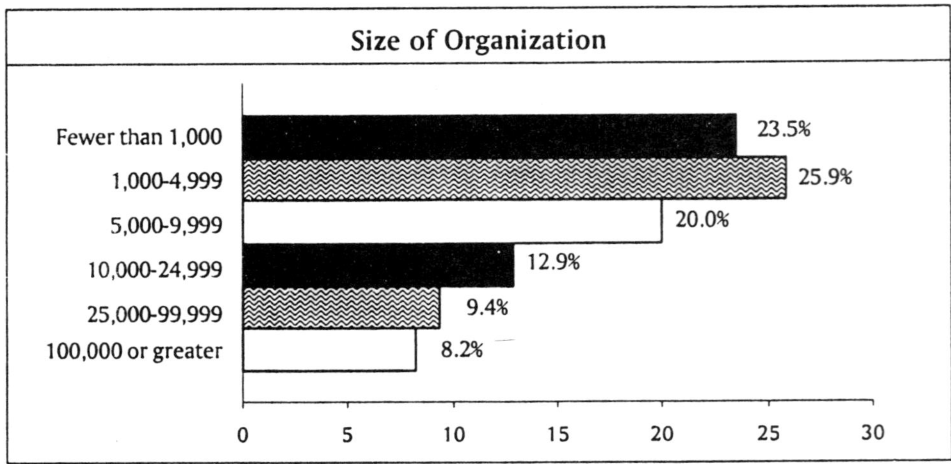

Industry Sector

While employers in virtually all types of industries responded, 23.5 percent of the respondents represented companies in the manufacturing industry.

Government and non-profit groups accounted for 18.8 percent of respondents, and financial services firms accounted for 9.4 percent. Natural resources and retail industries were each represented by 8.2 percent of respondents. Technology, communications, and entertainment accounted for 5.9 percent of respondents, followed by health sciences and transportation, each with 4.7 percent, and energy, consumer products, and industrial products, each with 3.5 percent. Other industries represented were: real estate, professional services, hospitality, construction, and aerospace.

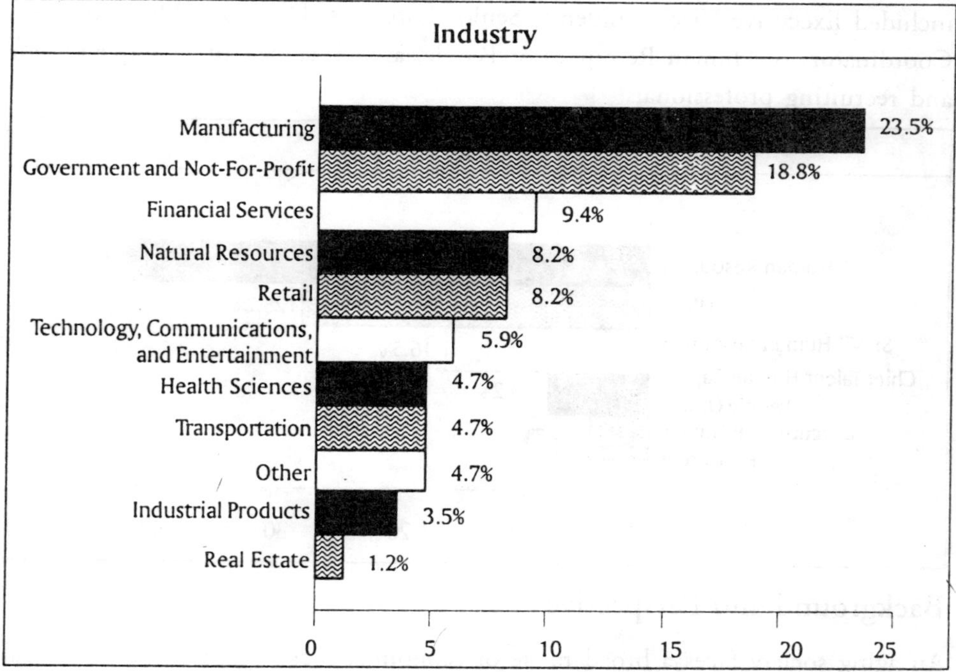

Respondents to our survey do not represent a statistical sampling weighted according to the proportions of older workers in each industry. According to the US Bureau of Labor Statistics (BLS), more than 20 percent of the nation's 3.2 million federal employees were aged 55 or older in 2004, and, within the next five years, half of the federal government's civilian workforce will be eligible to retire. Nearly 20 percent of 16.7 million state and local government employees were age 55 or older in 2004. In comparison, just over 14 percent of private sector workers were 55 years or older in 2004.

These statistics illustrate the significant challenge facing the public sector workforce in the next five years.

Respondents' Roles in their Organizations

The most common leadership role held by individual respondents—just over 42 percent—was Vice President of Human Resources. Another 16.5 percent of respondents were Senior Vice Presidents of Human Resources and just over 8 percent were Chief Talent, Human Capital, People Officers. The remainder included Executive Vice Presidents, Senior Directors, Directors, Managers, and Coordinators of Human Resources or People, as well as benefits, compensation, and recruiting professionals.

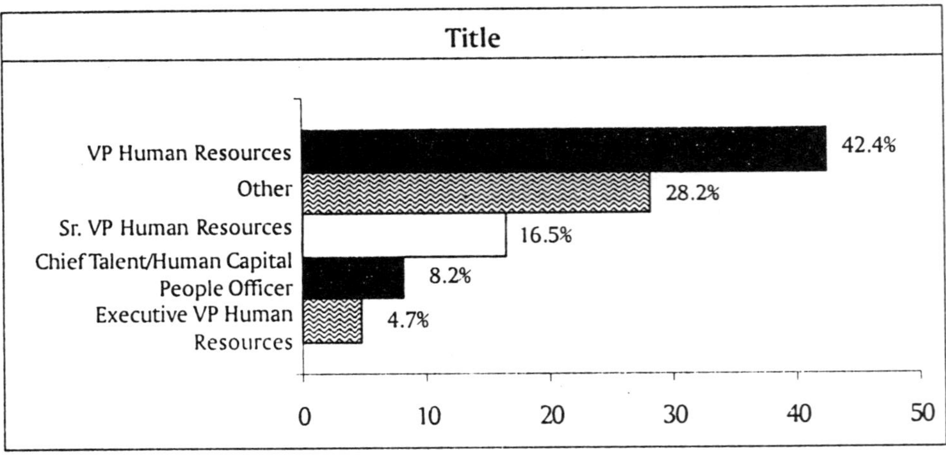

Background and Perspective

An aging society faces a broad range of economic, social, political, and cultural challenges. One critical dimension is the impact on national productivity, economic growth, and global competitiveness. The deployment and contributions of older workers affect not only the economic and social well-being of the workers themselves, but also the standard of living enjoyed by current and future generations.

Aging of the US Population

The United States is undergoing a profound shift in the distribution of older people in the overall population, with the primary factor being an increase in life expectancy. An American male born in 2000 has an estimated life expectancy of 74 years. For American women, life expectancy is 80 years. Men reaching age 65 have an average life expectancy of an additional 16 years; women have an additional 19 years. As a result of increases in life expectancy, the number of Americans aged 65 and over is projected to more than double by the year 2030. As noted by Robert Friedland and Laura Summer in *Demography is Not Destiny, Revisited,* "The population is anticipated to grow older than it is now, but the population already is older now than it has ever been."

The "baby boom" in the United States from 1946 through 1964 resulted in approximately 12 million more births than the country had experienced in the 18 years prior (1928 through 1945) and over 6 million more births than in the subsequent 18 years (1965 through 1983). In the next 18 years (1984 through 2002), however, there were almost as many births as in the baby boom (74.9 million vs. 75.9 million).

Today, out of a total US population of nearly 300 million, approximately 35.9 million people are age 65 or older. This number represents approximately 12 percent of the nation's population, or about 1 of every 8 Americans. By the year 2030, people age 65 and older are projected to constitute as much as 24 percent of the country's population, or nearly one of every four Americans.

An aging population is not just an American phenomenon. The United States ranks 32nd among countries with high proportions of people age 65 and older. The world's population age 65 and older is growing by an estimated 800,000 people a month. Demographers project that, by mid-century, people age 65 and over will comprise about 15 percent of the world's population, up from about 7 percent today.

Older Workers

In the United States today, there are approximately 22.8 million people aged 55 and older who are working. They comprise approximately 16 percent of the workforce. The number of workers age 55 and over is growing four times faster than the workforce as a whole.

Because of the relative size of their group, as the Baby Boomers age, they will have a disproportionate impact on the overall age distribution of the nation's population in general and its workforce in particular. Baby Boomers, who in 2006 range in age from 42 to 60, currently represent nearly one-half of the US workforce. This is slightly more than the combined number of workers from the succeeding two generations (Generation X, currently ages 23-41, and the Millennial Generation, currently ages 4-22).

Between 2000 and 2010, the number of US workers ages 45-54 is projected to grow by just over 20 percent, while the number of those ages 55-64 is projected to grow more than 50 percent. In contrast, the number of workers ages 35-44 is projected to decrease by 10 percent over the same period of time. By 2012, the median age of the US workforce is projected to reach an all-time high of 41.4 years and nearly 20 percent of workers in the nation will be aged 55 and over. In the same period, people in what has traditionally been viewed as the prime working years (ages 25-44) will fall to 43 percent of the US workforce, down from 46 percent today.

Projected annual growth rates of segments of the population also differ significantly. From 2010 to 2020, the annual growth rate of the US population ages 15-64 (traditionally viewed as the total working-age population) is projected at 0.3 percent, while the comparable rate for ages 65 and over is projected at 3.1 percent. Furthermore, almost 90 percent of the net increase in the traditional working-age population is projected to occur in the age 55-64 group.

Improved health, the need for income and health insurance coverage, the shift to a knowledge-based service economy, and advances in technology are among the primary contributors to the labor force participation rate of older Americans and to prospects for an increasingly productive aging of the nation. As a result, traditional notions of the expected "working" vs. "retirement" ages of the population are changing, as are the very concepts of work and retirement themselves. For example, nearly two in five American men and three in ten American women ages 55-64 who have pension income are also employed.

Increasing research attention is being given to the older segment of the nation's working population. Recent studies have explored various aspects of the aging of the workforce from the vantage point of both older employees themselves and of employers. The "Sources" section of this White Paper identifies many of the most significant recent studies on this topic, largely from the employer's perspective.

In 2005, for example, The Conference Board issued a report on the "mature workforce." The report was the result of a survey of a working group consisting of executives from a cross-section of industries, staff and line functions, and job titles. Ernst & Young LLP's Human Capital Practice was represented in this working group.

The Conference Board report's key findings were the following:

Shortages

- In industries in which a labor or skills shortage is already apparent, new recruitment, retention and work-time arrangements are being tested and implemented.
- Industries currently feeling the greatest pain in terms of skill shortages are oil, gas, energy, health care, and government.

Perceptions

- The maturing workforce is often seen as an issue to be dealt with, instead of an opportunity to be leveraged.
- Generational views differ on the concept of retirement. This affects knowledge transfer and mentoring opportunities.
- Stereotypes and assumptions exist about the mature workers' ability to stay innovative and productive, yet companies fear doing research.
- Forward-thinking organizations view mature workers within the framework of talent management.

Realities

- The maturing workforce is often isolated and couched in:
  - Work/life.
  - Elder care.

- Diversity.
- Disability.

- Retirement-eligible employees are not necessarily retirement prone. Employees want to continue working for both personal fulfillment and financial reasons.
- A corporate culture can limit or enhance views on the mature worker as being critical human capital and part of an integrated whole.
- It is not "politically correct" to discuss perceived or real cost concerns relating to the maturing workforce, so many companies don't discuss related issues or opportunities at all.
- "Tough issues" have to be acknowledged and researched if progress is to be made on fully integrating mature workers into the workforce.
- Both mature workers and younger workers can "retire in place" (i.e., remain on the job, but not working).

Practices

- Phased retirement practices are currently being done ad hoc and "under the table."
- Companies are recognizing that a maturing workforce can have a positive impact on customer satisfaction and profitability, but not necessarily without effective intergenerational inclusion initiatives.

Even more recently, the US Government Accountability Office (GAO), issued a December 2005 report to Congressional committees on older workers. The GAO stated that it issued this report because "(d)emographic changes pose serious challenges for employers, the economy, and older Americans." In particular, the GAO noted that "the loss of experienced workers could have adverse effects on productivity and economic growth." The GAO warned that "(p)otential skill gaps from impending retirements and a slowdown in the growth of the labor supply may make older workers a resource of growing importance."

The GAO recommended that "the Secretary of Labor design a comprehensive and highly visible public awareness campaign as a way to help employers and employees plan better for the future and by doing so bridge the gap between employer and employee needs."

Our survey and this White Paper elaborate on many of these and other recent findings.

Aging Workforce Profiles

Of our survey respondents, 13.3 percent reported that greater than one-quarter of their current workforce is over the age of 55. Another 18.1 percent reported that nearly one-quarter (21-25 percent) of their workforce is over age 55. For 31.4 percent of respondents, more than one-fifth of their current workforce is over age 55.

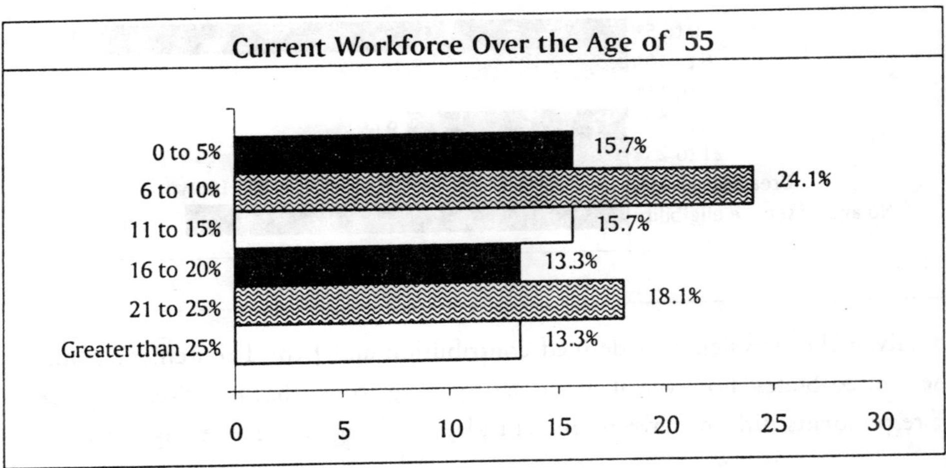

For 27.4 percent of respondents, workers over age 50 comprise more than one-quarter of their workforce. Another 15.5 percent of respondents reported that 21-25 percent of their workforce is over age 50. For 42.9 percent of respondents, more than one-fifth of their workforce is over age 50.

Defining eligibility to retire as meeting the age and/or years of service rules in their retirement plans, 16.9 percent of respondents reported that more than one-quarter of their current workforce will be eligible to retire over the next five years. Other studies have estimated that nationwide just over 40 percent of the US workforce will be eligible to retire during the next ten years.

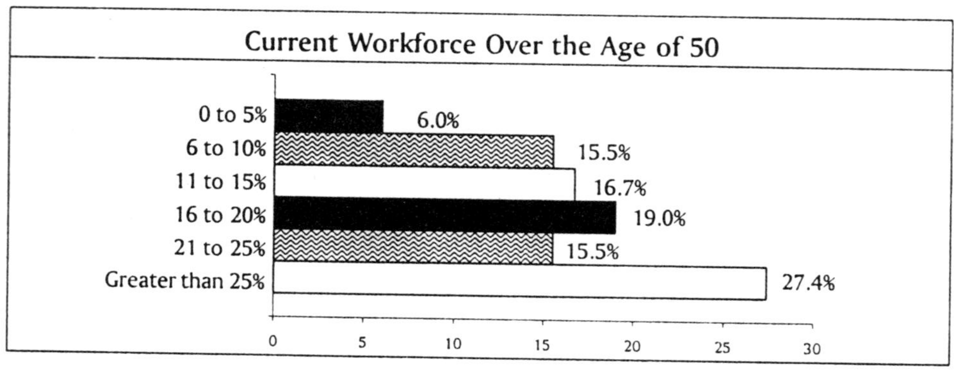

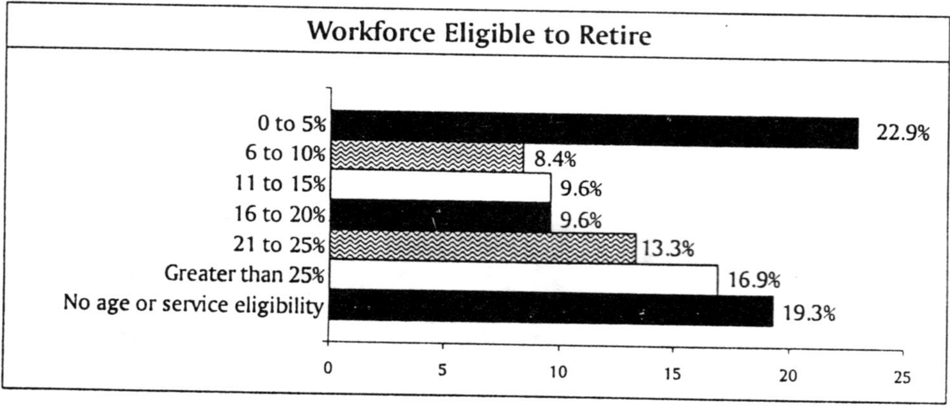

Given the prevalence of defined contribution and hybrid retirement plans in the United States, however, it was not surprising to see that just over 19 percent of respondents did not have retirement plans with age or service eligibility rules.

These responses indicate that employers have access to basic data about older workers as part of their workforce segmentation analyses. Whether employers are using such workforce profiles to monitor and project changes in their future workforces and their emerging human capital needs is another matter.

When asked what percentage of their workforce was likely to retire over the next five years, only 4.8 percent responded with an estimate of greater than one-quarter, and another 9.5 percent estimated that 21-25 percent would retire. For 14.3 percent of respondents, more than one-fifth of their workforce is likely to retire over the next five years. Over 8 percent of respondents did not know.

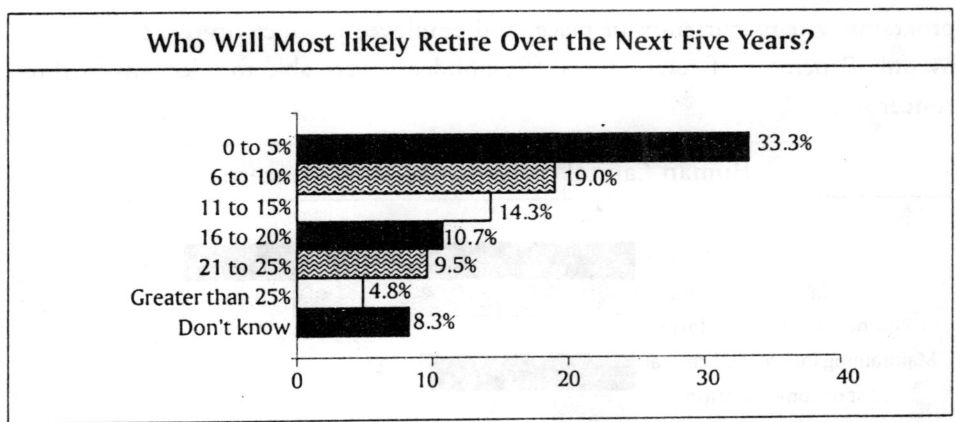

Just over 19 percent of respondents reported that the average age of those workers who had retired from their organization during the last 12 months was 65 or older. Another 22.9 percent reported the average age at 63-64 and 21.7 percent reported the average age at 61-62. Only 2.4 percent reported the average age at 55-56. Almost 23 percent of respondents, however, did not know the average age of recent retirees.

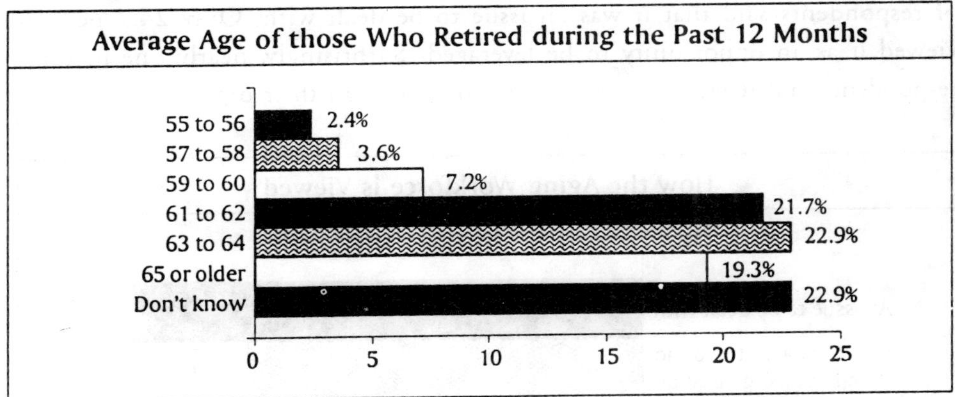

Attitudes Toward Human Capital

The availability of talent was rated as a top human capital concern (just over 38 percent). Talent management (right employees/right positions) was cited by 29.1 percent of respondents. Retention of key employees was cited by 20.9 percent and maintaining intellectual capital by 17.4 percent. The cost of compensation and benefit programs, people not taking advantage of benefits and related programs/systems currently in place, and employee productivity were each cited by only 7 percent of respondents. (Respondents were able to select up to three concerns.)

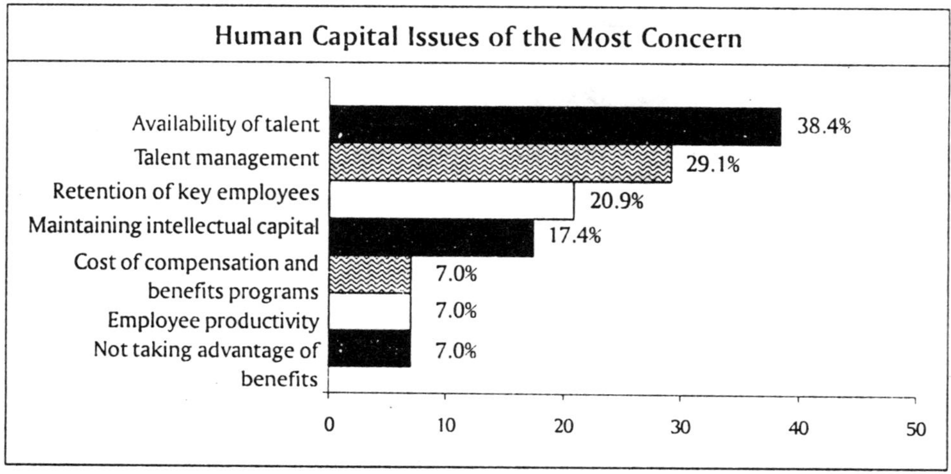

When asked how their organization viewed its aging workforce, 42.4 percent of respondents said that it was an issue to be dealt with. Only 24.7 percent viewed it as an opportunity to be leveraged. Surprisingly, nearly one in three respondents said it would have little or no impact on their organization.

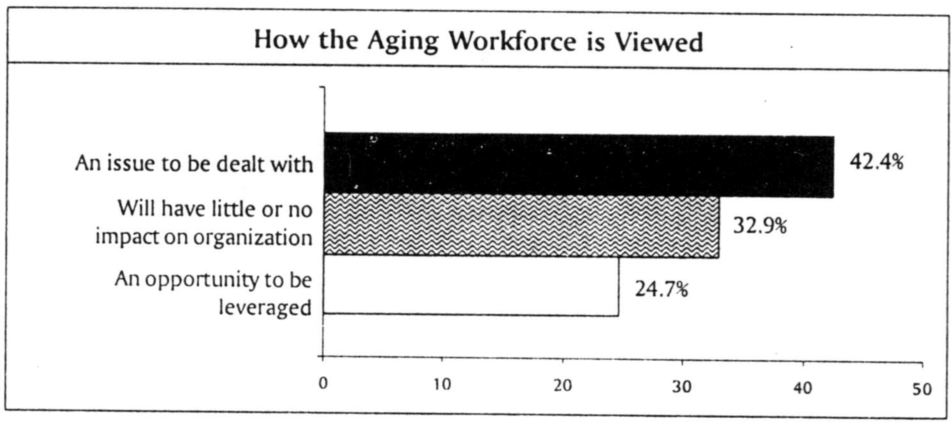

Of those respondents who described their aging workforce as an issue to be dealt with, 52.9 percent identified it as likely to lead to a workforce shortage. Only 8.8 percent expected it to lead to an excess of older workers who would like to keep working. Just over 11 percent said that they could not deal with this issue due to legal statutes, e.g., the Employee Retirement Income Security Act (ERISA) and the Age Discrimination in Employment Act (ADEA). Just over 10 percent cited costs associated with the aging workforce as a barrier to dealing with it and just under 8 percent cited cultural concerns as a barrier.

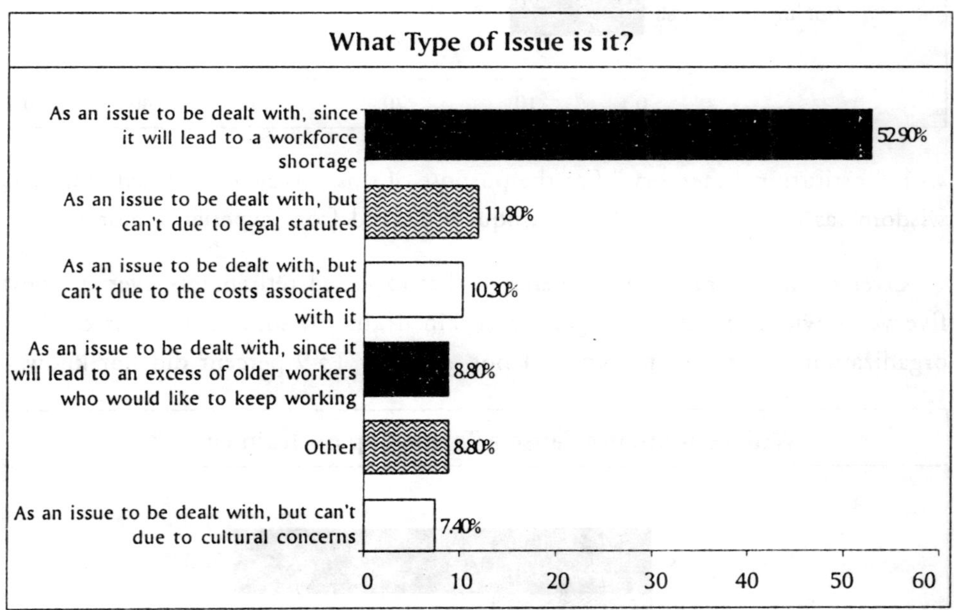

Almost half of the respondents rated the aging of their workforce as *very important* or *important* to their organization's goals and strategy over the next five years. Another 41.1 percent rated it *somewhat important.* The remaining 11 percent rated it *not important at all.*

Identification and Transmission of "Business Wisdom"

Wisdom has been denned in various ways. For historian Theodore Roszak, it is "the hard-won result of experience and reflection." Others have equated wisdom

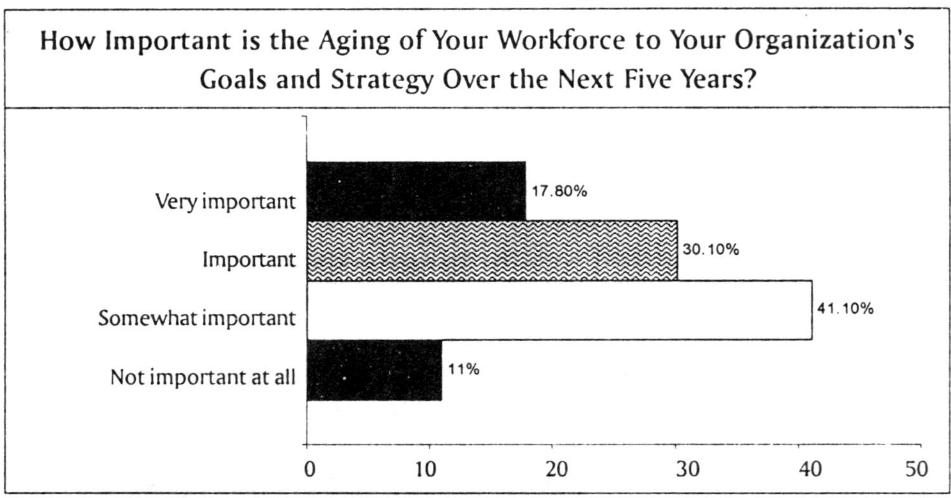

with "institutional memory." For the purpose of this survey, we defined "business wisdom" as business value that is uniquely derived from experience alone.

Over six in ten respondents believed that expected retirements over the next five years will cause a talent gap or "brain drain" in some functions of their organization. Nearly 24 percent did not. Another 13.9 percent did not know.

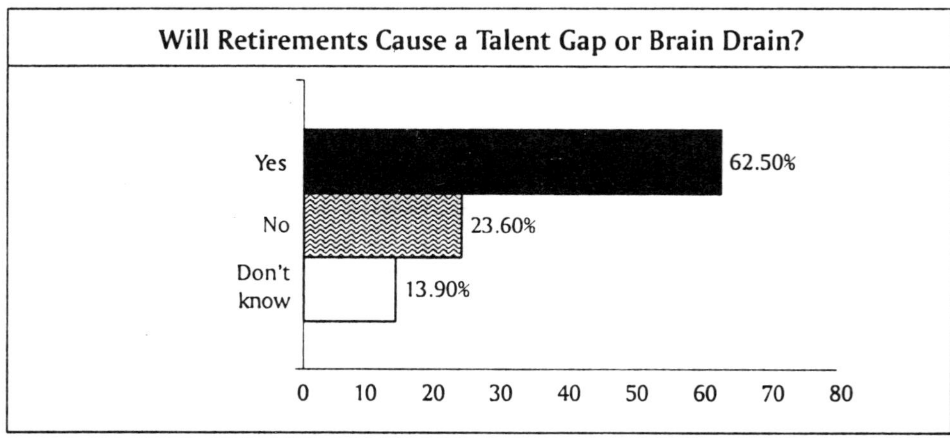

When asked which levels of their organization will be most affected, 25.4 percent identified middle management and 22.1 percent identified senior management other than at the C-level (e.g., chief executive officer, chief operating officer, chief financial officer). For 18.9 percent of respondents, supervisory positions will be most affected, and for 15.6 percent of respondents, hourly employee levels will be most affected. Only 12.3 percent of respondents identified C-level management positions as most affected. (Respondents were able to select all that applied.)

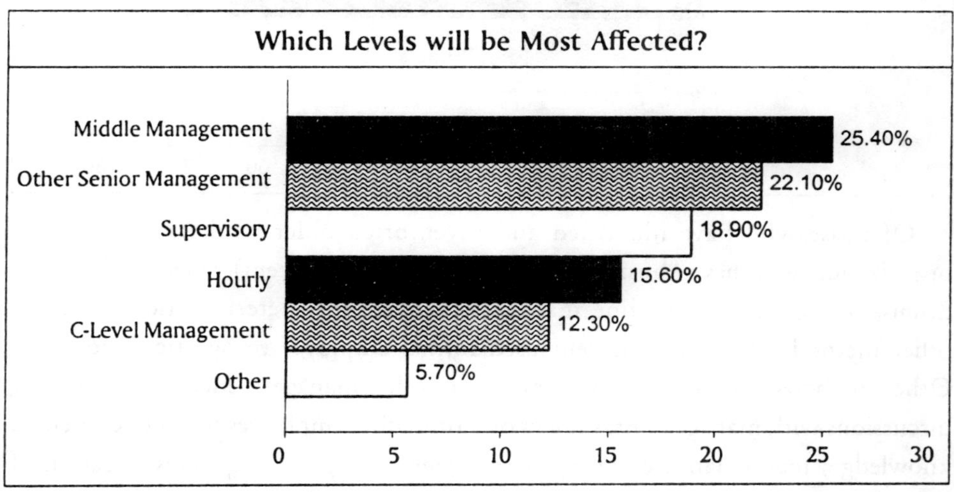

This response should be placed in the broader context of what is known nationally about today's older workers. The vast majority of US workers ages 55-74 today are employed in professional, management, service, office and administrative support and sales occupations. The number and proportion of older workers in each of these occupations is projected to grow considerably over the next decade.

While a higher percentage of professional/service-related jobs are held by older workers, blue-collar jobs are less likely to be held by older workers. Those blue-collar occupations with higher numbers of older workers are primarily in production and transportation.

Only 29.8 percent of respondents said their organization attempted to define "business wisdom" and identify where it resides.

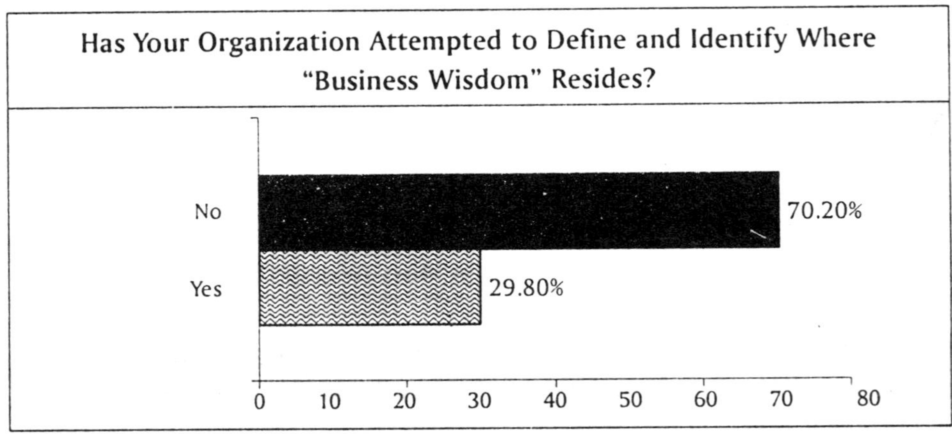

Of those who have identified and inventoried older workers within their organization who have "business wisdom," more (50 percent) relied on informal discussions with business line managers to make this determination than any other method. Only 22.7 percent used formal employee recognition programs. Other methods cited were: surveys of business line managers; succession planning discussions with management; surveys of terminating employees for undocumented knowledge; maintenance of formal knowledge management systems; creation of development plans based on input by incumbents; annual performance and talent

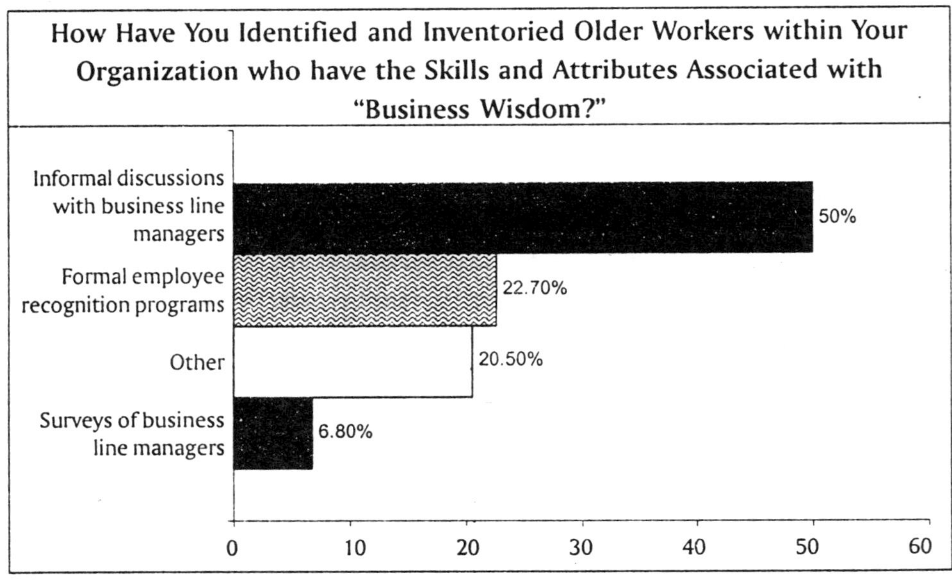

review process; and mentoring programs with younger personnel. Only one respondent stated that he or she used "business wisdom inventory sessions with incumbents."

Of those who attempted to define and identify "business wisdom," two-thirds stated that their organization has formal processes to capture and transmit "business wisdom" in place.

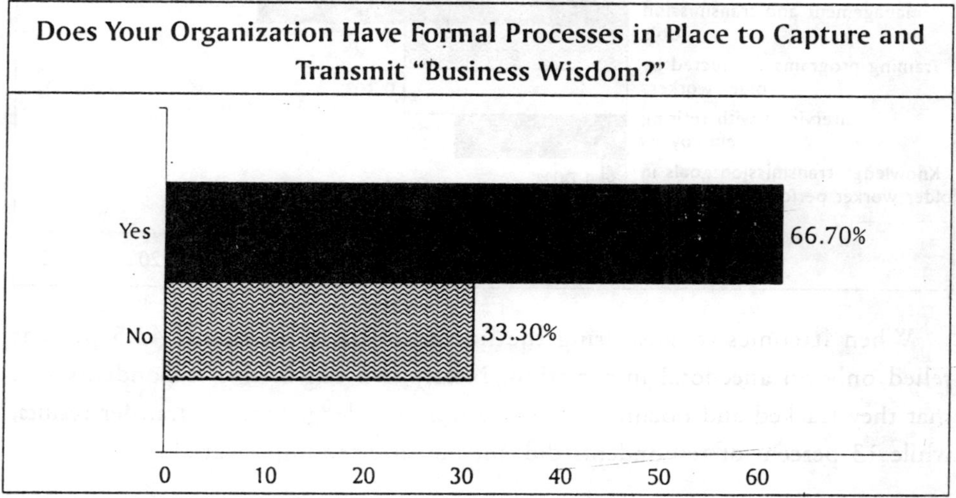

The most popular process was leadership succession planning (cited by 21.6 percent of respondents), followed by mentoring of younger workers by older workers (18.6 percent), informal knowledge networks (17.5 percent), and Web-based knowledge management and transmission tools (15.5 percent). Interviews with retiring employees were used by 9.3 percent to capture and transmit "business wisdom" and training programs conducted by older workers were used by 9.3 percent of respondents. Only 7.2 percent put knowledge transmission goals in the performance reviews of older workers. (Respondents were able to select all that applied.)

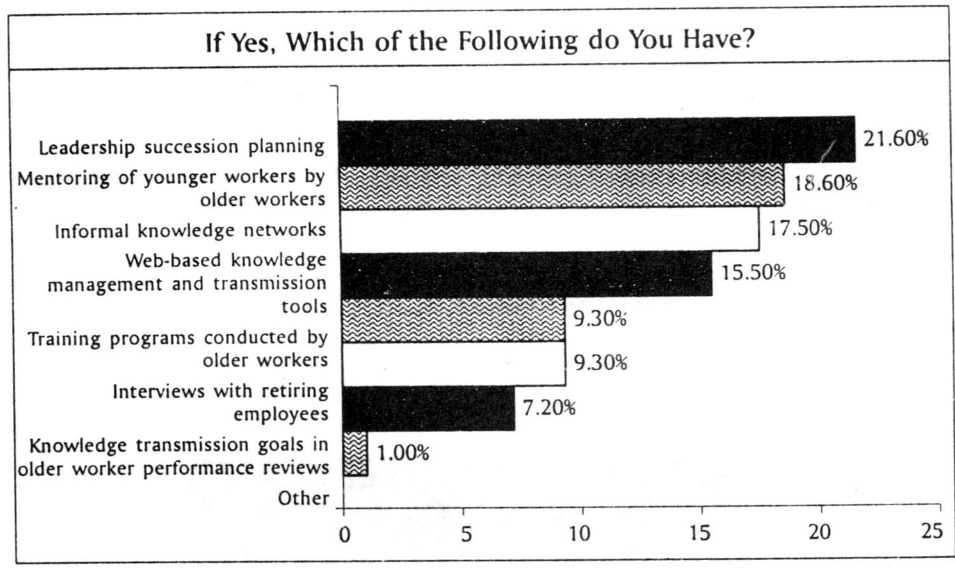

When it comes to measuring the impact of these programs, 43.5 percent relied only on anecdotal information. Nearly two out of five respondents said that they tracked and documented successful knowledge/wisdom transfer results, while 13 percent of respondents did not measure the impact at all.

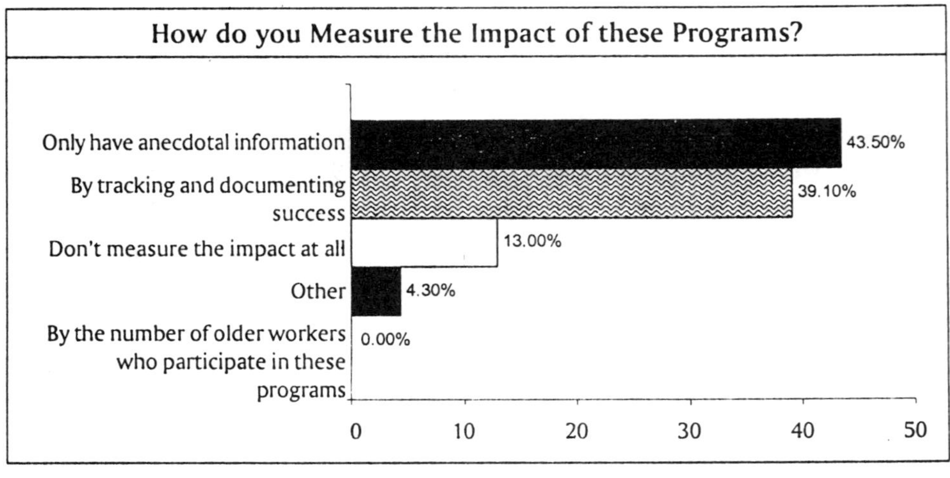

Respondents who did measure the performance of these programs found only three which they rated as high-impact efforts. Mentoring was rated highest by 47.6 percent. Leadership succession planning was rated highest by 19 percent and informal knowledge networks were rated highest by 14.3 percent of respondents. None of the other programs was rated highest by as many as 5 percent of respondents.

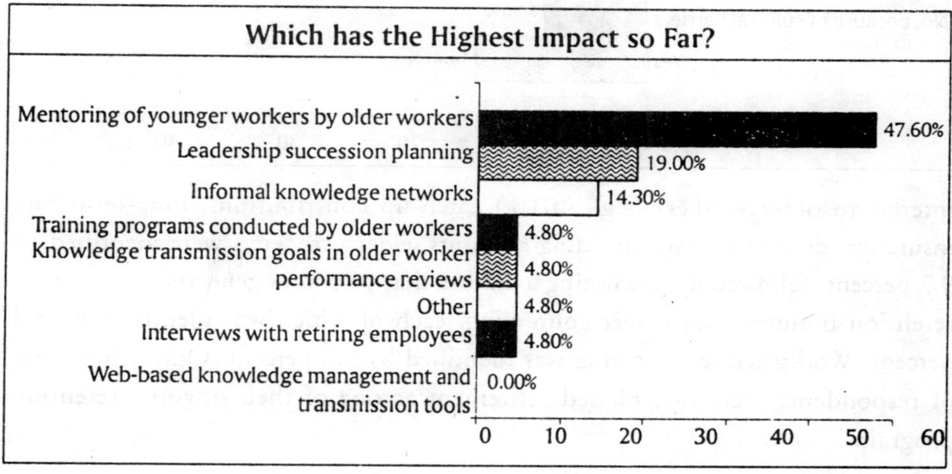

Retention of Key Employees

Few employers are undertaking programs aimed specifically at retaining older workers. Only 14.3 percent of survey respondents said that their organization had any ongoing and formal programs to retain key employees based on "business wisdom." Of those that did not (42.9 percent), the most frequent reason given was that such programs were not a priority. Costs were cited by another 18.6 percent and cultural barriers by another 8.6 percent.

Of those that did have programs to retain key employees based on "business wisdom," the most popular were continuous learning and training (12.9 percent). Next in popularity was a flexible work schedule (such as job-sharing, telecommuting, and work-life balance), identified by 11 percent. Pre-retirement planning was identified by 10.3 percent of respondents, as was hiring retirees as consultants, contractors, or mentors. Flexible or special benefits of particular

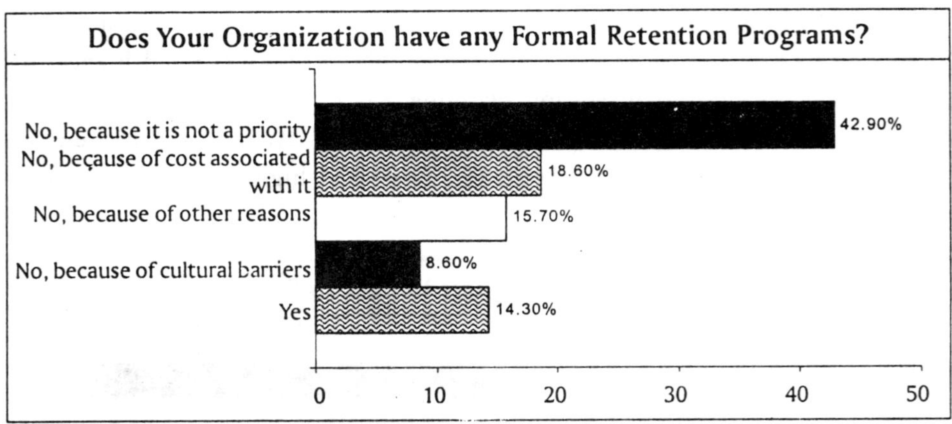

interest to older workers (e.g., 401(k) catch-up contributions, long-term care insurance, dependent care spending accounts, elder care, etc.) were identified by 9.7 percent, followed by promoting a culture that promotes generational diversity, retention bonuses, and career counseling, each of which was identified by 8.4 percent. Workplace restructuring was identified by 5.2 percent. Only 2.6 percent of respondents identified phased retirement as one of their ongoing retention programs.

When it comes to measuring the impact of these programs, 40 percent of respondents said that they tracked the number of workers who continue to work beyond the age of retirement eligibility under their organization's retirement plan. Another 36.7 percent rely only on anecdotal information and 23.3 percent do not measure the impact at all.

Of these programs, 25.9 percent of respondents said that hiring retirees had the highest impact. Creating and maintaining a culture that promotes generational diversity was rated by 14.8 percent as having the highest impact, as were retention bonuses. Pre-retirement planning was rated highest by 11.1 percent of respondents.

Looking ahead to the next few years, 11.2 percent said that they are considering hiring retirees as consultants or contractors or using on-call pools of retirees.

If Yes, Does Your Organization Have any of the Following Ongoing and Formal Retention Programs?

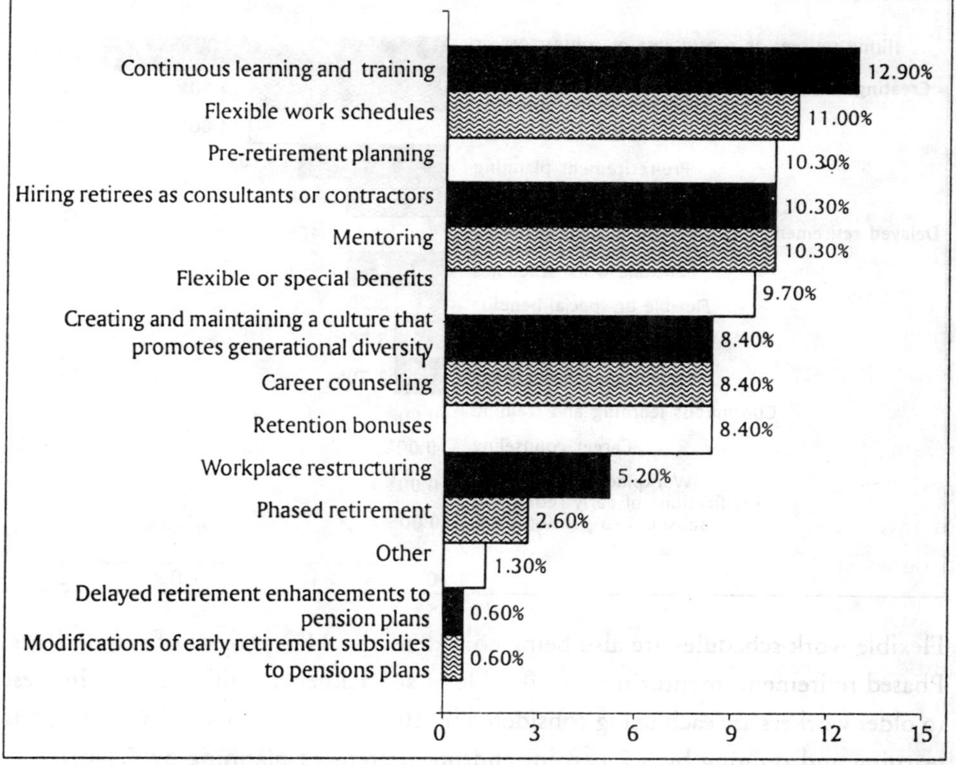

Program	%
Continuous learning and training	12.90%
Flexible work schedules	11.00%
Pre-retirement planning	10.30%
Hiring retirees as consultants or contractors	10.30%
Mentoring	10.30%
Flexible or special benefits	9.70%
Creating and maintaining a culture that promotes generational diversity	8.40%
Career counseling	8.40%
Retention bonuses	8.40%
Workplace restructuring	5.20%
Phased retirement	2.60%
Other	1.30%
Delayed retirement enhancements to pension plans	0.60%
Modifications of early retirement subsidies to pensions plans	0.60%

0 3 6 9 12 15

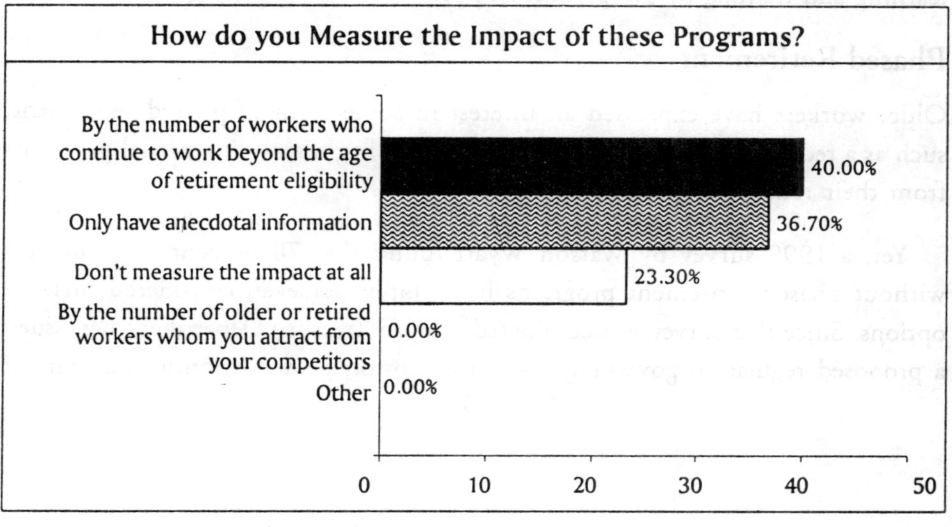

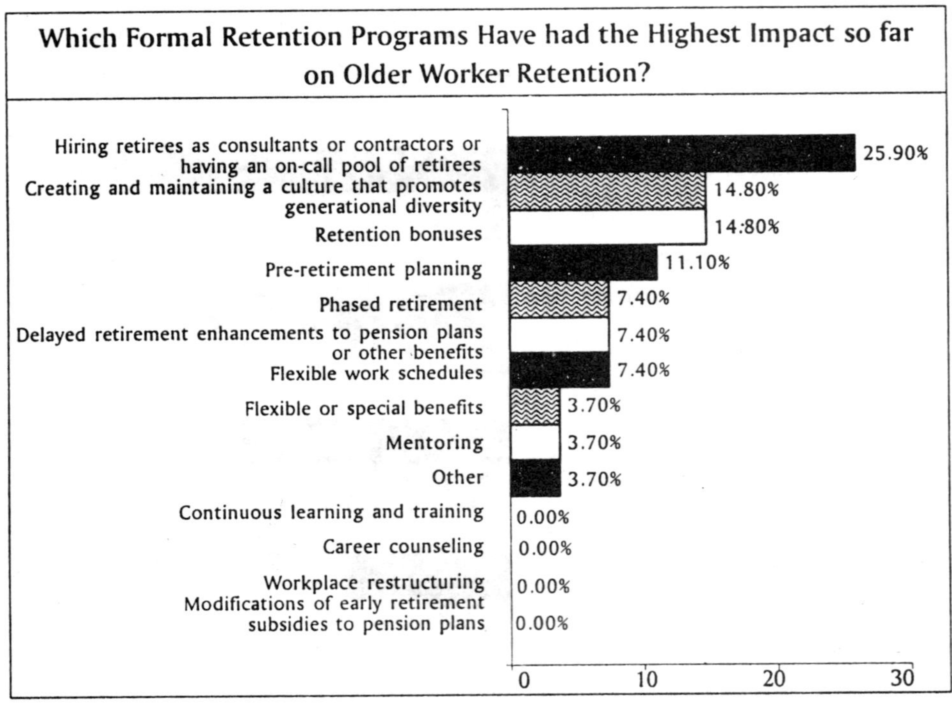

Flexible work schedules are also being considered by 11.2 percent of respondents. Phased retirement, mentoring, and flexible or special benefits of particular interest to older workers are each being considered by 10.2 percent, followed by continuous learning and training by 9.2 percent and pre-retirement planning by 7.1 percent.

Phased Retirement

Older workers have expressed an interest in some form of phased retirement, such as a reduced work schedule so that they can begin receiving partial payments from their retirement program(s).

Yet, a 1999 survey by Watson Wyatt found that 70 percent of employers without phased retirement programs had simply not even considered them as options. Since that survey was conducted, the US Treasury Department has issued a proposed regulation governing in-service pension plan distributions as part of

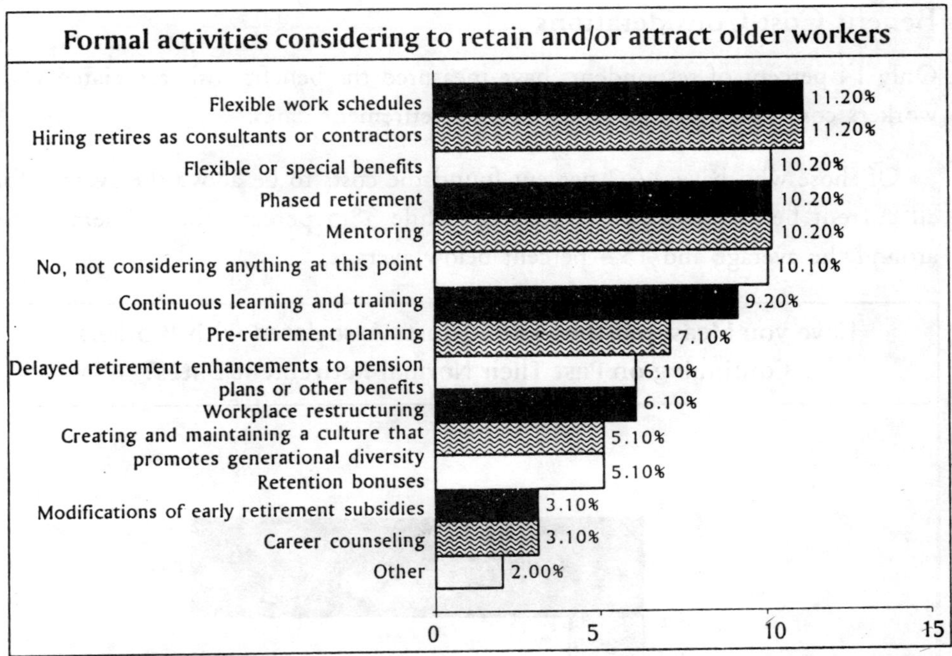

such programs. Older workers who reduce their work schedules by at least 20 percent would be eligible to receive a pro-rated portion of their pension benefits. Phased retirement arrangements would be required to be voluntary and in writing. Despite having the guidance of this proposed regulation since November 9, 2004, few employers have implemented phased retirement programs. Some, in comments to the Treasury Department, have expressed their concern that the proposed regulation is too administratively cumbersome. Final regulations have not yet been issued.

State and local governments have the most experience with one form of phased retirement—the Deferred Retirement Option Program (DROP). A DROP enables eligible older workers, typically teachers, to continue to work for a government employer beyond normal retirement ages and build additional retirement plan income.

Benefit Cost Considerations

Only 14 percent of respondents have measured the benefit costs associated with workers continuing on past their normal retirement dates.

Of those who have, 46.2 percent found the costs to be above the average for all current benefit costs per employee, while 38.5 percent found them to be around the average and 15.4 percent below average.

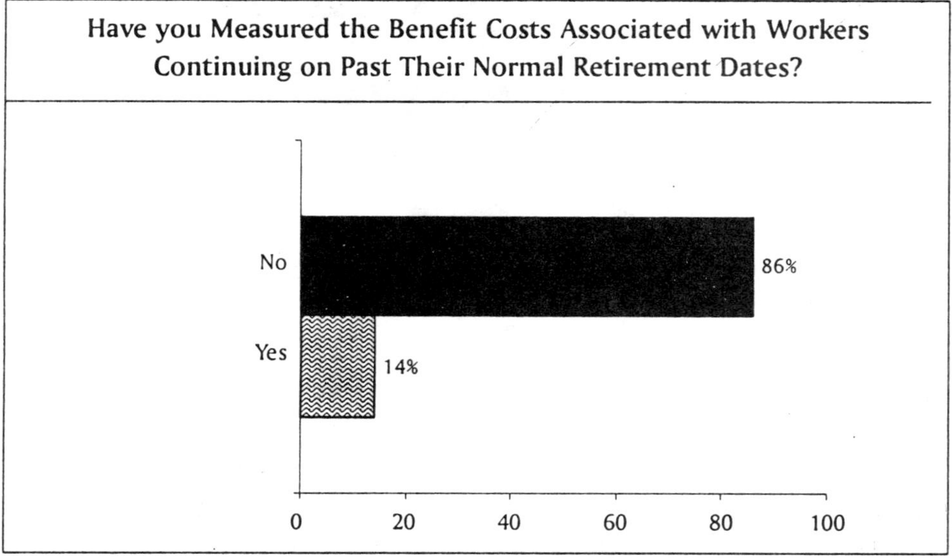

The health care costs of an aging workforce should concern employers. As people age, they tend to utilize more, and more costly, health care services. The treatment costs for conditions such as cardiovascular disease and diabetes are significantly more, on average, for older patients, due to progression of the disease. Additionally, the usage of prescription drugs increases dramatically with age.

Annual health care costs can increase by as much as 3 percent as a result solely of a one-year increase in the average age of an employee population. This increase is in addition to increases based on other factors influencing an employer's health care costs, such as increases in the cost of services, increases in the number of

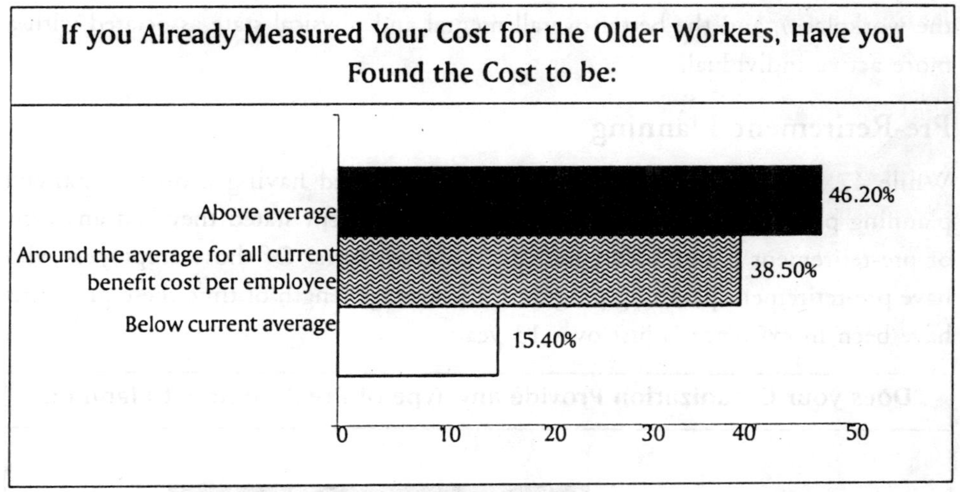

services utilized, the mix of services utilized, and any cost shifting by providers of services (e.g., hospitals, physicians, etc.) from mandated, fixed-price programs (e.g., Medicare, Medicaid) to the programs typically offered to employees.

According to the Kaiser/HRET Survey of Employer-Sponsored Health Benefits 2005, health care costs for single and family coverage averaged $4,024 and $10,880, respectively, in 2005. These numbers imply that a typical employer with 1,000 employees covered under its health care plan can expect an increase of as much as $250,000 annually, if the average age of its employee population increases by just one year.

Employers that offer retiree medical benefits, however, often find that it costs less to maintain an individual as an active employee than of as a retired member of the health plan. Costs associated with a retiree who is not yet eligible for Medicare (i.e., under age 65) can be 2.5 times as much as an active employee's health care costs. Although a significant portion of this difference is attributable to aging, other factors may influence the cost differential between an active and a retired employee, including time available to seek treatment (active employees are more likely to seek self-care treatments to reduce the time needed to leave work to visit a physician), social needs (some retirees see physician office visits as an opportunity to compensate for the loss of social interactions that occurred in the workplace), and the better overall mental and physical state associated with a more active individual.

Pre-Retirement Planning

While 47.1 percent of survey respondents reported having a broad financial planning program for all employees, only 16.5 percent stated they had any type of pre-retirement planning program for older workers. Of those employers who have pre-retirement planning programs, the average length of time these programs have been in existence is just over 13 years.

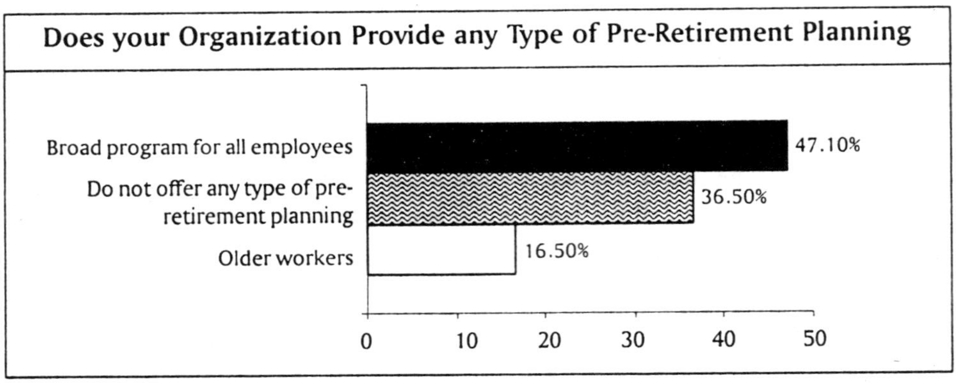

Respondents identified as the most popular components of these programs: group seminars/workshops (48.8 percent); on-line tools, such as Web-based calculators (46.5 percent); generic print publications (45.3 percent); personalized plan statements and projections of retirement benefits at different retirement ages (44.2 percent); and on-line information (40.7 percent). Only 17.4 percent of respondents offer older workers individual counseling in person and 16.3 percent by telephone. (Respondents were able to select all that applied.)

Just over one in four respondents reported that more than 20 percent of eligible employees used one or more of these program components during the past 12 months. Usage by 5 percent or lower was reported by 17 percent of respondents. Nearly one-third of respondents did not know what the actual usage was at their organization.

What are the Components of Your Pre-Retirement Planning Program?

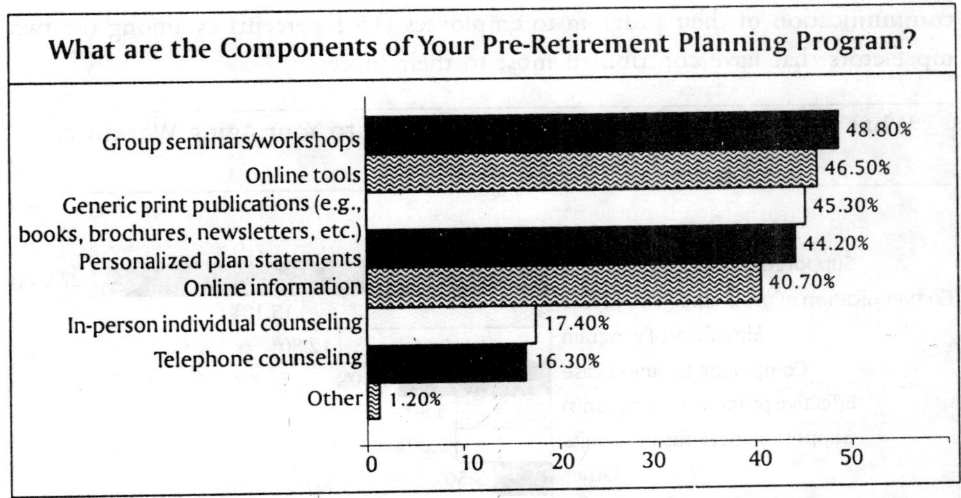

Of those respondents who have a broader program for all employees that includes pre-retirement planning, 15.2 percent reported that workers over age 55 comprised greater than 50 percent of program users over the past 12 months. Over 54 percent of respondents, however, did not know the extent to which older workers used these programs.

Respondents with pre-retirement planning programs reported relying most often on their 401(k) or other plan provider to deliver program components. While 38.4 percent of respondents used their plan providers for their pre-retirement planning program, 34.9 percent used their internal HR or benefits staff and 27.9 percent used an independent third-party pre-retirement or financial education/counseling firm. Only 11.6 percent reported using local individual financial planners, investment brokers, and/or insurance agents. (Respondents were able to select all that applied.)

Just over 44 percent of respondents stated that they planned to enhance or expand their pre-retirement planning program over the next one to two years.

Overall Success

Respondents who viewed any of their aging workforce activities as successful most frequently rated support of senior management (27.9 percent) and the communication of their program to employees (15.1 percent) as among the two top factors that have contributed most to their success.

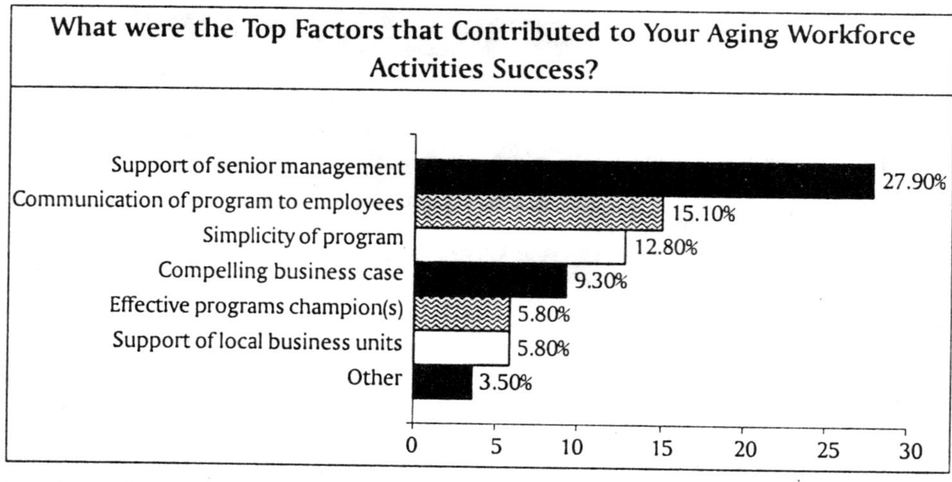

In Conclusion

One need not accept dire predictions of a looming talent shortage in order to make the business case for attracting and retaining older workers. If there is, in fact, such a shortage, then workforce planning is no longer a zero-sum game in which jobs for young workers depend on moving older workers out. Regardless of future workforce demographics, employers need to assess the attributes of certain older workers that will translate into unique contributions to their enterprise and that will complement, rather than compete with, what younger workers offer. Such an assessment may be particularly critical for those businesses where the prime market is also aging, as older customer-serving and market-facing workers may offer added value. This perspective is consistent with a human capital framework that views people as a differential investment, not an undifferentiated expense.

The age-old concept of wisdom is critical to this assessment. The notion of "business wisdom" must be systematically applied by HR professionals as part of overall workforce planning. Starting with a definition of "business wisdom" that is specific to their industry, employers need to conduct an inventory of their workforce, with a goal of identifing those individuals whose employment and life experiences have endowed them with unique business insights, and who have demonstrated the rare capacity to make sage judgments in changing environments. This effort should not be limited to the executive suite or managerial ranks.

Without a deliberate and carefully executed plan to retain the right individuals in the aging segment of their workforces, employers run the risk of a significant "business wisdom" withdrawal due to early retirements. The consequences of such a loss of human capital are likely to harm both the employer (especially if such high-value workers deploy their capabilities and relationships on behalf of competitors) and individual workers who will not be engaged in productive work, perhaps at peak performance. Our nation will also suffer from the wasting away of those older Americans who still have so much to offer.

There is much that employers can do to manage the risk of "business wisdom" withdrawal, including:

- Instituting flexible work and phased retirement arrangements.
- Bringing their own retirees back on a contractual basis through other entities.
- Redesigning compensation and benefit plans.
- Establishing sound pre-retirement planning programs.
- Initiating training and leadership development activities that explicitly focus on wisdom as a recognized and transferable quality.

Time is running out as millions of Baby Boomers reach early retirement ages. Employers need to act now to develop and implement strategies that focus on this vital segment of their workforce.

(Ernst & Young's Human Capital practice includes an Employee Financial Services group that designs and delivers employee financial education and counseling programs, including pre-retirement planning, to large employers in a range of industries. It also includes a Performance and Reward group that assists employers with all aspects of their retirement, health, and other benefit plans.)

Sources

AARP, *Maximizing Your Workforce: Employees Over 50 in Today's Global Economy,* University of Pennsylvania, Wharton Impact Conference (2004).

Burtless, Gary and Joseph F Quinn, *Is Working Longer the Answer for an Aging Workforce?* Center for Retirement Research (2002).

Cappelli, Peter, *Will There Really Be a Labor Shortage?* Organizational Dynamics (2003).

Coleman, Dennis R, *Baby Boom to Baby Bust: Flexible Work Options for Older Workers,* Benefits Quarterly (Fourth quarter 1998).

Collison, Jessica, *Older Workers Survey.* Society for Human Resource Management (2003).

DeLong, David W, *Lost Knowledge: Confronting the Threat of an Aging Workforce* (2004).

Dychtwald, Ken, Tamara Erickson, and Bob Morison. *It's Time to Retire Retirement,* Harvard Business Review (March 2004).

Employment Policy Foundation, *The American Workplace Report 2001: Building America's Workforce for the 21st Century* (2001).

Friedland, Robert B and Laura Summer, *Demography Is Not Destiny, Revisited.* Center on an Aging Society, Georgetown University (2005).

Goldberg, Beverly, *Age Works: What Corporate America Must Do to Survive the Graying of the Workforce* (2000).

Gornick, Mary Ellen, *A Proactive Approach to Retaining "Wisdom Workers," International Foundation of Employee Benefit Plans,* Benefits & Compensation Digest (March 2005).

Hoops, F and N Stoops, *Demographic Trends in the Twentieth Century,* US Census Bureau (2002).

Horrigan, Michael W, *Employment Projections to 2012: Concepts and Context.* Monthly Labor Review (February 2004).

Hutchens, Robert M, *The Cornell Study of Employer Phased Retirement Policies: A Report on Key Findings,* Faculty Publications, Labor Economics (2003).

Kaiser/HRET, *Survey of Employer-Sponsored Health Benefits* (2005).

Leonard, Dorothy and Walter C, Swap, *Deep Smarts: How to Cultivate and Transfer Enduring Business Wisdom* (2005).

Lockwood, Nancy, *The Aging Workforce, HR Magazine,* (December 2003), McCafferty, Joseph *A Human Inventory, CFO Magazine* (April 2005).

Morton, Lynne, Lorrie Foster, and Jeri Sedlar, *Managing the Mature Workforce,* The Conference Board (2005).

Muson, Howard, *Valuing Experience: How to Motivate and Retain Mature Workers,* The Conference Board (2003).

Purcell, Patrick, *Older Workers: Employment and Retirement Trends,* Congressional Research Service (2005).

Robson, William B P, *Aging Populations and the Workforce: Challenges for Employers,* British-North American Committee (2001).

Roper Starch Worldwide, *Baby Boomers Envision Their Retirement: An AARP Segmentation Analysis,* AARP (2000).

Roszak, Theodore, *America the Wise* (1998).

Rix, Sarah E, *Update on the Older Worker,* AARP Public Policy Institute (2003).

Society for Human Resource Management, *Generational Differences* (2004).

Society for Human Resource Management, *Future of the US Labor Pool Survey Report* (2005).

Toosi, Mitra, *A Century of Change: The US Labor Force, 1950-2050, Monthly Labor Review* (May 2002).

UnumProvident, *Health and Productivity in the Aging American Work Force: Realities and Opportunities* (2005).

Index

M

P

R

S

T

V

W